# ABOUT THE AUTHOR

Stevyn Colgan is an author, artist, songwriter, public speaker and oddly-spelled Cornishman. He is one of the 'elves' that contribute research to the popular BBC TV series *QI* and co-writes its sister show, *The Museum of* *sity*, for BBC Radio 4.

has also, among other things, been a chef, a potato picker, a milkman police officer. He has written briefing notes for two prime ministers and ipts for Gerry Anderson and *Doctor Who*. He's helped build dinosaur is for the Natural History Museum, movie monsters for Bruce Willis at, and was the official artist for the 2006 National Children's Book e has given hundreds of talks across the UK and USA on a variety of from problem solving to Cornish mythology to why he believes that 't intelligently designed.

the author of *Joined-Up Thinking* (Pan Macmillan, 2008) and *dhlow* (Kowethas, 2010). The latter (translated by Tony Hak) is a g of eight classic Cornish folk tales published in both English and i languages and is the largest collection of original Cornish prose in ice to date. He is currently writing a comedy novel and a book about cording an album of his own songs and developing an animated series on *Constable Colgan's Connectoscope®*.

stops inordinately frequently for tea.

## Praise for *Joined-Up Thinking*

'I found myself fascinated and somewhat dizzy. Most impressive.'
– Stephen Fry

'Dizzily intriguing.'
– *The Bookseller*

'Quite simply the best way to spend time when not shopping, sleeping or preparing food.'
– Tony Hawks (author of *Around Ireland with a Fridge*)

'This is not a stocking filler – this is a real book. Buy several copies and keep one.'
– *Daily Telegraph*

'The book's packed with great info, from the derivation of the phrase 'letting the cat out of the bag' to the name for the thin bits of a cricket bail. Spigots, since you ask.'
– Mark Mason (author of *The Importance of Being Trivial*)

'If you've ever looked at the Eiffel Tower and wondered how it's related to Dracula, then Stevyn Colgan is your man. Yes, it's trivia porn.'
– *London Lite*

'He connects each piece of his puzzle in a concise, chatty, easy to follow, even logical, manner. Colgan has the knack of making it all sound intensely fascinating.'
– *New Zealand Herald*

'Stevyn Colgan has a theory; everything in the world can be connected through "six degrees of information". Trying to prove it takes us up some strange alleys but his engaging style means we don't get stuck down the road of intellectual whimsy.'
– *Maxim*

## Praise for *Henhwedhlow*

'All power to Stevyn Colgan and his project to preserve Cornish myth, legend and song. Who knows; as a result some Penzance Wagner may write the Cornish Ring Cycle and won't the world be pleased? There's more to Cornwall than Padstow, pasties and "Piss off you grockles" and Colgan is doing the ancient kingdom a great service.'
– Stephen Fry

'Jumping from the 19th to the 21st century, Stevyn Colgan is taking an essential element of our Cornish culture and bringing it bang up-to-date.'
– Bard Howard Curnow

'The best book I've ever seen for helping you to learn the Cornish language or practice reading it. Brilliant fun too.
– *Cornish Voice*

'The best bilingual English/Cornish book out there, wonderful stories, great for learners of the Cornish Language, and for English speakers who want to read good Cornish stories.'
– An Tala

CONSTABLE COLGAN'S CONNECTOSCOPE®

# CONSTABLE

# COLGAN'S

# CONNECTOSCOPE®

STEVYN COLGAN

unbound

This edition first published in 2013

Unbound
4–7 Manchester Street, Marylebone, London, w1u 2ae
www.unbound.co.uk

A CIP record for this book
is available from the
British Library

isbn 978-1-908717-83-2

Typeset by Bracketpress
Cover design by Tom Gauld

Printed in England by Clays Ltd, Bungay, Suffolk

For Dawn, Sarah, Kerys, Liam, Leah and Tyler

Dedicated to all of the authors, philanthropists, scientists,
researchers, detectives, librarians, explorers, journalists,
biographers, analysts, inventors, comedians, physicians,
adventurers, artists, philosophers and anyone
else who ever thought to ask
'Why?'

Without them we'd still all be living in the Oldupai Gorge.

# INTRODUCTION

The ability to relate and to connect, sometimes in odd and yet striking fashion, lies at the very heart of any creative use of the mind, no matter in what field or discipline.
– George J. Seidel

Making mental connections is our most crucial learning tool, the essence of human intelligence; to forge links; to go beyond the given; to see patterns, relationships, context.
– Marilyn Ferguson

I believe that all things are fundamentally interconnected, as anyone who follows the principles of quantum mechanics to their logical extremes cannot, if they are honest, help but accept.
– Dirk Gently[1]

It's a fact (the first of many in this book) that I am horribly unskilled in a great many areas of human endeavour. I'm a sporting disaster: I can't run, swim, kick, dive, throw, hit, crawl, twist, hurl, lob, leap or thump with any degree of grace, speed or accuracy. I'm even worse at DIY. Any shelf I put up could double as a ski-jump for kittens and recently, while attempting to repair my reading glasses, I somehow succeeded in superglueing them to my nose. My panoply of incompetence is really quite impressive. However, it's not all doom and gloom. There are a few – a very few – things at which I'm not too shabby. For example, I'm pretty good at remembering things. And I'm not too bad with a pencil and paintbrush. So while I may not be able to fix your carburettor or help you win the local football derby, I can at least draw you an ostrich and tell you that its taxonomic name is *Struthio camelus*. Not terribly useful, I'll admit. Which is why, for most of my childhood, it seemed to me that all Nature had equipped me for was winning quizzes while starving in a garret.

1. From Douglas Adams's *Dirk Gently's Holistic Detective Agency* (William Heinemann Ltd., 1987).

Upon leaving school I embarked on a number of poorly paid jobs, and a stint as a trainee chef, before joining the police service as the result of a £50 bet (true) with my late father, himself a homicide detective. And I quickly discovered that I was pretty rubbish at that too. I couldn't have spotted a villain if he'd painted his bottom *smalt* in colour (see Investigation 9) and lapdanced in my face to the tune of The Clash's 'Bankrobber'. I was deemed psychologically unsuitable for anything involving weapons. I had the leadership skills of Captain Bligh. And my short legs, long body and large head meant that any uniform I wore fitted like a glove on a dolphin.[2] Things weren't looking too rosy for me in my (nearly) chosen career. But rather than throw me out on my incompetent arse, the London Metropolitan Police Service was sufficiently large[3] and flexible enough to find a niche for me (or maybe they simply weren't prepared to throw away the investment they'd made in tailoring a uniform to fit me). Whatever the reason, someone noticed that I was: (a) quite good at remembering things; and (b) of a creative bent. These things combined meant that I often found the links between facts that others hadn't spotted. This led to me being brought into the fascinating world of intelligence work.

Criminal intelligence works rather like a mosaic or a jigsaw for which you have no guiding picture and just a suspicion of what the finished article looks like. You start with lots of apparently unrelated pieces and, over time, you spot connections and form the pieces into clumps. Then you try to merge them into bigger clumps by finding out what links them together. Eventually the big picture starts to emerge. And, with luck, it's the one you suspected it would be and you get to catch the bad guys.

So that's what I did for most of my 30-year police career ... I joined things up. I helped match the bad guys to the bad things they'd done. But it went further than that; finding connections helped me to research and analyse crimes and community problems and subsequently design creative solutions that were more permanent and sustainable than the usual short-term enforcement-based tactics. And

2. The man at the police uniform stores told me that I was 'Sooty shaped' (as in the glove puppet) and that I had a head like 'a fucking watermelon'.
3. The Met has more employees than the Royal Navy; around 45,000 to the Navy's 43,000. Sources: Met Police and Royal Navy websites.

I got pretty good at it. I won awards and ended up sitting on Home Office consultative groups and lecturing all over the UK and USA. Of course, I was just one tiny, tiny cog in a very big, multi-organisational machine. But just as the flick of a guppy's tail can be an infinitessimally small part of a tsunami, so my modest contribution helped to get some bad people off the streets and, more importantly perhaps, made good people feel safer in their homes.

So it's maybe no surprise that I came to write *Constable Colgan's Connectoscope®* and my previous book, *Joined-Up Thinking* (Pan Macmillan, 2008). Spotting connections is in my DNA. And connections are all around us.

For many years, we have known about something called *Six Degrees of Separation*; the idea that every person on this planet can be linked by a chain of just six, or fewer, individuals (You can read a lot more about it in Investigation 7). So maybe I shouldn't have been surprised when I found that I could do the same thing with facts; a kind of *Six Degrees of Information*.

Everything really can be connected to everything else. You've undoubtedly experienced this for yourself when surfing the net; how one website leads you to another and another and, after a very short time, you find yourself some way away from the topic you started with. So imagine how great it would be to have a device that helped you to make those connections; a portable hand-held *Connectoscope®* that could access and search every possible database, encyclopaedia and online resource. But more than that, it could spot the connections, no matter how obscure or bizarre, between any one fact, object, person or event and any other fact, object, person or event. It would revolutionise so many areas of human endeavour.

Sadly, the real *Connectoscope®* doesn't exist yet. But I can, at least, give you a sense of what such a device would be like. In this wireless, battery-free, paper-based *Connectoscope®* that you hold in your hand,[4] you'll find the results of 32 'investigations' each starting off from a simple question asking me to connect three apparently unrelated items. All 32 investigations are stuffed full of fascinating facts linked together into small circular chains by the connections that the *Connectoscope®* has found.

If you fancy a challenge, why not have a go at finding the con-

4. Unless you're reading the e-book or listening to the audiobook of course.

nections yourself? At the start of each investigation, I'll give you the same list of three things that I started with. Your challenge (if you choose to play along) is to build a circular chain of connections that includes those three things. You can use as many other facts as you like to form each chain. The only rules are that:

(1) each fact has to connect to the one before and the one after it; and (2) the very last fact must link back to the first, thus completing the circle.

Have a read through one of the investigations first to get a feel for how the *Connectoscope®* works.

I wonder if you'll find the same connections that I did?

This isn't a textbook or an encyclopaedia. It's not even very serious. This is a book for those dull commutes to work on the train; for reading on the beach on holiday; for that little shelf near the loo. My aim in writing it is to provide you with an entertaining and informative read, spiced with a soupçon of challenge, if you fancy it.

That said, I hope that it will occasionally surprise you too. It would be grand if at least one fact in each investigation made you exclaim, 'Crikey!' or some possibly ruder words to that effect.

If that happens, then the *Connectoscope®* will have done its job.

Stevyn Colgan
(Ex-Constable 174702 Metropolitan Police Service, London)
A pub somewhere in Soho, probably
January 2013

# INVESTIGATIONS

# INVESTIGATION I

## How do you connect the **Yakuza** to the **Pendle Hill Witches** and **LSD**?

### *Bob the Builder gets the Finger*

The author **Jerome K. Jerome**'s middle name was Klapka. Or, at least, his nom de plume contained the name Klapka. It is most likely that Jerome was christened with the same names as his father – Jerome Clapp Jerome – and that he later adopted 'Klapka' to sound more exotic. Some evidence for this lies in the fact that his mother's death certificate contains the words 'J. C. Jerome, son, present at the death'.

Jerome Snr was an eccentric parson who obviously had a thing for unusual names as his other children were named Paulina Deodata, Blandina Dominica and Milton Melancthon. There is a commonly told story that he was friends with an exiled Hungarian General called György Klapka and that this friendship was honoured by his son adopting the name. However, research shows that it's far more likely that Jerome K. made the story up.

The family was very poor (due to a series of bad investments) and Jerome Jnr's parents died when he was a teenager. He therefore sought work on the railways and then later as a jobbing actor using the stage name of Harold Crichton.[5] He also began to write and, in

---

5. Pronounced Cry-ten, it's a name often associated with butlers and manservants. It was popularised by Kenneth More's character in the 1957 movie *The Admirable Crichton*, which was, in turn, based on a play written in 1902 by *Peter Pan* author J. M. Barrie. Barrie's character later inspired the name of Kryten, the service droid in the BBC TV comedy series *Red Dwarf*. Unrelated but curiously coincidentally, *Red Dwarf* starred Chris Barrie (whose real surname is Brown). Also coincidentally, all four of the show's main cast members – Barrie, Craig Charles, Danny John-Jules and Robert Llewellyn (Kryten) were born in leap years (1960, 1964, 1960 and 1956 respectively). Yup, that's the kind of book this is.

1889, he wrote the book that would make his name: *Three Men in a Boat*. The book has been in publication ever since.

In 2005, comedians Dara O Briain, Griff Rhys Jones and Rory McGrath re-enacted Jerome's journey along the Thames for a television series called *Three Men in a Boat* made for the **BBC**, the world's first national broadcaster.

The British Broadcasting Corporation was founded in 1922 (but got its charter and current name in 1927). It is now the world's largest such organisation, employing 23,000 staff and has an annual budget in the region of £4.26 billion (based on 2011/12 figures). Starting with (and still broadcasting) radio programmes, it has followed the development of new media as time has gone by and has embraced television, digital television, interactive services and the internet. Its website (bbc.co.uk) is the 45th most popular website in the world and the 5th most popular in the UK.[6]

In 2000 the BBC reported that its television series **Bob the Builder** was being 'doctored' before export to Japan by giving all the characters five fingers instead of the original four.[7] The reason given was the fear that people would associate the characters with the Japanese 'mafia' – the **Yakuza** – because of their tradition of cutting off the little finger, or part of the little finger, as a punishment. This sounds like an urban myth but the story was, and still is, posted on the BBC website and claims that the doctoring would be done by HIT Entertainment. It's also notable that the characters in Japanese cartoons or anime do traditionally have five fingers on each hand. However, *Bob the Builder* eventually went out undoctored in Japan along with other four-fingered shows such as *Postman Pat* and *The Simpsons*.[8]

The cutting off of part of a finger, or *yubitsume*, is an act of penance or apology to the Yakuza boss or *Oyabun*. Upon first transgression, the Yakuza member is required to cut off the tip of the smallest finger of the left hand (at the first joint) and present it to his Oyabun. On second offence, it's more of the same finger to the next

6. Stats taken on October 28th 2011 from www.alexa.com.
7. The tradition of animated characters only having four fingers is as old as animation itself and is simply about making the characters as easy to animate as possible without the hands looking too 'weird'. A traditional, non computer-based cartoon short involves something like 50,000 individual drawings. By removing one digit, that's 100,000 fewer fingers to draw. Time, as they say, is money.
8. In Japan, *Bob the Builder* is called *Hataraku Buubuuzu*. Meanwhile, BBC TV show *Teletubbies* is translated as *Teretabīzu* or 'Antenna Babies'. I rather prefer that.

joint. And so on. When the pinkie is completely gone, attention moves to the right hand. Yubitsume originated in a time when the sword was the weapon of choice. The Japanese style of grip relies heavily on the strength of the little finger so losing it, or a part of it, would adversely affect swordplay performance. The penitent was therefore forced to rely more upon the group or family for protection.

The name Yakuza comes from a card game called *Oichu-Kabu* and literally translates (in old Japanese) as 'eight nine three' (*ya ku sa*). This is the worst hand of cards you can have during the game. Consequently, if a player finds themself landed with it, they have to exhibit extraordinary skill to outmanoeuvre their opponent(s). The hand is sometimes called 'good for nothing'.

Yakuza are organised crime groups, many of which enjoy a degree of respectability within society. Some have histories spanning hundreds of years but their origins are confused. It may be that the early Yakusa were Robin Hood type figures; community vigilantes that enforced order and protected the people. Other evidence suggests that they were town bullies or local criminals. Another theory suggests that they were groups of *Rōnin* (masterless Samurai) who operated as soldiers of fortune. Samurai were, at that time, the only people allowed to lawfully carry swords.

**Samurai Jack** was a cartoon series created by Genndy Tartakovsky that ran from 2001 to 2004. The Emmy Award-winning series was an immediate hit because of its cinematic style, wit, clever stories, striking graphics and excellent musical scores. The series follows the adventures of a Samurai warrior (with five fingers on each hand) who fights an apocalyptic battle with Aku, a shape-shifting demon.[9] At the last minute, Aku opens a hole in time and hurls him into the far future to an earth where the demon has reigned for millennia. It is a desolate, subjugated place ... some people have reverted to mediaeval lifestyles, others to societies mirroring different eras. There are bounty-hunting aliens and mercenary robots, strange mutants and even stranger creatures from mythology that have somehow been brought back to life. We follow the Samurai's adventures – some epic and deadly serious, others very funny or light-hearted – as he searches for a way to return to the past to defeat Aku and prevent this terrible

9. *Aku* means 'evil' or 'wickedness' in Japanese and there is a demon with burning eyes in Japanese mythology called Akuma.

dystopian future. On his journey, he collects the nickname of 'Jack' and uses it thereafter.

A male donkey is called a Jack. A female donkey is called a Jenny, or a Jennet. Jennet is also: (a) another word for a mule; (b) a breed of small Spanish horse with a distinctive spotted coat; and (c) an old-English girl's name originally derived from John.

Jennet Preston was one of the 13 **Pendle Hill Witches** who, in 1612, were accused of killing 17 people by witchcraft. Following a series of sensational trials, ten of them were hanged at Lancaster Gaol. They were: Alizon Device, Elizabeth Device, James Device, Anne Whittle (known as 'Chattox'), Anne Redferne, Alice Nutter, Katherine Hewitt, John Bulcock, Jane Bulcock and Isobel Robey. Jennet Preston was hanged in York. Margaret Pearson was found guilty of witchcraft but was acquitted of murder. As a result she was the only survivor and served just a year in prison. The 13th alleged witch, Elizabeth Southerns (known as 'Demdike'), died in Lancaster Gaol while awaiting her trial.

In Demdike's written confession, most likely extracted under duress, she claimed that she and her associates had sold their souls to the Devil and had murdered the 17 by making 'pictures of clay'; small voodoo-doll type effigies of their intended victims that were then stuck with a pin or slowly crumbled or burned over time, causing pain, illness, degeneration and ultimately death. Demdike also claimed that each of the witches had a familiar; a spirit companion of hellish origin. Alizon Device's familiar was a black **demon dog**, whom she allowed to suck on her breast.

Demon dogs are fairly commonplace in British mythology and folklore. In Cornish legend, the wicked clerk Jan Tregeagle is pursued across Bodmin Moor by a pack of demonic hounds whose 'heads blazed with the fires of Hell'. Yorkshire's 'Hellhound' is called Barguest, and the Norfok, Suffolk and Essex coastline is reputedly haunted by Black Shuck. The Isle of Man's demon dog is Moddey Dhoo, Wales has Gwyllgi and Devon has the Yeth Hound. In the North of England, there was a spirit called Gytrash that could assume the form of several types of animal (it is mentioned in Charlotte Bronte's *Jane Eyre*) including a large black demon dog.[10]

Demon Dogs was the name of a famous hot dog restaurant in

10. There is a long tradition of demon dogs in literature. One of the earliest is Cerberus which guarded the gates to Hades, the hell of Greek mythology. However, the most

Chicago that was closed in 2003 to make way for development work at Fullerton Station on the Brown Line Railway. However, it did not go without a fight as Demon Dogs was a piece of rock and roll history. Owner Pete Schivarelli discovered a local band nearly 40 years previously and called them Chicago Transit Authority. The real CTA objected to the name, so it was shortened by producer James Guercio to Chicago. Under Schivarelli's management, the band went on to make millions and Demon Dogs became a shrine to them, its walls boasting gold and platinum Chicago albums, and also signed guitars from fellow rockers Steven Tyler and Eddie Van Halen and countless photos of Schivarelli with major celebrities.

The **hot dog** sausage was invented in the 17th century by a German butcher from Coburg named Johann Georghehner. At least, that's the claim of the American National Hot Dog and Sausage Council. However, the first appearance of the sausage in a bun is difficult to trace. Some sources state that Charles Feltman of Coney Island, New York was the first when, in 1867, he started selling Vienna sausages[11] in buns as 'Coney Island Red-Hots'. By 1874 he had gone from a small cart to a full-sized restaurant at West 10th Street and Surf Avenue. Others state that he started selling pies in 1867 and opened the hotdog stand in 1871. Still others claim the invention as belonging to Antoine Feuchtwanger, a German sausage-maker who served hot dogs at the 1904 St Louis World's Fair, with his brother baking the buns.

The term 'hot dog' itself also has a confused origin. It may have started as a sarcastic comment on the provenance of the meat. Or it may relate to the fact that German sausages and Dachshunds arrived in the USA at around the same time (Germans called frankfurters 'little-dog' or 'dachshund' sausages). Or it may have an origin in the phrase 'hot dog', used to describe a stylish dresser. To get dressed in a sharp suit was known as 'putting on the dog'. The term 'hot dog' for the finger snack may possibly stem (though it sounds dubious to me) from the idea that the sausage is 'clothed' or 'dressed' by the bread.

Nathan's Famous Hot Dog Eating Contest is an annual event that

famous is probably found in the Sherlock Holmes adventure *The Hound of the Baskervilles* by Sir Arthur Conan Doyle.
11. *Wiener* is Austrian for 'Viennese', which is why some hot dog sausages are called wieners to this day.

takes place on July 4th in Coney Island, New York. Tradition has it that the origin of the competition can be traced to 1916 when four immigrants staged an impromptu hot dog-eating contest at the site of the first Nathan's Famous Hot Dog stand to settle an argument about who was the most patriotic.[12] After 12 minutes, James Mullen had eaten 13 hot dogs and was crowned the victor. A 12-minute contest has been held on the site on Independence Day every year since (although it changed to ten minutes in 2008). The mustard-coloured champion's belt[13] is currently held by the excellently named Joey Chestnut, who has won every competition since 2007. His current record is a gut-busting 68 hotdogs (2012) in ten minutes... and that includes the bread buns. In 2011, a separate women's competition was inaugurated and was won by Sonya Thomas who ate 40 hotdogs in the required time. She also won in 2012 with 45.

'Hot dog, jumping frog, Albuquerque' (sung twice) is the rather odd chorus of the 1988 hit song 'The King of Rock and Roll' by Prefab Sprout. The somewhat surprising lyric has since become a common **mondegreen** with people singing things like 'almond cookie' or 'Albert Turkey' instead of Albuquerque.[14] A mondegreen is a misheard phrase or lyric. It is named after a line in the ballad 'The Bonny Earl O'Moray' that should have been, 'And laid him on the green' but which was often misheard as 'And Lady Mondegreen'. The term was coined by American writer Sylvia Wright.[15]

Talk of frogs, jumping or otherwise, brings us to *Phyllobates terribilis*, the **golden poison-dart frog.** There is enough poison in one small frog to potentially kill at least two elephants, ten people or 10,000 mice. Their skin produces a poison called a batrachotoxin

12. Although veteran publicist Mortimer Matz claims that he invented the idea with a friend, Max Rosey. Nathan's admit that they have no records of such an event before the 1970s.

13. Contestants also win two crates of hot dogs and $10,000.

14. Albuquerque is the largest city in the US state New Mexico and is named after Don Francisco Fernández de la Cueva, Duke of Alburquerque (Spain) and viceroy of New Spain (New Mexico) from 1653 to 1660.

15. There is an urban myth that Prefab Sprout's name is also a mondegreen. Various sources state that the band was named after the opening line of Nancy Sinatra's and Lee Hazelwood's 1967 hit single, 'Jackson'. It's said that Sprout frontman Paddy McAloon misheard the line 'We got married in a fever, hotter than a pepper sprout' as 'hotter than a prefab sprout'. He didn't. He simply made the name up along with other rejected possibles like Chrysalis Cognosci, Dry Axe and The Village Bus.

that affects the nerves, heart and repiratory systems. The Embre and Choco Indians from Colombia use the poison for their blowgun darts. Once a dart is poisoned it remains lethal for up to two years.

This is not the only dangerous chemical produced by an amphibian. The Colorado river toad, or Sonoran desert toad (*Bufo alvarius*) from the Southwestern USA and northern Mexico produces a psychoactive called 5-MeO-DMT (a tryptamine related to seratonin, melatonin and the psylocibin found in so-called 'magic mushrooms') and bufotenin, a chemical that can produce an hallucinogenic effect similar to **LSD**.

LSD or lysergic acid diethylamide was a popular drug during the 1960s and 1970s when many prominent self-experimenting artists and musicians 'dropped acid' in an attempt to enhance their creativity, spirituality and consciousness. And it may have had something to do with the curious title of the 1968 single 'In-A-Gadda-Da-Vida' by **Iron Butterfly**. A commonly repeated story states that the song's title was originally 'In the Garden of Eden' but was slurred by singer Doug Ingle when he was high. However, the sleeve notes for their 'Best of' album state that drummer Ron Bushy was listening to the track through headphones, and couldn't hear the lyrics clearly and therefore wrote down what he thought he'd heard. To add to the confusion, a different set of sleeve notes (from the 1995 re-release of the *In-A-Gadda-Da-Vida* album) claims that Ingle was drunk when he first told Bushy the title. One final theory claims that that all of the above may be true but the title was supposed to be *Bhagavad Gita*, the name of a Hindu book of scripture, and nothing to do with the **Garden of Eden** at all.

There have been many claims as to the geographic location of the Garden of Eden, if indeed it ever existed at all and is not simply an allegory. Most often, it is placed in the Middle East near Mesopotamia or Israel. However, some researchers, scholars and writers have suggested locations as diverse as Adam's Peak in Sri Lanka, the Seychelles, Ethiopia and even Missouri and Florida.

The long-lived writer **Eden Phillpotts** (he was 98 when he died in 1960) was an English novelist, poet and dramatist whose work mostly centred upon Dartmoor in Devon where he lived and grew up as a child (and, hopefully, avoided the Yeth Hound). He loved the area and, for many years, was President of the Dartmoor Preservation Association. He produced 18 Dartmoor novels and two volumes of short stories. One novel, *Widecombe Fair*, became the play *The Farmer's Wife*, which was later filmed by Alfred Hitchcock. Phillpotts was a great friend of Agatha Christie[16] who encouraged him to also write mystery and horror novels (which he did under the pseudonym of Harrington Hext). Among his other friends, he counted many contemporary writers including J.M. Barrie, H. Rider Haggard, H.G. Wells, Arthur Conan Doyle, W.W. Jacobs, Hall Caine, Thomas Hardy, Israel Zangwill, Rudyard Kipling and Jerome K. Jerome. In fact, Phillpotts and Jerome co-wrote a farce with the excellent name of *The McHaggis*.

The author **Jerome K. Jerome**'s middle name was …

16. Agatha Christie may have been one of the very first people in the UK to stand up while surfing. In a recently published book of her travel diaries, *The Grand Tour* (Harper Collins 2011), she describes learning the technique in Waikiki in 1922. She says she had 'a moment of complete triumph on the day that I kept my balance and came right into shore standing upright on my board!' The only account I could find of a Briton standing up before this related to Prince Edward, also in the early 1920s.

# INVESTIGATION 2

## How do you connect **Terry Scott** to the **Battle of Marathon** and **Fennel**?

### *Terry and Chewin'*

**Fennel** (*Foeniculum vulgare*) is an edible plant with a gentle aniseed-like flavour. This can be found in its feathery shoots but is concentrated in the bulb, which can be cooked and eaten as a vegetable or used like a herb to flavour food – particularly fish. It is a primary ingredient in making the spirit Absinthe. The word 'fennel' comes from the Anglo-Saxon *fenol* or *finol* and means 'little hay' as it smells sweet and often grows in hay fields. In mediaeval times, it was used as a medicinal herb in conjunction with St John's Wort as a charm against witchcraft and other evils. It was also once said that eating fennel improves the bust and/or milk production. Modern chemistry has revealed that the plant does contain phytoestrogens that can promote growth of breast tissue so it's maybe not so much of an Old Wives' Tale after all.

In mythology, Prometheus used the stalk of a fennel plant to steal fire from the Gods of Olympus. The ancient Greeks called the plant **Marathon** and the town of Marathon – North East of Athens – took its name from the plant. It was the site of a famous battle in 490 BCE; the final battle, in fact, in a long campaign by King Darius I of Persia to conquer Greece. When the battle was won, the legend goes that a herald named Pheidippides ran from Marathon to Athens to announce the Greek victory. As he entered Athens with the cry 'Nenikékamen!' ('We were victorious!'), he suddenly dropped dead, his heart having given out after such a swift and lengthy run.[17] His extraordinary feat

---

17. Pheidippides' cry was in praise of Niké, the Greek goddess of victory – the sports shoe manufacturer is appropriately named after her. That said, the story isn't exactly true as it confuses and combines two separate sources: Herodotus' tale of

was immortalised in the 'marathon' long-distance running race, which was first staged at the 1896 Olympic Games.

The 1896 **Olympics** were the first international games to be staged in 1500 years, having been banned by the Roman Emperor Theodosius in 393 AD. They were a far cry from the huge events we know today. There were fewer sports and many of the athletes played for themselves or their clubs rather than for a national team.[18] The facilities were poor and the athletes were a mix of amateurs, professionals and people who entered solely for the sporting fun. For example, an Irishman called John Pius Boland, who was on holiday in Greece at the time, was entered for the tennis competition by a friend and ultimately won first prize. He also won the men's doubles event by selecting a German called Friedrich Traun – who was actually an 800m runner – as his partner. Boland walked away with two silver medals because silver was awarded for first, bronze for second and nothing for third. The gold/silver/bronze medal system that we know today wasn't introduced until the 1904 Olympics.

The 1904 St Louis Olympics formed part of the larger Louisiana Purchase Exposition being held in the city. The bid to host the Olympics had actually been won by Chicago but the St Louis event was so huge that it threatened to split the visitor count so the Olympic Committee agreed to its relocation.

The marathon that year was extraordinary – but for all the wrong reasons. The day was hot – over 32°C/90°F – and very humid and the entire course was wreathed in choking clouds of dust. The first man over the finishing line was New York bricklayer Fred Lorz ... but he was disqualified when officials discovered he'd completed most of the race in a car. He had dropped out after nine miles due to exhaustion and had been collected by his manager. According to one source, he was actually going to collect his clothes when he walked past the

Pheidippedes who ran between Athens and Sparta, and Plutarch's story of a soldier who marched the 26 miles between Marathon and Athens. The legend as we know it was popularised by Robert Browning in his poem *Pheidippides*.

18. Some sports have since fallen by the wayside. The Olympics no longer boast live pigeon shooting, pistol duelling, tug-of-war, club swinging, rope climbing or long jump for horses events. Between 1912 and 1952 there were also medals awarded for literature, architecture, music, painting and sculpture. They were dropped when the Olympics went fully amateur. No one wants an amateur architect building their office block.

finishing line and was accidentally hailed as the winner. However, another states that Alice Roosevelt, daughter of President Theodore Roosevelt, was just about to award him his prize when the truth was revealed. Lorz then claimed he had never really intended to accept the prize and that he had only crossed the finishing line 'as a joke'.[19] So the prize then went to British-born Thomas Hicks, who'd nearly died in the attempt. About ten miles from the finishing line, Hicks had begged his trainers to let him stop running as he needed a rest. Rather than pop him in a car, they gave him a dose of strychnine sulphate mixed with raw egg white and brandy instead. Strychnine was often used, in small doses, as a stimulant. In larger doses, however, it is also used as rat poison. Regular doses continued to be administered for the rest of the race and Hicks was eventually carried across the finishing line, very close to death. It took the efforts of four doctors to revive him enough to leave the stadium. As it was, he fell asleep on a trolley during the awards ceremony.

Another runner was a Cuban postman called Felix Carvajal. He raised the money to get to America by pleading for donations but then lost it all en route in a craps game in New Orleans. He got to St Louis by hitching a lift but had no money for running gear, so the marathon was put back by several minutes to give him time to cut the sleeves off his shirt and the legs off his trousers. During the race, he ate some apples from an orchard that turned out to be rotten and eventually came in fourth, doubled over with stomach cramps. The marathon also boasted the first two black African Olympic runners although they were not officially competitors. They were actually part of the Boer War cultural exhibit at the Exposition. That said, Jan Mashiani came in 12th and Len Taunyane came in 9th and might have done even better had he not been chased almost a mile off course by aggressive dogs.

The word 'marathon' is now used to describe any long-distance running race. Many are held around the world every year but perhaps the best known take place in New York, which began in 1970, and London, which began in 1981. Both races attract around 40,000 runners per year, the majority of which are running to raise money for charity. A marathon covers a distance of 26 miles and 385 yards. This curious distance was set at the 1908 Olympics in the UK when

19. He did, however, go on to win the 1905 Boston Marathon.

the additional yardage was reduced from 585 yards so that Queen Alexandra and others could clearly see the finishing line.

Marathon was also the name originally given to the British version of the American **Snickers** bar, produced by the Mars confectionary company. The Marathon Bar had its name changed to Snickers in 1990, which brought it in line with the rest of the world.[20] The bar was named 'Snickers' after the Mars family's favourite horse. It got a chocolate coating in 1930 and has gone from strength to strength ever since, becoming the best-selling chocolate bar of all time with annual global sales of US$2 billion.[21] The reason it was originally branded Marathon in the UK is probably because Snickers sounded so close to 'knickers', a word not used so much in the USA (who favour 'panties') and still considered a bit rude in polite 1930s British society.

The name Marathon was used in the US for a braided chocolate and toffee bar very similar to what the Canadians know as a Cadbury's Wig Wag and what we in the UK call a Cadbury's **Curly Wurly**. The first British Curly Wurly TV adverts featured comedian **Terry Scott** dressed as a schoolboy – a cheeky character he created for his 1962 novelty song *My Brother* (aka *My Bruvva*).

Terry Scott was a veteran of many British comedy films during the 1960s and 70s and starred in seven of the *Carry On* films. In the 1980s, he achieved further fame as the voice of Penfold, idiot sidekick of the animated super spy Danger Mouse.[22] But most famously, he was partnered with screen wife June Whitfield in two long-running British sitcoms, *Happy Ever After* and *Terry and June*.

*Terry and June*'s depiction of bland suburbia and use of gentle and predictable jokes made it an easy target for people who liked their comedy a bit more 'edgy'. However, the show regularly pulled in audiences of ten million or more; three times the ratings of its more alternative competitors. Sixty-five episodes and four Christmas

---

20. There was a trade-off for this; the bar that had been known as Raider elsewhere got to be renamed globally as Twix. Not a bad swap.

21. At the start, its main rival was a very similar bar produced by the Sperry Candy Company called, bizarrely, the Chicken Dinner Bar because it filled you up like a full cooked meal. The name may have contributed to its demise.

22. Penfold's first name was Ernest and he was a hamster. Dangermouse's boss, Colonel K, was a chinchilla and DM's iconic eye-patch was an affectation and 'part of the uniform'. He had sight in both eyes.

specials were made and a movie was planned but, for various reasons, never happened. Throughout them all, Terry Scott portrayed bumbling middle class Terry Medford from Purley in Surrey, who worked for Playsafe Fire Extinguishers and Appliances. The head of the company was the bombastic Sir Dennis Hodge (played by Reginald Marsh). Hodge's long-suffering secretary was played by Joanna Henderson and was called Nora or, as she was most commonly referred to, Miss Fennel.

Fennel (*Foeniculum vulgare*) is an edible plant...

# INVESTIGATION 3

How do you connect **naturism** to
**cannibalism** and
**Sigue Sigue Sputnik**?

## *Yummy Yummy Yummy I got Man in my Tummy*

The term 'cannibal' describes a living thing that eats members of its
own species. Many animals and plants indulge in **cannibalism**, and
we humans are no exception. It was certainly practiced by some
ancient societies and rumours persist to this day of such things going
on.[23] Human cannibalism is more properly called *anthropophagy*.

The word 'cannibal' comes from Columbus's early voyages to the
Lesser Antilles (part of the West Indies) where he suspected that the
local Carib people ate human flesh. Some confusion between the
spelling and pronunciation of Carib – the letters 'R' and 'N' were
interchangeable to a degree – mixed with the Spanish word *canibales*
(meaning 'thirsty and cruel') led to the term 'cannibal' appearing.

There are allegations of regular cannibalism in the UK within
recorded history. In the 13th-century chronicles known as the
*Trioedd Ynys Prydein* or *Welsh Triads*,[24] the Saxon King Ethelfrith is
said to have encouraged cannibalism at his court. One courtier called
Gwrgi was said to have developed such a taste for it that he wouldn't
eat anything else. It was his custom to have a 'male and female Kymry
[or Cymry – a Welsh person] killed for his own eating every day,
except Saturday, when he slaughtered two of each, in order to be
spared the sin of breaking the Sabbath'. And in 1339, when a large

---

23. In her excellent book *Stiff* (Penguin 2003), Mary Roach investigates several modern
    cannibalism stories including some from China where it's alleged that people have
    surrendered parts of themselves to be turned into medicine for relatives. She also
    chases up the macabre story of a mortuary assistant who sold dead people's but-
    tocks to be made into dumplings ...
24. Sadly, not a Cardiff-based Yakuza.

part of Scotland had been desolated by the armies of Edward III, there were allegations of hungry Scots who, 'when hunting in the woods, preferred the shepherd to his flocks'.

So what does human meat taste like? The most commonly reported description is that it's similar to pork. Certainly, the local word that cannibal Polynesian islanders once used for white men translates as 'Long Pig'. And, in 2006, researchers at NEC System technologies and Mie University, Japan, unveiled a robot that seemed to back this claim. The robot can taste and identify a whole range of flavours and the ultimate aim is to produce a machine so accurate that it can identify individual vintages of wine. At present it can identify cheeses, meats and some other flavours. When a reporter placed his hand in the robot's mouth it identified the 'food' as bacon. When a photographer repeated the action, his hand was identified as prosciutto ham.

Cannibalism is a common theme in popular culture. The name of Shakespeare's monster *Caliban* (from *The Tempest*) is a misspelled anagram.[25] Hannibal 'the cannibal' Lecter is the villainous star of several books by Thomas Harris and a string of successful movies. State-controlled industrial-scale cannibalism is the central theme of the 1973 film *Soylent Green*. Set in a dystopian future where resources are few and global warming has gone mad, the hero, played by Charlton Heston, discovers that the government has solved food shortages by recycling the dead as a protein rich food tablet which is then issued to the people. And cannibalism of a far more gruesome kind was exhibited in the story of **Sweeney Todd**, the 'demon barber of Fleet Street'. After murdering his victims and robbing them, Todd's sidekick Mrs Lovett would carve them up and use the meat in pies that were then fed to the unwitting public. Sweeney Todd is a fictional character who first appeared in a Victorian 'penny dreadful'[26] serial called 'The String of Pearls: A Romance' in 1846–1847. Although exact authorship is unknown, it was probably written, in

25. The Elizabethans had no dictionaries or rules to standardise spelling. Therefore, they spelled things as they sounded – and that varied from accent to accent. Shakespeare famously spelled his own name several different ways and it turns up on registers and legal documents in a blizzard of variants. They include: *Shakesspere, Shaksper, Shakysper, Shaxpeer, Schakespeire, Shackper, Shexpere, Shaxkspere, Shakspeyre, Shakespere, Shakspeare, Shakspere, Shackspeare* and *Shakespeare*.
26. The magazine in question was Edward Lloyd's *The People's Periodical and Family Library*, issues 7–24, November 21st 1846 to March 20th 1847.

alternating episodes, by James Malcolm Rymer and Thomas Peckett Prest.

Sweeney Todd is Cockney Rhyming Slang for 'Flying Squad', a branch of the police concerned with tackling armed robberies and other serious organised crime. The 1970s TV series *The Sweeney* made household names of Dennis Waterman and the late John Thaw and was one of the first 'warts and all' British police shows that portrayed coppers as fallible human beings. The series won many awards and spawned two feature films and a 2012 remake staring Ray Winstone[27] as DI Jack Regan and Ben Drew (better known as musician Plan B) as DS George Carter.

During the opening credits for series 1 to 3, a set of fingerprints is clearly seen displayed behind Sweeney boss Haskins's head. The prints belonged to actor and model **Pamela Green** who pioneered nudity in non-pornographic British cinema and was the lead in the controversial films *Peeping Tom* and *Naked As Nature Intended*. In the latter film, the spurious plot device of a naturist holiday in Cornwall was used to allow as much on-screen nudity as possible. She was also co-founder of the glamour magazine *Kamera*. Her connection with *The Sweeney* came from her relationship with photographer Douglas Webb who created the programme's title sequence.

Before he became a photographer, Webb was in the RAF where he served as an air gunner with 49 and 617 Squadrons. In 1943, he took part in the famous **Dambusters**'s raid on the dam at Ennepe. His plane was the last to return from this legendary mission, for which he received the Distinguished Flying Medal. The raid – properly called Operation Chastise – took place on May 17th 1943 and consisted of three waves of adapted Avro Lancaster bomber aircraft targeting specific dams on the German mainland. The aircraft carried the famous 'bouncing bombs' designed by scientist **Barnes Wallis** to overcome the problem of the dams' underwater anti-submarine netting. To stand any chance of destroying the dams, the bombs had to detonate very close to the dam walls and at water level, something the netting prevented.

Barnes Wallis was a quite brilliant man and, in his time, designed airships, various types of bomb, submarine oil tankers, remote controlled vehicles and variable geometry ('swing-wing') aircraft. His

27. Winstone also played Sweeney Todd in a BBC drama in 2006.

designs led to the creation of America's General Dynamics **F-111** 'Aardvark' strategic bomber. The aircraft was retired by the US Air Force in 1996 although the Australian Air Force did not retire their F-111s until 2010. The plane was immortalised in UK rock band **Sigue Sigue Sputnik**'s 1986 hit 'Love Missile F-111'. The song was made popular by appearing in the soundtrack to the film *Ferris Bueller's Day Off.*

*Ferris Bueller's Day Off* was one the most popular comedies of the 1980s. Directed by John 'Home Alone' Hughes and starring Matthew Broderick and Jennifer Grey, it told the story of Ferris's misadventures as the result of bunking off school. Much of the comedy revolved around a borrowed Ferrari and its subsequent accidental destruction. The film spawned a short-lived TV series starring Charlie Schlatter (later to achieve success as Dr Jesse Travis in *Diagnosis Murder*) as Ferris and **Jennifer Aniston** taking the Jennifer Grey role as Ferris's sister Jeannie.

Jennifer Aniston is one of the rare few celebrities to have actually provided a voice for a character in the anarchic cartoon series *South Park.* Most celebrities are imitated – usually quite badly – and are the subjects of ridicule. Tom Cruise, for example, was taunted over allegations about his sexuality and Paris Hilton was portrayed as a depressing, alcohol-raddled, promiscuous man hunter whose pets serially commit suicide. Jennifer Aniston provided the voice of choir leader Miss Stevens in the episode *Rainforest Schmainforest.*

*South Park* was the brainchild of Trey Parker and Matt Stone, who have made a number of other animated and live action films including *Orgazmo* (1997) about a devout Mormon who becomes a porn star and *Team America: World Police* (2004). They also wrote the stage musical *The Book of Mormon* (2011) with Robert Lopez, and another based upon the life of Alferd Packer, the first man to be convicted of cannibalism in the USA. The film was *Cannibal! The Musical* (1996).

The term 'cannibal' describes a living thing ...

# INVESTIGATION 4

How do you connect **Halley's Comet** to
**DCI Gene Hunt** and
the **Goblin King** from *Labyrinth*?

## *Disaster!*

In Greek mythology **Icarus** was the son of a brilliant engineer called **Daedalus** who famously built a complex maze for King Minos at Knossos. Minos had upset the Gods and so, as punishment, they arranged for his wife Pasiphae to develop an unnatural sexual attraction to a bull. Daedalus helped her to satisfy her urges by building a hollow wooden cow for her to hide inside while the bull ... did what bulls do. The result of this bizarre union was a bull-headed child called Asterius ('Starry One') who later became known as 'Minos's Bull' or **Minotaur**. When the creature became too hard to handle, Minos had Daedalus build the labyrinth to keep it in. Some time later, Daedalus fell out of favour with Minos (understandable when you consider what he arranged for the man's wife) and was imprisoned in a tall tower on an island with his son. But he soon hit upon a plan to escape. He built a pair of wings by sewing large feathers together into a curved surface and then attaching smaller feathers with wax. After a couple of successful test flights, he built a similar pair for Icarus and soon, they were off, flying over the sea towards freedom. But Icarus got cocky and flew too high. The sun melted the wax on his wings and the feathers wore loose. He subsequently plunged into the sea and was drowned. Daedalus arrived safely in Sicily and built a temple to Apollo, and hung up his wings as an offering.

The story of Icarus and Daedalus is frequently referenced in popular culture. The Daedalus is an earth spaceship that appeared regularly in TV series *Stargate SG1* and *Stargate Atlantis*. In the original 1968 version of *Planet of the Apes*, Charlton Heston and his buddies crash-land in the future in an unnamed ship that has since become known as the Icarus among fans.[28] And Greece's Olympic Airlines paradoxically used 'Icarus' for the name of its frequent flyer program.

The story of Icarus is also used as a warning against hubris – exaggerated self-pride or over-confidence (cockiness, in other words). However that didn't stop the story inspiring an 11th-century Westcountry monk, **Eilmer of Malmesbury**, to try his own hand at man-powered flight.

According to fellow monk William of Malmesbury, Eilmer had studied mathematics and astrology and had read the fable of Icarus and Daedalus and was captivated by it. So much so that, mistaking fable for truth, he fixed wings to his hands and feet and jumped off the tower of Malmesbury Abbey in Wiltshire. He is supposed to have travelled for some 600 feet (about 1/10th of a mile) before crashing to earth and badly breaking both legs. He never quite recovered from his injuries and was lame for life. But this didn't put him off and, just a few years later, he prepared to repeat the experiment, this time with a tail attached to his wing assembly. However, when the abbot of Malmesbury found out, he banned Eilmer from all such future adventures.

Scientists seeking to understand what Eilmer achieved have noted that, had the wings stayed rigid, the airborne monk might have achieved greater distances and a safer landing. However, it is recorded that Eilmer started to flap the wings once he started losing altitude and this lost him his gliding ability. His astoundingly brave (or foolish) feat is commemorated in a 1920 stained glass window at the abbey.

Eilmer must have been an old man at the time of the Norman invasion because, in his *Gesta regum Anglorum* (Deeds of the English Kings), William of Malmesbury suggested that Eilmer had seen **Halley's Comet** (although it wasn't called that then) in both 1066 and as a young child in 989. Eilmer is supposed to have declared: 'You've come, have you? You've come, you source of tears to many mothers, you evil. I hate you! It is long since I saw you; but as I see you now you are much more terrible, for I see you brandishing the downfall of my country. I hate you!'

Eilmer reacted this way because comets were seen as omens of bad

28. The name was coined by a fan called Larry Evans in 1972 and, despite being non-canonical, is used extensively for model kits, toys and in comic adaptations.

fortune. In fact, the word disaster comes from the Latin for 'bad star' (*Aster* means 'star', as in the aster flower, the shape of an asterisk, the words 'asteroid', 'astrology', 'astronomy' and 'astronaut' and, as you saw earlier, the name Asterius). At the time of Eilmer's second sighting the comet truly did presage disaster for England with the arrival of William the Bastard (later known by the kinder title of 'The Conqueror').

Halley's Comet is a periodical comet; a large rock encrusted with ice that passes by the earth while travelling on a huge elliptical orbit that takes 74 to 79 years to complete. It last visited us in 1986 and will be back again in 2061. Its appearance has been recorded in the literature and art of many cultures including The Talmud in 66CE, the Bayeux Tapestry in 1066 and Giotto's painting of the Nativity in 1301. During the 1986 pass, close-up photographs were taken using the Giotto unmanned space probe. Two Space Shuttle missions were also planned to coincide with this visit: Mission STS-51-L was scheduled to observe the comet from earth's orbit, while mission STS-61-E was scheduled to do the same and also launch the ASTRO-1 scientific platform carrying a variety of ultraviolet and X-ray cameras to photograph the comet. Neither mission was completed for the most tragic of reasons. Mission STS-51-L became the **Challenger disaster** in which the shuttle disintegrated shortly after launch on January 28th 1986, killing all onboard. Consequently, all shuttle missions were put on hold and mission STS-61-E was cancelled. The shuttle that had been due to undertake STS-61-E was the equally ill-starred **Columbia**, which broke up on re-entry into earth's atmosphere in 2003. Again, all onboard were killed as the unique launch and return system of the shuttle did not allow for an escape system to be installed. The curse of the comet?

Various memorials exist to the crew of the Columbia, some, appropriately, not on earth. NASA named seven asteroids after the crew[29] and a range of hills on Mars were named the Columbia Hills. The landing site of the Mars rover *Spirit* was named Columbia Memorial Station and the Spirit lander carried a memorial plaque to the Columbia crew mounted on the back of its high gain antenna. One of *Spirit*'s roles was to search for evidence of life on Mars.

29. 51823 Rickhusband, 51824 Mikeanderson, 51825 Davidbrown, 51826 Kalpanachawla, 51827 Laurelclark, 51828 Ilanramon and 51829 Williemccool.

The BBC television series *Life on Mars* was hugely successful from the start. Its curious mix of sci-fi, comedy and hard-hitting detective drama was an instant hit. In the series, 21st-century Detective Inspector Sam Tyler (John Simm) is knocked down by a car and wakes to find himself back in 1973. Much of the humour and tension comes from the huge gulf between Tyler's modern political correctness and the 1973 sensibilities of Detective Chief Inspector Gene Hunt (Philip Glenister). The series owes much of its visual look and plotlines to 1970's cop series like *Special Branch* and *The Sweeney*. Curiously, there is a direct link between this time travel story and the BBC's other great time travel success, *Doctor Who*. When Matthew Graham, one of the writers, was trying to decide on the hero's surname, his daughter suggested Tyler. It was only later that he found out his daughter had picked the name after seeing Rose Tyler, The Doctor's companion played by Billie Piper, on TV. And, of course, John Simm went on to play The Doctor's arch nemesis The Master in the 2007 and 2008 seasons of *Doctor Who*. The series takes its name from the song that was playing on Tyler's iPod in 2006 and on an eight track stereo when he wakes in 1973. It was, of course, *Life on Mars* by **David Bowie**.

David Bowie is arguably one of the UK's most successful recording artists. But he has also had a successful career as an actor. He has played, among many other roles, Andy Warhol in *Basquiat* (1996), Pontius Pilate in Martin Scorcese's *The Last Temptation of Christ* (1988) and Jareth the Goblin King in *Labyrinth* (1986), which featured creatures (but no Minotaurs) produced by Jim 'Muppet' Henson's Creature Workshop. However, the roles he is most praised for are Major Jack 'Strafer' Celliers in the wartime drama *Merry Christmas Mr Lawrence* (1983) and the enigmatic being called Thomas Jerome Newton in Nicholas Roeg's *The Man Who Fell to Earth* (1976). In the latter, Bowie's character is an alien trapped on earth who is searching for a way to get water back to his dying home planet. In the film, and in Walter Tevis's original novel of the same name, there are frequent references to the legend of Icarus (hence the film's title). Newton even has a copy of Brueghel's painting *Landscape with the Fall of Icarus* on his wall as a constant visual reference.

In Greek mythology **Icarus** was ...

How do you connect **Darth Vader** to
**palm civet dung** and the
**Black Death?**

## *Mork and Monkey*

The Capuchin order of friars was formed sometime around 1525 and
was a major player in establishing Catholicism in Reformation
Europe.[30] The Capuchins wore robes with long, pointed cowls, which
is how they got their name as '**cappuccino**' means 'hood' in Italian.
The French version of the word is 'capuchin'. The friars' robes were
a rich brown – the same colour that you get when you add milk or
cream to espresso **coffee**. Hence the origin of the term 'cappuccino',
which sounds infinitely better than 'monk's hood brown'.

Coffee is grown commercially in over 40 countries but Brazil grows
the most, producing over seven billion pounds of coffee every year –
that's almost a third of all coffee produced. It has been estimated that
over 400 billion cups per annum are drunk worldwide. Originally,
coffee was touted as a medicine. It contains caffeine, which is the
stimulant that gets us going in the morning. Caffeine does no real
harm as long as you don't drink too much of it. However, just ten
grams (equivalent to 100 cups of coffee) over four hours, could kill
the average human.[31]

---

30. The Capuchin Crypt in Rome contains the skeletons of more than 4000 monks.
The walls and ceilings of the crypt itself are ghoulishly decorated with bosses and
borders made from human bones.
31. You can die from drinking too much water too quickly. Water intoxication or
*hyponatremia* can result in death because of over-dilution of sodium in the body.
Infants are very succeptible to it and, in 2007, a lady called Jennifer Strange died
while participating in a 'Hold your wee for a Wii' competition at her local KDND
radio station in Sacramento, California.

The world's most expensive coffees go through an unusual process before they get to the drinker; they are first passed through the digestive system of an animal. Black Ivory coffee, from Thailand, costs £30 per cup and £300 per pound and is made from coffee beans picked out of elephant dung. The animals are fed coffee cherries and the enzymes in their stomachs digest the outer fruit. They then break down the protein in the seed (the coffee bean), which reduces the bitterness of the flavour. Similarly priced is Kopi Luwak, which comes from the Philippines and which is harvested from the poo of the Asian **Palm civet** (*Paradoxurus hermaphroditus*).

Palm civets, badgers, raccoon dogs and other animals are often sold at street markets in Southern China – and there is some evidence that this may have been responsible for the spread of the **SARS** virus to the human population.

The SARS (Severe Acute Respiratory Syndrome) coronavirus is a bit of a mystery. It appeared as if from nowhere in 2003 and has since killed hundreds of people and infected thousands more (mainly in Asia). The virus causes symptoms that include high fever, aches, a dry cough and a shortness of breath. Current theories suggest that it mutated from a disease found only in animals and was passed to human shoppers buying live animals.

SARS is spread among people by 'droplet transmission'. When an infected person coughs or **sneezes**, they release a cloud of droplets into the air, which can then be inhaled by others. However, you need to be quite close as the large droplet size (0.5 to 5 micrometres in diameter) means that they only travel about three feet despite the explosive force of the cough or sneeze (although the virus can live for several hours on surfaces even after the droplet has dried out). About 40,000 such droplets can be produced by a single sneeze. A sneeze, or sternutation or sternutatory reflex, can exceed 155 mph.

In many cultures, a person who sneezes will be 'blessed' by those nearby – often complete strangers. The Romans used to say 'Absit omen!' (May there be no evil omen). The saying 'Bless you' may stem from an old belief that the soul leaves the body during a sneeze. A deity is therefore called upon to protect the sneezer from evil spirits while allowing time for the soul to return home. There is an alternative story that, during the 17th-century Great Plague, Pope Alexander VII passed a law requiring people to bless anyone who sneezed. At the same time, the sneezer was expected to cover their mouth with their hand or a cloth to prevent the spread of the illness.[32] The Great Plague, or Black Death, was a form of **bubonic plague**, so called because the bacterial infection causes swollen lymph nodes or buboes under the skin.

Bubo was the name chosen by pioneering stop-motion animator Ray Harryhausen for the golden mechanical owl that he built to be Perseus's companion in the 1981 film *Clash of the Titans*.[33] The name was almost certainly chosen because more than 20 species of owls, including the horned owls (America) and the eagle owls (Eurasia), belong to the genus *Bubo*. The genus gets its name not from any connection with 'swellings' but from a folk name based on the sound of its call. Many people have pointed out the similarity between the tweeting and beeping Bubo from *Clash of the Titans* and **R2-D2**, the tweeting and beeping robot in *Star Wars* who performs a similar comic sidekick role. There have even been suggestions that Harryhausen 'copied' George Lucas's character and gangs of rival fans can be quite vociferous about the subject. However, while *Star Wars* may have made it to the cinema first, *Clash of the Titans* was already in production before *Star Wars*. So which came first – the owl or the droid?

The *Star Wars* character of Darth Vader has been played by at least ten actors.[34] As Anakin Skywalker, he was played first by Jake Lloyd and then by Hayden Christensen. In Genndy Tartakovsky's animated *Clone Wars* series (2003–2005) he is voiced by Mat Lucas and in the 2008 *Clone Wars* movie and subsequent CGI series by Matt Lanter.

32. It should be noted that germs, viruses and bacteria were unknown back then. Covering the mouth would have been to prevent the transmission of evil spirits or *miasma*. People believed that disease was transmitted by smells – *miasmata* – right up until the 19th century.

33. He is given the owl by the goddess Athena who had an owl of her own. In Greek myth, her owl represented all-seeing wisdom and had no name. Bubo the mechanical owl also makes a cameo in the 2010 re-make of *Clash of the Titans*.

34. I've just listed appearances in the films and series. In some live footage used in video games and adverts, the Vader suit is worn by C Andrew Nelson. In video games he was voiced by Matt Sloan and Scott Lawrence. Brock Peters did Vader's voice in the radio dramas. Bob Anderson was Vader's stunt double and Ben Cooke was Anakin's. Sound engineer Ben Burtt provided the laboured breathing noise for Vader's suit by manipulating a recording of scuba equipment (it sounded like he had SARS ...). And then there are all of the fan movies and videos and film studio and theme park Vaders ...

As the adult Vader, he was played by 1970s 'Green Cross Man' body builder Dave Prowse and, when Vader was unmasked at the end of *Return of the Jedi*, the actor we saw was Sebastian Shaw. However, Vader's voice was provided by veteran actor **James Earl Jones** as it was felt that his deep, sonorous tones were more fitting than Prowse's West Country accent. Because Jones' lines were dubbed afterwards, Prowse was not always aware of what his character would be saying in the final edit. He certainly didn't know about the iconic 'Luke, I am your father' line uttered near the end of *The Empire Strikes Back* and stated that he was as shocked as everyone else when he saw the film at the cinema.

James Earl Jones performed a cameo of his Vader voice in the 2005 animated film *Robots*. The star of *Robots* was Ewan McGregor... who coincidentally played Anakin Skywalker's mentor, the younger Obi Wan Kenobi in *Star Wars* Episodes 1, 2 and 3. *Robots* also starred prolific comedian and actor **Robin Williams** who shot to fame as the alien Mork in the *Happy Days* TV series and the spin-off *Mork and Mindy* series with Pam Dawber.

In 2006 Williams played a living waxwork of President Theodore Roosevelt in the comedy movie *Night at the Museum* and its sequel. In the film, Ben Stiller plays the caretaker in a museum where all of the exhibits come to life once the sun goes down. His job is made all the more difficult by the mischievous actions of Dexter, a monkey from the Hall of African Mammals taxidermy exhibit. In the film Dexter is described as a **capuchin monkey** but this is an error as capuchins are from South America, not Africa.

The capuchins are a group of New World monkeys of the genus *Cebus*. They inhabit areas of Honduras, Paraguay, Peru and Brazil – where the coffee comes from. The monkeys get their name from the fur patterns on their heads that resemble the cowls worn by the Capuchin order of Roman Catholic friars.

The Capuchin order of friars was formed...

# INVESTIGATION 6

How do you connect **Buffalo Bill** to
the **French Revolution** and
**Julius Caesar**?

## *Hairy Salad? Not Tonight Josephine...*

The **Caesar salad** was first served in a bar in Tijuana, Mexico, on July 4th 1924 by its inventor, Cesare Cardini, an Italian hotelier, restaurateur and chef. The name Cesare is the Italian version of the Greek 'Caesar' and means 'long-haired' or 'hairy'.

Cesare Borgia was the son of Pope Alexander VI and his mistress Vannozza dei Cattanei. His sister was **Lucrezia Borgia** and, if historical rumour is true, Lucrezia was often a player in the machinations and crimes perpertrated by her father and notorious brother. Certainly, they arranged several of her marriages to important or powerful men in order to advance their own political ambitions. It is rumoured that Lucrezia was in possession of a hollow ring that she frequently used to poison drinks. She was commemorated in a curious way by the world famous Wild West showman and bison hunter **Buffalo Bill,** who named his favourite rifle after her because it was so deadly.

William Frederick Cody gained his famous nickname by supplying the Kansas Pacific Railroad workers with bison meat (and should, therefore, technically be called Bison Bill). Curiously, he had to fight for the right to use the nickname. William 'Billy' Averill Comstock was a grand-nephew of James Fenimore Cooper and General Custer's favourite tracker. Also known as Buffalo Bill or 'Medicine Bill', he claimed to be the best bison hunter in the USA, a fact that threatened Cody's reputation. Therefore, a shooting competition was held to decide who should be the one and only Buffalo Bill. The two men had to shoot as many bison as possible in an eight-hour period from horseback. Cody killed 69 bison to Comstock's 46 and won not only the right to exclusive use of the name but a substantial $500 wager too. Comstock's weapon was a 16-shot Henry rifle, while Cody was armed with his beloved Lucretia Borgia, an 1866 Springfield Model .50 calibre breechloading 'needle gun' rifle.[35] The likelihood is that Cody learned of Lucrezia Borgia by watching the play about her life written by Victor Hugo – author of that other great epic *Les Misérables*.

*Les Misérables* (1862) is set in the early 19th century and follows the lives of ex-convict Jean Valjean and several other characters over a 20-year period. The action ends with student revolts that mark the start of the Paris Uprising of 1832. Many important dates in Valjean's life coincide with dates in the life of **Napoleon** Bonaparte. For instance, both were born in 1769. Valjean's 19-year imprisonment matches the dates of Napoleon's rise and fall (from 1796 to 1815) and Valjean's escape attempts take place in the same years as the more important battles of Napoleon's military career.

Napoleon Bonaparte was 20 years old and already a general when the French Revolution began.[36] Ten years later, in 1799, he had risen to become ruler of France as Premier Consul of the French Republic. It was he who, on January 1st 1806, abolished the ill-fated **French Revolutionary Calendar** (or Republican Calendar).

Under the French Revolutionary Calendar, a year consisted of 12 months of 30 days each. The months were: Vendémiaire, Brumaire, Frimaire, Nivôse, Pluviôse, Ventôse, Germinal, Floréal, Prairial, Messidor, Thermidor and Fructidor. Following Fructidor every year, there were five Festival Days making the year up to 365 days. They were the Celebration of Virtue, the Celebration of Genius, the Celebration of Labour, the Celebration of Opinion and the Celebration of Rewards. Then, on Leap Years, an extra Festival called the *Jour de la Revolution* (Day of the Revolution) was added.

Each month was divided into three *décades* of ten days. The ten days of each décade were uninspiringly called Primidi, Duodi, Tridi, Quartidi, Quintidi, Sextidi, Septidi, Octidi, Nonidi and Decadi.

---

35. Lucretia was, until relatively recently, the more common spelling. However, the accepted version is now Lucrezia (pronounced loo-cret-see-ah).

36. The song that became the French national anthem, *La Marseillaise*, originated with the men of Marseilles who sang it as they marched into Paris at the start of the Revolution. The song's composer, Rouget de l'Isle, was an artillery officer who claimed that he fell asleep at a harpsichord and dreamt the words and the music.

Decadi was a day of rest. But the workers of the new republic were quick to note this meant nine working days per 'week' and only one day off, which is very probably why the calendar ultimately failed.[37]

The calendar began with the establishment of the first French Republic on September 22nd 1792 or, as it became, the 1st of Vendemiaire, Year 1 of the Republic.[38] Incidentally, the French also attempted to establish a new clock, in which the day was divided into ten hours of a hundred minutes, each with a hundred seconds – exactly 100,000 seconds per day. That failed too.

You can take decimalisation too far.

Upon abandoning the French Revolutionary Calendar, the French returned to using the Gregorian Calendar that we use today. The Gregorian system counts days as the basic unit of time, grouping them into years of 365 or 366 days. Leap Years are added because the average year length is 365.2425 days – or 365 days, 5 hours, 49 minutes and 12 seconds. The addition of February 29th every four years mops up the accumulated extra hours and minutes. Any further anomaly is dealt with by the fact that Leap Years are missed when they fall on a year that is a multiple of 100 e.g. 1900. As clumsy as this is, the Gregorian Calendar was a big improvement upon the earlier Julian Calendar. And the Julian Calendar was a massive improvement on what the Romans used before. Their calendar looked like this:

| | |
|---|---|
| Martius | (31 days) |
| Aprilis | (29 days) |
| Maius | (31 days) |
| Iunius | (29 days)[39] |
| Quintilis | (31 days) |
| Sextilis | (29 days) |
| September | (29 days) |
| October | (31 days) |

37. It's probably true to say that no one really had 'days off' in pre-industrial societies. However, a 'day of rest' for religious observances was common.
38. If you want to know today's date in the French Revolutionary Calendar, there are several websites that do the calculation for you including the excellent Fourmilab site (www.fourmilab.ch/documents/calendar) that allows you to convert today's date into the date in many different calendar systems.
39. The letter 'J' wasn't invented until the 16th century.

November  (29 days)
December  (29 days)
Ianuarius  (29 days)
Februarius (28 days)

In addition, an extra 'month' – the *Mensis Intercalaris* – was some-times inserted between the 23rd of February and the 24th making the year 377 or 378 days long. It was all quite bizarre. It was a rubbish system.

Then **Julius Caesar** came along in 46 BCE and redesigned it (or, at least, he got his advisers to redesign it). His version became known as the Julian Calendar and was very close to our present day calendar with 365 days and a leap day added to February every four years. Meanwhile, the beginning of the year was moved back several months, which explains why our modern months are now wrongly named. Anything beginning with 'octo' usually means 'eight'. Octo-ber means 8th month but is now our 10th. Similarly 'dec' means 'ten' (decimal, decathlon etc.) but December is now month 12.[40] However, despite its faults, the Julian Calendar was used for nigh on 2,000 years; a fitting tribute to Julius 'Hairy' Caesar.

The **Caesar Salad** was first served in ...

40. A curious social fossil of this is that in the UK and some other countries the financial year still begins in April.

# INVESTIGATION 7

## How do you connect **werewolves** to **Rick Wakeman** and **Facebook**?

### *Yes ... I'll have a Bacon Curry*

Six Degrees of Kevin Bacon is a game based upon the **Six Degrees of Separation** theory[41] first put forward in a short story by Hungarian writer Frigyes Karinthy in 1929. It states that every person on the planet is connected, however loosely, to every other person on the planet by a chain of six or fewer people. The concept was popularised in 1967 when Stanley Milgram, the famed American psychologist, decided to test a theory of his own that he called The Small World Effect. He randomly selected people from the Midwest of America and told them that he wanted each of them to get a letter to a complete stranger. The only information they were given was the stranger's name, occupation and general location in the USA. The method they were then asked to use was to pick a person who they thought was most likely, out of all their friends, to know the target personally, then pass the letter to that friend with instructions for them to do the same. That person would pass the letter on, and so on, and so on, until the letter was personally delivered to the intended recipient. Amazingly, a number of the letters got through. Everyone involved expected the various chains of people between sender and target to include at least a hundred or more people each. In fact, it mostly took an average of six intermediaries to get each letter deliv-

---

41. The idea for this book and its prequel grew from me noticing connections between facts while researching a book about superstition. I then turned it into a game with friends where, in the spirit of Six Degrees of Separation theory, we would challenge each other to link two apparently unconnected facts using the least possible number of other facts. From this silly but fun game the idea of *Joined-Up Thinking* and, eventually, the *Connectoscope*®, was born.

ered. The experiment has since been repeated several times with similar results.

The results aren't really so surprising. We all know approximately 150 people quite well.[42] Assuming that each of these 'friends' also has 150 friends, by mathematical progression we all have up to 22,500 possible 'friends of a friend'. If we now extend this by a further multiple, there are a potential 3,375,000 'friends of a friend of a friend'. Just one more step and the figure reaches a staggering 506,250,000 people. That's almost ten times the population of the UK and that's from a chain of only four people. Naturally, these figures are not wholly accurate as there will be some overlap in the people that you and your friends know. But even $\frac{1}{10}$th of that figure is an entire nation of connections after just four 'separations'.

Interestingly, social network Facebook suggests that there are now only three to five degrees of separation. Working with a team of researchers from a university in Milan, Italy, Facebook analysed the links between 721,000,000 of its users (that's around 10% of the world's population or 69 billion virtual friendships) and discovered that the average number of 'hops' that connect everyone is 4.74. Meanwhile, analysts at the BBC have suggested that the number is even lower. They say that Facebook's figures are skewed because they are based on global connections while 84% of all connections are between users in the same country. Therefore, if you just use the country a user lives in the degrees of separation shrink to 3.74.

The Facebook study also found that the average number of 'friends' a person has is 190, that people tend to have friends their own age, and that 84% of people think they have more friends than they do.

All of which brings us back to Six Degrees of Kevin Bacon, a game that dictates the individual **Bacon Number** of any actor. Kevin Bacon has appeared in a great many films with a wide range of different actors.[43] A person's Bacon Number is determined by linking them to

42. This is known as Dunbar's Number. British anthropologist Robin Dunbar was the first to suggest that human beings have a limit to the number of stable relationships that they are able to maintain. This has since been supported by research and evidence. Although an exact number was not specified, most scientists agree on an average of 150. In pre-industrial societies, most tribes do seem to have around 150 members all known to each other.

43. The fact that Kevin is so 'connectible' is the reason why he was chosen to front a 2012 advertising campaign for the mobile phone company EE.

the ubiquitous Mr Bacon via a chain of people and the movies in which they've appeared. The shortest chain gives the Bacon Number. For example, Steve Martin has a Bacon Number of One (BN1) as both he and Kevin Bacon appeared in *Trains, Planes and Automobiles* (1987). Meanwhile, Marilyn Monroe has a Bacon Number of Two (BN2) because, even though she died when Bacon was only four years old, she was in *The Misfits* (1961) with Eli Wallach who was in *Mystic River* (2003) with Kevin Bacon. Eli Wallach (BN1) is one step removed, Marilyn is two.

Almost anyone who has ever appeared in a movie seems to have a Bacon Number of One or Two. However, as the Oracle of Bacon (Yes, there is such a thing)[44] points out: 'About 12% of all actors cannot be linked to the rest of the movie universe, either because they have appeared only in video games or straight-to-video releases that the Oracle doesn't count, or because they have not appeared in any films with actors from the Hollywood mainstream.' Many porn stars fit this description, for example. These people cannot be connected to Kevin Bacon and therefore get a Bacon Number of Infinity (BN∞). But then there are people who have made a mainstream film but who still cannot be connected; people like the excellently named **Fred Ott** who appears in the late 19th-century films *Edison Kinetoscopic Record of a Sneeze* and *Fred Ott Holding a Bird*. As he was the only actor in those films and never made any others, he has the very rare distinction of having a Bacon Number of Zero (BN0). Don't you want to rush out now and find a copy of *Fred Ott Holding a Bird*?[45]

The name Ott is very old and has variants like Odda, Oda, Odo and Otto. It may have its origin in the Old Norse word 'odd' (point of a weapon) or the Old Germanic word 'od' meaning possessions or riches. 'OTT' is also an acronym for *Over The Top*, the name of an ITV show hosted by Chris Tarrant (BN2), Lenny Henry (BN2), Bob Carolgees (BN∞), John Gorman (BN3), Helen Atkinson-Wood (BN∞) and Alexei Sayle (BN2) in the early 1980s. *OTT* was a late-night adult version of the popular Saturday morning children's show *Tiswas*.

*Tiswas* regularly attracted as many adult viewers as children with

---

44. www.oracleofbacon.org

45. Ott may possibly be the uncredited man in Thomas Edison's 1896 film *The Kiss* also featuring actress May Irwin. If it is him, he rises to BN3.

its anarchic humour, custard-pie violence and great jokes. Soon, celebrities were queuing up to be gunged, doused, sprayed or abused by the cast or by the mysterious masked 'Phantom Flan-Flinger'. The more adult *OTT* show featured material that was often sexist (Alexei Sayle had some discomfort with this and was later replaced with, of all people, Bernard Manning [BN3]) and included topless dancers, a large breasted stripper who never quite got naked before the credits rolled, and 'The Greatest Show on Legs'; three dancing men naked but for strategically placed balloons. The show was cancelled after 12 episodes.

The show was apparently named after an elite showbiz club. **Rick Wakeman** (BN2), keyboard wizard with Prog Rock band Yes, was chairman of the Over The Top Club in the late 1970s. The president was a record plugger called Allan James (BN∞) who supplied some of the music acts for *Tiswas*. The OTT Club consisted of 20 or so hard-drinking hell-raisers who would meet for a meal and a few drinks but, as the evening wore on would exhibit more and more bad behaviour until the evening ended in ejection or, occasionally, arrest.

Wakeman was always the odd man out of Yes. He was the only non-vegetarian and didn't fall in with the band's interest in spiritual and New Age philosophies. Famously, during the *Tales from Topographic Oceans* tour, he ate a curry on stage during an extended trance-like instrumental section. It was at the Manchester Free Trade Hall, and Wakeman had little to do except an occasional keyboard twiddle. At this point, his roadie asked if he fancied a curry. Wakeman, assuming that he meant after the show, agreed. The curry arrived a short while later so Wakeman ate it on stage. 'It was chicken vindaloo, bombay aloo, popadom,' explains Wakeman, 'So I was eating away whilst Chris (Squire) and Steve (Howe) did some intricate parts. Jon (Anderson) starts sniffing the air and comes over and says "You're eating a curry!"' Following the tour, as the band began work on what would become *Relayer*, Wakeman felt further alienated from the group and was already enjoying a successful solo career so decided it was time to go. He was to rejoin the band several times in the nineties and in 2006 undertook an acoustic tour with his friend Jon Anderson (BN3). Without on-stage curries.

Wakeman is a self-confessed former alcoholic and suffered several heart attacks in his twenties. The first occurred just after he left Yes in early 1974, during the release of his solo album *Journey to the*

*Centre of the Earth*. He is now a committed Christian. He was married for 20 years to ex-Page Three model **Nina Carter** (BN2).

Nina Carter was born Penny Mallett on October 4th 1952. She made regular appearances on Page Three of the *Sun* newspaper and in the softcore *Mayfair* magazine. In the 1980s, she teamed up with fellow glamour model Jilly Johnson (BN3) to form the pop duo Blonde on Blonde. Carter had a brief cameo in the movie *An American Werewolf in London* when she is seen on television in a newspaper advertisement – 'The Naked Truth About Naughty Nina'. Other cameos in the film included ex-wrestler Brian Glover (BN2) and comedian Rik Mayall (BN2) – who would later appear in the anarchic TV sitcom *The Young Ones* with Alexei Sayle from *OTT*. The film was directed by John Landis (BN1) and produced by Lycanthrope Productions.

**Lycanthropy** is the ability or power of a human being to transform into a wolf. It is a term sometimes used for any human/animal transformation but that is more properly called *Therianthropy* or *Zoanthropy*. The term 'Lycanthrope' comes from the story of canniballistic King Lycaon of **Arcadia** who was turned into a wolf for attempting to disprove Zeus' divinity by serving the god with the cooked flesh of his own son.

Arcadia is a rural area of central Greece which includes present-day Tripolis where you will find Mount Lycaeum, one of the reported birth-places of Zeus. Because of the relaxed, pastoral country lifestyle of the area, the term 'Arcadian' has become synonymous with *Paradise* or *Utopia*, meaning a peaceful, uncomplicated, even perfect existence.

Arcadia was the name chosen by ex-**Duran Duran** members Simon LeBon (BN∞), Roger Taylor (BN∞) and Nick Rhodes (BN2) for their 1985 electro-pop band. They released only one album called *So Red the Rose*. Duran Duran took their name from a character in the 1968 Roger Vadim (BN2) film *Barbarella, Queen of the Galaxy* (in turn based upon the French comic book created by Jean-Claude Forest).[46] Professor Durand Durand was played by Milo O'Shea (BN2). He later reprised his role on stage with the band during their 1985 *Arena*

---

46. The experimental electronica duo Matmos, who have recorded and performed with artists such as Björk (BN2) took their name from the seething liquid entity that lived below the city of Sogo in *Barbarella*.

tour and film. The film starred Jane Fonda as the eponymous heroine. She has a Bacon Number of Two (BN2) by virtue of appearing in *Agnes of God* (1985) with Deborah Grover (BN1) who was in *Cavedweller* (2004) with Kevin Bacon.

Six Degrees of Kevin Bacon is a game ...

# INVESTIGATION 8

How do you connect the **Milky Way** to
**The Three Musketeers** and the
death of the dinosaurs?

## *All for One and One for MEE*

When the committee of **l'Académie Française** was updating its dictionary of the French language, it defined a crayfish as 'a red fish which walks backwards'. The definition was run past the naturalist and zoologist **Georges Cuvier** for his approval. His reply was, 'I will make one small observation in natural history. The crayfish is not a fish, it is not red, and it does not walk backward. With these exceptions your definition is excellent.'[47]

Baron Georges Léopold Chrétien Frédéric Dagobert Cuvier was instrumental in establishing the fields of modern comparative anatomy and palaeontology by comparing living animals with each other and with fossils. It was Cuvier who first classified animals into branches – four at first: *Vertebrata* (animals with backbones), *Articulata* (jointed animals like insects, spiders, crabs and segmented worms), *Mollusca* (snails, bivalves, etc.) and *Radiata* (starfish, sea urchins, etc.). These classifications have since been considerably amended and expanded. Cuvier's work became a cornerstone for later work by people like Charles Darwin, Alfred Russell Wallace and Charles Lyell in that he identified that function determines form; not the other way round.

47. The most common telling of this story features a crab instead of a crayfish. However, the oldest version of the story I have found dates from 1844 (just 12 years after Cuvier's death) and is published in French in the annual of the Société Archéologique et Historique des Côtes-du-Nord. It uses the word *ecrevisse* (crayfish) and not *crabe* (crab). Many versions of the story also state that the disputed definition was for the first dictionary produced by l'Academie. This would be impossible as that was published in 1694 and Cuvier wasn't born until 1769. It would most likely have been the 6th edition (1835) published three years after Cuvier's death.

Cuvier's other great contribution to science was establishing the existence of extinction as a fact. Fossils had been accepted for some time as the remains of once-living plants and animals. But, until Cuvier, people had had a problem accepting the idea that God had firstly created all things and pronounced them good, but then allowed whole species to be wiped out. Much carnage was attributed to The Great Flood but that didn't explain why some fossils looked like creatures that no longer existed. After all, Noah was supposed to have kept representatives of every species safe on his ark. Cuvier suggested the idea of periodic 'revolutions' during which a great many species were wiped out by natural causes. These days we know such revolutions as **Mass Extinction Events** (MEE) or Extinction Level Events (ELE).

An MEE (or ELE) is when a large number of species suddenly disappear in a short period of time without evolving into new forms. The normal rate of extinction is approximately two to five families of animals every million years (a family consists of a number of related species, e.g. all types of ants or cats). In a Mass Extinction Event thousands of species disappear. The most well-known MEE was the K-Pg Extinction (formerly known as the K-T Extinction) of 65.5 million years ago that killed off 70% of all life on Earth.[48] This included all of the great sea reptiles, the flying pterosaurs, the ammonites, the marsupials in the northern hemisphere, many species of birds and mammals and, of course, nearly all of the dinosaurs.[49]

There have been a number of MEEs since life began on Earth, several of which can be seen in the fossil record. Older MEEs are harder to prove as life back then was soft-bodied and it tends to be hard items like bones, teeth and shells that fossilise. Some scientists believe that there may have been as many as 25 MEEs in the past 540 million years, but more conservative estimates put the figure as low as five.

So what causes a mass extinction? In the case of the K-Pg Extinction,

48. K-Pg stands for Cretaceous-Paleogene (K being the abbreviation of *Kreide*, the German term for the Cretaceous). Formerly, the term Cretaceous-Tertiary (K-T) was used but the term 'Tertiary' (meaning 65 to 2.6 million years ago) is no longer used as a formal unit by the International Commission on Stratigraphy.
49. It is now accepted that birds are a branch of the dinosaur family tree as many species of feathered dinosaur fossils have now been found, especially in China. Therefore, it can be argued that it was only the 'non-avian dinosaurs' that became extinct.

current best theories suggest that it was caused by a meteor hitting the earth, probably at Chicxulub (pronounced *Chicks-ah-lube*) on the Yucatan Peninsula, Mexico. But other MEEs could have been caused by the earth passing through clouds of interstellar gas, climate change, cosmic rays, exploding stars, increased volcanic activity, global warming or a combination of several factors. One thing that it probably wasn't was a blast of gamma radiation. For many years it was suspected that this was the cause of MEEs, but recent research suggests that the probability of such an event occurring in our galaxy is very low. Gamma-ray bursts – the most powerful explosions in the universe – only tend to occur in small galaxies that are low in metallic elements. And the galaxy we live in – the **Milky Way** – has lots of heavy metals.

In other cultures the Milky Way is called The Hay Merchants' Way (Arabic), The Straw Thief's Way (Armenian), The Road to Santiago (Catalan), The Way the Dog Ran Away (Cherokee), the Silver River (Chinese), the Deer Jump (Georgian), the Fair Cow's Path (Irish) and the Way of the White Elephant (Thai), to list just a few.

Milky Way is also the British name of a popular chocolate bar made by the Mars confectionary company and consists of a light nougat covered in chocolate and marketed as 'the sweet you can eat between meals without ruining your appetite'. The bar was first produced in 1923 in the USA and was called the 3 Musketeers bar, a name it has kept there until the present day.[50]

In the novel **The Three Musketeers** (*Les Trois Mousquetaires*) by Alexandre Dumas, the musketeers in question – Aramis, Porthos and Athos – are joined by the young and inexperienced d'Artagnan who wants to become a musketeer too. Dumas continued the story of d'Artagnan in *Twenty Years After* and *The Vicomte de Bragelonne*. All three books featured a host of real historical characters including King Louis XIII, his wife Anne and **Cardinal Richelieu**.

Cardinal Armand Jean du Plessis de Richelieu was King Louis XIII's chief minister and is considered by many to be the first ever prime minister. He consolidated the power of the king and crushed anyone who opposed the crown. By restraining the power of the

---

50. The bar comes in four varieties including a fun size bar. 'Fun-sized' chocolate bars arrived in the UK during the 1980s but they were invented in the USA in the 1960s for the benefit of trick or treaters on Halloween Night.

nobility and bringing them under a single leader, he transformed France into a stronger nation. He also founded l'Académie Française, an eminent body of intellectuals to oversee the purity of the French language and culture. It was officially established in 1635 but was suspended in 1793 during the French Revolution. It was re-established in 1803 by Napoleon Bonaparte.

L'Académie consists of 40 Immortels who are elected by existing members when a position becomes free. Cuvier was elected as an Immortel in 1818 and remained so until his death (Immortels hold their positions for life unless dismissed for misconduct). Part of the work of l'Académie is to publish the official dictionary of the French language.

When the committee of **l'Académie Française** was updating its dictionary...

# INVESTIGATION 9

How do you connect **polar bears** to
**shopping trolleys** and
**The Six Million Dollar Man?**

## *Oranges and Linnaeans*

When **Leo Tolstoy** and his brother were children, they created a club
with a peculiar initiation ceremony. In order to become a member,
you had to stand in a corner for a half an hour and not think of anything **white**. But how would you know?

White is a very curious thing. Is it a colour or not? A scientist might
tell you that it is a colour because it's formed by blending the three
primary colours of light: red, green and blue. Black, meanwhile,
wouldn't be a colour as it results from a complete absence of light.
However, an artist would say that black is a colour because it can be
mixed using other colours, but white isn't because you cannot make
it by mixing; white is a lack of pigmentation and many things are
made white by bleaching away the colour (e.g. paper). This is why
white and black are sometimes called 'achromatic' colours – colours
without colour.

Physical objects that are 'white' are generally not white at all;
rather, they reflect back all of the colours of the spectrum, which the
eye blends into white. A polar bear's fur, for example, is actually
transparent, each hair being a hollow tube.[51] It's the same story for
things like sugar, snow, clouds etc. They have no physical colour; they
are transparent. Our eyes create the 'white'. White paints and other

---

51. Captive polar bears occasionally turn green. It happened recently at Higashiyama
    Zoo in Tokyo and at the Singapore Zoo. It is caused by a form of algae that lives in
    their swimming pools (usually fresh water) that gets inside the hollow hairs. The
    warm humid weather causes it to grow very rapidly. However, the algae is harmless
    and is easily dealt with using salt water, which kills it. That's why sea-dwelling polar
    bears stay white. Or look white to us anyway.

pigments are created by taking highly refractive substances and suspending them in a binder agent.

'White' is also the wholly inadequate descriptor for caucasian people – just as 'black', 'yellow' and 'red' are also inadequate and innaccurate skin colours. This state of affairs arose partly from the fact that many of the colours we know today were only named in the past few hundred years. For example, in the older Celtic languages of Wales, Cornwall and Brittany, the word *glas* could mean blue or green or a grayish version of either as there was no distinction made between them. *Glas* was simply 'the colour of the sea'.[52] Mauve only appeared as recently as 1856. Pink appeared in the 17th century. Orange is first recorded in 1512. Brown has been around since 1000 CE but its many variants – burnt umber, bronze, taupe, liver, bistre, sepia, auburn, sienna, chestnut, etc. – are all relatively recent inventions.[53]

Anthropologists during The Enlightenment (which began in the mid-1600s) defined five human races: Yellows (East Asians), Reds (Native Americans), Whites (Europeans), Browns (indigenous Australians, Asian Indians, Southeast Asians like Malays, Filipinos, Indonesians, Hispanics and Thais) and Blacks (Africans). Before this, Linnaeus had suggested just four races: white, yellow, red and black.

Carl von Linné, or **Carolus Linnaeus** as he called himself in Latin, was the father of modern taxonomy – the biological classification labels we use to identify individual species. It was his idea to define each individual species by way of a family name and a species name. Therefore, all bears can be shown to be related by belonging to the family *Ursus*, and the Polar Bear (*Ursus Maritimus*) can be differentiated from the Brown Bear (*Ursus Arctos*). And a subspecies of Brown Bear – the Grizzly Bear – becomes *Ursus Arctos Horribilis*. There is a handy mnemonic that you can use to remember the various levels of Linnaean Classification: *King Philip Came Over From Greece Singing Songs*. Here it is, using the African wildcat as an example:

---

52. Modern Welsh now makes the distinction of *glas* as blue and *gwyrdd* as green.
53. Some once popular paint colours now seem to have disappeared. They include Realgar (a kind of orange), Smalt (a kind of blue), Feldgrau (Nazi uniform grey) and Caput Mortuum (a kind of brown made from ground-up Egyptian mummies).

| King | Kingdom | *Animalia* |
|------|---------|-----------|
| Philip | Phylum | *Chordata* (sub-phylum *Vertebrata*) |
| Came | Class | *Mammalia* |
| Over | Order | *Carnivora* |
| From | Family | *Felidae* |
| Greece | Genus | *Felis* |
| Singing | Species | *Felis Silvestris* |
| Songs | Sub-species | *Felis Silvestris Lybica* |

Quite which King Philip this mnemonic refers to is unknown. Queen Elizabeth II's husband certainly came over from Greece but, as the consort of a reigning female monarch, his title is Prince Philip. Maybe it refers to King Phillip II of Spain or any of the King Philips of Macedon?

**King Philip II of Macedon,** who ruled from 359 BCE until his assassination in 336 BCE, was the father of Alexander the Great, Philip III Arrhidaeus and possibly Ptolemy I, founder of the Ptolemaic dynasty of Egypt, although this is disputed.

**Ptolemy Elrington** is an award-winning Brighton-based artist known chiefly for his ability to transform refuse into fine art. He creates dynamic, realistic and anatomically correct fish from discarded hubcaps. He turns broken electrical goods into biplanes and jet fighters. And he transforms abandoned **shopping trolleys** pulled from rivers into dragonflies, frogs, water voles and herons.[54]

Shopping trolleys, or shopping carts, or shopping carriages, first appeared in the 1930s. There are several contenders for first use but one of the better known is Sylvan Goldman who used them for the very first time on June 4th 1937 at the brilliantly named Piggly-Wiggly supermarket chain in Oklahoma City. Goldman claimed they were his invention (though he was a notorious self-publicist) and employed a mechanic called Fred Young to build them, based upon the design of a wooden folding chair. They built a prototype with a metal frame and added wheels and wire baskets. Not long afterwards, Arthur Kosted developed a way of mass-producing the trolleys on an assembly line. They did not catch on immediately as men found them effiminate and women thought they were too similar to a pram (which made younger unmarried women in particular feel uncom-

54. www.hubcapcreatures.com

fortable). But ultimately, the practicality of trolleys became apparent and Goldman went on to become a multi-millionaire.

The name Goldman may have its origins in mediaeval England. It could mean 'goldsmith' or it may be descriptive of someone's hair colour as *golda* originally meant 'fair'. Another theory states that it may derive from the Yiddish woman's name *Golde* as it is a popular Jewish surname. It may also be an Anglicised version of German family names such as *Goltmann*, *Geldman* or *Coltman*. It is the 868th most common surname in North America.

Oscar Goldman (played by Richard Anderson) was the government agent who authorised the specialised 'bionic' implants and replacement limbs to be given to Steve Austin and Jaimie Sommers – *The Six Million Dollar Man* and *The Bionic Woman* respectively. These popular 1970s television series, based on the novel *Cyborg* by Martin Caidin, featured cybernetic organisms – humans augmented with electronic or mechanical prosthetics – as agents working for the US Secret Service. Jaimie Sommers was played by Lindsay Wagner and Steve Austin was played by Lee Majors who subsequently became a pop culture icon of the 1970s. An image of Austin appears in a mosaic by artist Eduardo Paolozzi on the walls of the 'rotunda' area of Tottenham Court Road Tube Station in London. This station can be found at St Giles' Circus at the meeting of four major streets: Oxford Street, New Oxford Street, Tottenham Court Road and Charing Cross Road.

The **Charing Cross** area is considered to be the absolute centre of London and is marked by Charing Cross railway station and the *Eleanor Cross*; a monument that King Edward I built for his wife, Eleanor of Castile. A 100-metre-long mural (designed by David Gentleman) runs along the Northern Line platforms at Charing Cross underground station and depicts scenes from Eleanor's funeral journey from Nottinghamshire to Westminster Abbey. The Jubilee Line platforms at this station are no longer in use, except as film sets. Transport for London (TfL) maintains them just for this purpose. Recently, they were used in the BBC TV series *Spooks* and the films *Creep* (2004) and *28 Weeks Later* (2007). In 2010 they were used to hold auditions for licensed London Underground buskers.

The most imposing church in the Charing Cross area is St Martin's in the Field, close to Charing Cross on the boundary of Trafalgar Square. It's a common mistake to think that this is the St Martin's mentioned in the children's rhyme *Oranges and Lemons* – some books even claim so. However, the actual church bells were at the now-derelict St Martin Orgar, most of which was destroyed during the Great Fire of 1666 (only the spire remains). The other church bells mentioned in the rhyme are: St Clement Eastcheap, St Sepulchre-without-Newgate (opposite the Old Bailey), St Leonard's Shoreditch, St Dunstan's Stepney and St Mary-le-Bow. Some believe that the rhyme relates to the shouts of tradespeople who clustered around the churches selling their wares. Others claim that the words relate to executions ('Here comes the chopper to chop off your head'), specifically the execution of King Charles I. Executions at Newgate Prison began at nine o'clock on Monday morning following the first toll of the tenor bell of St Sepulchre-without-Newgate. This does seem unlikely as the final three lines have a different metre and don't appear in earlier published versions of the rhyme. It may simply be a singalong that was created to match the tunes made by the 'change ringing' of campanologists.

There were once a lot more verses and a lot more churches included as well. They include:

> *Bull's eyes and targets say the bells of St Marg'ret's.*
> *Brickbats and tiles say the bells of St Giles'.*
> *Halfpence and farthings say the bells of St Martin's.*
> *Pancakes and fritters say the bells of St Peter's.*
> *Two sticks and an apple say the bells of Whitechapel.*
> *Pokers and tongs say the bells of St John's.*
> *Kettles and pans say the bells of St Ann's.*
> *Old Father Baldpate say the slow bells of Aldgate.*
> *You owe me ten shillings say the bells of St Helen's.*

The song often accompanied a game where pairs of players file through an tunnel of arches each made by two children facing each other, with their arms raised over their heads and clasping each other's hands. As the last three lines are sung...

> *Here comes the candle to light you to bed.*
> *Here comes the chopper to chop off your head.*
> *Chop! Chop! Chop! The last man's dead.*

... the children forming the arches drop their arms to catch the pair of children currently passing through. The captured pair are then 'out' and must form the next section of arch. As the game progresses, the number of participants dwindles as the tunnel gets longer and longer. Consequently, the game gets faster and faster as the participants have to get through the arches more quickly. Older children have sometimes used a more violent variant of this game (minus the rhyme) as a 'rite of passage' type initiation ceremony. The most common is a form of 'kicking arch' or 'tunnel of pain' where the applicant has to endure a protracted bout of kicking and kneeing as they pass through the tunnel. Success without tears means acceptance into the gang or club.

When **Leo Tolstoy** and his brother were children, they created a club ...

## INVESTIGATION 10

How do you connect **General Custer**
to **toothpaste** and
**pygmy shrews**?

## *Of Mice, Massacres and Molars*

Fifty humans could comfortably stand inside a **blue whale**'s mouth although its throat is so small that the largest thing it can swallow is about the size of a basketball. This is because, despite being around 110 feet long and 200 tons in weight, the blue whale (*Balaenoptera musculus*) feeds almost exclusively on tiny shrimp-like crustaceans called krill. It does this by swallowing huge shoals and sieving them from the water by pushing its tongue against the baleen – thick sheets of keratin arranged like the teeth of a comb – that grows around the edges of the mouth. Thus, the water is pushed out of the mouth but the krill is left behind. An adult blue whale consumes 6.5 tons of food (approximately six million individual krill) per day.

The blue whale is the biggest creature ever to have lived, as far as we know. An adult's heart weighs a ton and is the size of a Mini Cooper; a slim adult or child could slide through its aorta. Its testicles weigh half a ton each and its penis is eight feet long (however, its brain weighs just 12.5lbs). Its tongue weighs approximately about the same as half an adult **Asian elephant** (*Elephas maximus*). The young of both elephants and whales are called calves[55] and adults are called cows and bulls.

**Sitting Bull** was a Native American chief of the Sioux *Hunkpapa Lakota* tribe. His name was the English translation of his tribal name *Tatanka Lyotanka*. Following the defeat of the Sioux at the Battle of Killdeer Mountain, many Native American tribes decided to acquiesce and enter reservations. But not Sitting Bull. He was a warrior, a

55. Even their kids are huge; a blue whale calf (which can weigh 50 tons at birth) can drink 100 gallons of milk per day and gain 11lbs in weight per hour.

medicine man and a great statesman, attempting on several occasions to negotiate a peaceful truce with the white men. However, when his people were driven out of the Black Hills, a place sacred to them, by the discovery of gold in 1876, Sitting Bull refused to capitulate and declared that he would defend his people. He soon became something of a hero figure to the disheartened tribes and many started to band with him.

On June 25th 1876, the US 7th Cavalry led by General George Armstrong Custer attacked a group of tribes who were camped by the Little Big Horn River. However, Custer had seriously misjudged their numbers and capabilities. Sitting Bull had by now inspired and mobilised more than 3000 native warriors who not only held their camp but also launched a counter-attack against the soldiers on a nearby ridge, ultimately annihilating them. The victory made Sitting Bull even more of a revered figure among the Native Americans – on a par with Crazy Horse and Geronimo. The US Army, outraged by defeat and spurred on by scared settlers who feared a massacre, came back in much larger, and much more heavily-armed, numbers. Sitting Bull refused to surrender and was pushed ever northwards, eventually finding refuge in Canada where he would stay in exile for many years, steadfastly refusing all pardons offered.

He eventually did return to a much-changed America and lived for a number of years on a reservation. In time, he made friends with Buffalo Bill Cody and joined his travelling Wild West show. But even this was a small act of defiance as he would often ride around the arena hurling abuse in his own language at the American audiences while they applauded and cheered in blissful ignorance. Among the other stars of Cody's show were the real Annie Oakley and her husband Frank Butler, Gabriel Dumont and 'Calamity Jane' (Martha Jane Cannary-Burke). Buffalo Bill and his performers would re-enact the riding of the Pony Express, Indian attacks on wagon trains, and stagecoach robberies. The show typically ended with a melodramatic and rather poor taste re-enactment of Custer's Last Stand in which Cody portrayed General Custer and Sitting Bull played himself.

Around this time, Sitting Bull became interested in the **Ghost Dance** movement. This began with a Native American prophet called Wovoka who took a 'white man's name' – **Jack Wilson** – and claimed to have had a vision from God that the red man would once more rule the land. He implored all native Americans to perform the ancient circle dances – sometimes called Spirit Dances or Ghost Dances – in order to hasten the arrival of this wonderful new age. He also claimed that the native dead would rise from their graves to become part of this new 'Indian Nation'. Wilson was charismatic, credible and a clever magician, skilled at sleight of hand. He would often perform tricks for his audience including a version of the 'catching a bullet' illusion. This led to an erroneous belief among some tribes that if they followed his advice, bullets could not harm them.

While Sitting Bull is not known to have actually participated in this new pseudo-religious movement, he supported it and this scared the authorities. Some even believed he was its spiritual leader and panic set in among nearby white settlers. On December 15th 1890, government soldiers moved into Sitting Bull's reservation to arrest him. His loyal followers defended him and a short battle took place with shots being fired. In the ensuing chaos, Sitting Bull was shot in the head and killed. Many more natives also died in what became known as the Wounded Knee Massacre. Jack Wilson died in Yerington on September 20th 1932.

Two years later, influential American soul and R & B singer **Jackie Wilson** was born. He had a string of hits starting with 'Reet Petite' in 1957. In 1985, The Commodores paid tribute to him and the recently deceased Marvin Gaye by recording a song called 'Nightshift', and Van Morrison wrote and recorded a tribute song called 'Jackie Wilson Said (I'm In Heaven When You Smile)', which was later covered by Dexys Midnight Runners. When the band performed the song live on the BBC TV show *Top of the Pops* in October 1982, a large picture of darts player **Jocky Wilson** was displayed behind the performers. For some time, it was assumed to be a ghastly mistake but the band has since revealed that it was an intentional joke by them and the BBC production staff.

John Thomas 'Jocky' Wilson was a popular Scottish darts player from Kirkcaldy who won many titles in his career, most notably the British Professional Championship a record four times between 1981 and 1988 and the World Championship twice. He retired from the game in 1995 due to health problems, notably diabetes, depression and chronic obstructive pulmonary disease and died in 2012. For the final decade of his life he was a virtual recluse who lived in social housing and who refused all interviews. Wilson's other great health issue was his teeth. A self-confessed sweet addict, he claimed to have never brushed his teeth in his life (his Gran allegedly told him that 'the English poison the water'). Consequently, he had lost all of his teeth by the age of 28. He did invest in **dentures** but never got on with them. He mostly used them as a ball position marker in pool games with darts colleague and friend Eric Bristow.

US president George Washington wore dentures most of the time but, contrary to popular myth, they were not made of wood. He had sets made from ivory, hippopotamus teeth, gold and, extraordinarily, lead. At the time of his inauguration in 1790, he had only one tooth left in his head. The first European dentures date from the 15th century and were carved from bone or ivory, or made up from teeth sourced from graveyards and battlefields, or from living donors who exchanged their teeth for money.

In Western society, historical methods of cleaning teeth have included brushing with salt, soot, clay (anything with an abrasive grain helped to scour plaque away) or washing them with soap and water. The first commercially available mass-produced toothpaste was Colgate, which hit the shelves in 1873. However, a formula for toothpaste was recently found in a collection of papyrus documents at the National Library in Vienna, Austria, that dates from 4th-century Egypt. It was made from mint, salt, grains of pepper and dried iris flower ... which is quite interesting as dental scientists are only now discovering (or re-discovering) the beneficial properties of iris as an effective agent against gum disease.[56]

But the Egyptians can claim tooth care even older than that. There is documentary evidence that a chap called *Hesi-Re* was 'doctor of the tooth' to the pharaoh circa 3100 BCE. Egyptian dentistry rarely involved extraction in those days but there is evidence of fillings made from resin and chrysocolla (a copper bearing mineral) to combat 'the worm gnawing the tooth' and of holes drilled to drain abscesses. Magic was also a normal part of dentistry in those days and one of the more obscure cures for toothache was to split the body of a mouse and apply it to the side of the face where the pain was. This may have been because **mice** were sacred and associated with the Sun God.[57] In ancient Greece, the mouse was also sacred to their Sun God, Apollo,

---

56. The bulbs, leaves and stems contain a bacteria-killing poison called iridin.
57. According to Herodotus, the mouse became sacred after Sethos, a priest of King Ptah, fell asleep in the temple after praying for help against the invading forces of the Assyrian King Sennacherib (Xerxes). Sethos was told in a vision that all would

and mice were sometimes eaten by temple priests. In ancient China and some parts of India, mouse meat was considered a delicacy – albeit a frugal delicacy.

Mice (genus *Mus*) are, arguably, the most successful mammals on the planet after rats and Man. The best-known species is the common house mouse (*Mus musculus*), which is so adaptable that it can be found all over the world and happily coexisting alongside human society. The mouse is a small mammal but by no means the smallest. That honour goes to either the Etruscan **pygmy shrew** (*Suncus etruscus*) or Kitti's hog-nosed bat (*Craseonycteris thonglongyai*) depending upon what criteria you use for measurement. The pygmy shrew is the smallest mammal by mass, weighing only 0.07oz. However, it is 2.3 inches (including tail) in length while Kitti's bat, also known as the **bumblebee bat,** measures about 1.2 inches long but does weigh slightly more than the pygmy shrew. The largest mammal is, of course, the blue whale and, in order to match its mass you'd need to fill a very large bag with 457,142 pygmy shrews.[58]

Fifty humans could comfortably stand inside a **blue whale's** mouth...

be well. That night field mice gnawed the bowstrings, quivers and shield-handles of the foe, who fled upon finding themselves disarmed.

58. Such an extraordinary difference between largest and smallest is also seen in fish. The largest confirmed whale shark (*Rhincodon typus*) had a length of 41.5 feet and a weight of more than 21.5 tons although larger specimens are alleged to have been seen. Meanwhile, the smallest fish on earth is the recently discovered *Paedocypris progenetica* from Sumatra that is just 0.33 inches (7.9 millimetres) long fully grown and weighs in the region of 0.00007oz. There is a species of angler fish called *Photocorynus spiniceps* where the male is marginally smaller than *P. progenetica* but it is parasitic and cannot function as an individual animal. Also, the females are substantially larger so it cannot be said to be the smallest species. The smallest species of vertebrate is a frog – *Paedophryne amauensis* – discovered in Papua New Guinea in 2009 and described in January 2012. It is a tiny 7 to 7.7mm in length.

# INVESTIGATION II

How do you connect **Winston Churchill** to
**palindromes** and
**Finnish soapstone vendors?**

## Dammit I'm Mad

A **palindrome** is a word or sentence that is entirely reversible. Common palindromic words include: kayak, sees, toot, rotavator, gig, level, mum and refer. There is some argument over the longest palindromic word. *The Guinness Book of Records* states that it is detartrated (something that has had tartrates removed from it). However, the *Oxford English Dictionary* also suggests the onomatopoeic word tattarrattat, coined by James Joyce in *Ulysses* to denote a staccato knock on a door. Other excellent examples include redivider, kinnikinnik (a type of tobacco substitute), deleveled and Malayalam (an Indian language).

The Finnish language boasts the world's longest palindromic word still in use, which is saippuakivikauppias; a 'soapstone vendor' (I wonder if the reason it's still in use is because it is the longest palindromic word?). In Dutch we find koortsmeetsysteemstrook, a rather obscure term for a measuring strip used in calculating the severity of fevers, and Estonia offers us kuulilennuteetunneliluuk – a bullet flightway tunnel hatch, whatever that is. No one (that I can find a record of) has ever been terrified by palindromes but if they were, it has been suggested that they'd suffer from aibohphobia.[59]

Palindromic sentences are difficult to create without the sentence becoming nonsensical or non-grammatical. Here are just a few of the

---

59. Coined as a joke for the *Devil's DP Dictionary* (McGraw-Hill, 1981) by Stan Kelly-Bootle that listed cynical definitions of terms related to people working in the computer and data processing industry. It was later republished as *The Computer Contradictionary*. The inspiration was Ambrose Bierce's bestselling *Devil's Dictionary* (Arthur F. Bird, 1906).

better ones:

> He lived as a devil, eh?
> A Toyota's a Toyota!
> Was it a rat I saw?
> Ma is as selfless as I am.
> Madam, in Eden, I'm Adam.
> Nurse, I spy gypsies. Run!
> Stressed? Desserts!
> Rats live on no evil star.

But people have written longer pieces. Comedian Demetri Martin wrote a 224-word palindromic poem called *Dammit I'm mad* that does make grammatical sense and has no made-up words and Will Thomas wrote a 5000-word palindromic story called *A Gassy, Obese Boy's Saga*. And in 1986 Lawrence Levine wrote a 31,957-word novel called *Dr Awkward & Olson in Oslo: A Palindromic Novel*. But the daddy is the novel *Satire: Veritas* by David Stephens (1980) which contains over 50,000 words. According to his grandson, Daniel, Stephens has 'added to it fairly considerably over the years' and hopes to publish the expanded version in the near future.

The term 'palindrome' was coined by English writer **Ben Jonson** in the 1600s from the Latin *palin* (meaning 'back') and *dromos* (meaning 'direction'). Jonson had an extraordinary life. He was a bricklayer and a soldier but neither career suited him. He then joined the theatre with Philip Henslowe's company in London as an actor and playwright … and was almost immediately imprisoned for participating in a 'seditious satire' called *The Island of Dogs* in 1597. A year later, he killed a fellow actor, Gabriel Spencer, in a duel and was tried for murder. He was released from prison by forfeiting of all his possessions, and with a felon's brand on his thumb. He then wrote a second play called *Every Man in His Humour*, which was performed in 1598 at the Globe Theatre. Among the cast was a young actor called William Shakespeare. The play was a hit and Jonson followed it with others that made him a celebrity. Soon he was writing for the crown and was given the post of Court Poet. His most enduring works are his comedies written between 1605 and 1614, such as *Volpone – or The Fox*, *The Alchemist* and *Bartholomew Fair*.

Jonson was appointed City Chronologer of London in 1628, the same year in which he suffered a severe stroke. He died on August 6th 1637 and was buried in **Westminster Abbey** under a plain slab. The words, 'O Rare Ben Jonson!' were carved on it later. Other famous people interred at the Abbey include three King Henrys, five Edwards, a couple of Queen Marys, an Elizabeth or two, a Charles, a Richard, a William and a gaggle of Annes. There are also royal consorts and a number of famous politicians, scientists and other notables including Clement Attlee, Charles Darwin, Isaac Newton, Ernest Rutherford, William Pitts the Elder and Younger, Geoffrey Chaucer, Thomas Hardy, George Frederick Handel, Charles Dickens, Laurence Olivier and Henry Purcell. Various other people are commemorated like Robert Baden-Powell, Benjamin Disraeli, William Shakespeare, Oscar Wilde and **Winston Churchill**.

Sir Winston Leonard Spencer-Churchill KG OM CH TD FRS PC (Can), ex-prime minister of Great Britain, is actually buried at Bladon, Oxfordshire, near to his birthplace at Blenheim Palace. Churchill was born in 1874 to Lord Randolph Churchill, the third son of the 7th Duke of Marlborough, and Jeanette 'Jennie' Jerome, daughter of the prominent American businessman Leonard Jerome. Winston had one brother with the excellent name of John Strange Churchill. During his long and distinguished career Winston not only led the UK through World War II as prime minister, he became the first honorary citizen of America (granted by John F. Kennedy), won the Nobel Prize for literature in 1953 and was awarded another 37 orders and medals. He was also granted the highest honour of a State Funeral upon his death in 1965.

Churchill had a great fondness for hats and was rarely seen without one. Most photographs show him wearing a Homburg or his trademark **Bowker** (not Bowler as is often recorded although he did very occasionally wear one). He would, on occasions don a top hat, a sola topee (pith helmet) or a Panama. The **Panama hat** is made from the plaited leaves of the panama-hat palm (*Carludovica palmata*). Other famous Panama hat wearers include Humphrey Bogart, Gary Cooper and Harry S Truman.[60] Despite the name, genuine Panama hats are made in Ecuador.

60. Famously, the 'S' in Harry S Truman's name didn't stand for anything at all. It's just an 'S'. However, fellow US president Warren G. Harding's middle name was Gamaliel. C. S. Lewis's middle name was Staples, and Hunter S. Thompson's was Stockton. When Sir Elton John – born Reginald Kenneth Dwight – legally changed his name

And here's a great story from Ecuador. In July 1967, during a very dull mayoral election campaign in the coastal town of Picoaza, a foot deodorant manufacturer came out with the slogan 'Vote for any candidate, but if you want well-being and hygiene, vote for **Pulvapies**'. 'Pulvapies' was, of course the name of the product. And then, on the eve of the election, the clever advertisers circulated a leaflet to the townsfolk that said: '*For Mayor – Honourable Pulvapies!*' The next day, in one of the great electoral embarrassments of all time, the foot powder won the election by a landslide and performed well in elections in outlying areas.

But back to the erroneously named Panama hat ... the Ecuadorian town of Cuenca is the main producer of these hats (which are properly called *jipijapa* or *Montecristi* hats), but the finest are said to come from Montecristi. The misnaming of the hat goes back to the 19th century but was undoubtedly perpetuated by its association with President Teddy Roosevelt who often wore one while overseeing the construction of the **Panama Canal**.

The Panama Canal was built from coast to coast across the Republic of Panama, the southernmost country of Central America. Situated on an isthmus, Panama connects North America to South America. Until the canal was built, ships had to travel right around the southernmost tip of Cape Horn in order to travel from the west coast to the east, and vice versa. By building the canal, the journey from New York to San Francisco, for example, was cut from 14,000 miles to 6000 miles; well under half the distance.

The building of the Panama Canal was one of the toughest engineering projects ever undertaken. The French were the first to have a crack at it but, by 1904, had lost 22,000 workers to fatal illnesses like yellow fever and malaria. The USA picked up the project but, despite attempts to prevent illness and improve sanitation, the construction saw a further 5000 deaths. The number of deaths among black workers was ten times greater than among the white workers (who lost only 350). Many blame the fact that although medical care was

he chose the new middle name of Hercules. *Steptoe and Son* star Harry H Corbett adopted the 'H' to distinguish himself from *Sooty and Sweep* puppeteer Harry Corbett and claimed that the 'H' stood for 'Hennyfink' – a cheeky Cockney comment on the fact that he would do 'anything' for the money. Meanwhile, Michael J Fox's middle name is ... Andrew. He preferred the sound of 'J' to 'A' and claims he chose it in homage to fellow actor Michael J. Pollard.

provided for all, the white workers lived in houses while the black workers lived in tents outside of the mosquito controlled zone.

Every year more than 14,000 ships pass through the Panama Canal, carrying more than 200 million tons of cargo. The project to build it was commemorated by wordsmith Leigh Mercer in the well-known palindrome: *A man, a plan, a canal – Panama*.

A **palindrome** is a word or sentence that is entirely...

## INVESTIGATION 12

How do you connect **Cardinal Richlieu**
to **Jason and the Argonauts** and
**The British Rocket Group**?

### *Forbidden Playwright*

**Mooncalf** was a term used in past times to describe the aborted foetus of a cow or other farm animal. There was a belief that such incidents were caused by the influence of an evil Moon. The term has since found its way into popular culture. In the *Harry Potter* universe, a mooncalf is a giant creature with big feet that dances in fields at night making crop circles. In Gerald Durrell's *The Talking Parcel* (1974)[61] it is a monster with the head of a cow and the body of a snail that leaves a trail of 'mooncalf jelly' that can be formed into different shapes by mind-power. And mooncalves appear in H.G. Wells's novel **The First Men in the Moon** where they are described as creatures of monstrous size, 200 feet in length with 'a brainless head' and looking like 'stupendous slugs, huge, greasy hulls, eating greedily and noisily, with a sort of sobbing avidity. They seemed monsters of mere fatness, clumsy and overwhelmed to a degree that would make a Smithfield ox seem a model of agility.' In the 1964 movie of the book, the mooncalves encountered by Professor Cavor and Arnold Bedford take the form of huge caterpillar-like creatures with large compound eyes. These mooncalves were created by legendary animator and film-maker **Ray Harryhausen**. A pioneer of movie special effects, Harryhausen created the giant octopus in *It Came from Beneath the Sea*, the alien ships in *Earth versus the Flying Saucers* and the amazing skeleton fight at the end of *Jason and the Argonauts*.

Although Harryhausen began his film career with 1950s 'B-Movie' genre hits like *20 Million Miles to Earth*, *Mighty Joe Young* and *The*

61. Also known as *The Battle for Castle Cockatrice*.

*Beast from 20,000 Fathoms*, his groundbreaking stop-motion animation techniques and a string of awards soon enabled him to command
bigger budgets. He made a number of films about Sinbad the Sailor
and several dinosaur movies including *One Million Years BC* and
*Valley of Gwangi*. And he played with Greek mythology, firstly with
*Jason and the Argonauts* (1963) and then with his last and most
ambitious film, *Clash of the Titans* (1981).

The film portrayed Princess Andromeda (Judi Bowker – as in
Churchill's hat) being sacrificed to a sea beast called the Kraken.
However, the Kraken was a creature from the mythologies of
Norway and Greenland; in the original Greek legend it was a whale-
like creature called Cetus. Bubo the metal owl was a wholly invented
creature but has some resonance with the tin owl in Frank L. Baum's
*The Tin Woodman of Oz* (1918). The Stygian witches seem lifted
straight from Celtic lore or Shakespeare's *Macbeth*. And while on the
Shakespearean theme, it also seems obvious that the deformed
Calibos (another invention that never featured in Greek myth) is a
thinly-veiled take on *The Tempest*'s **Caliban.**

Caliban was the child of **Sycorax**, a witch from Algiers who was
banished to an island after being accused of witchcraft 'so powerful
as could control the moon'.

The name 'Sycorax' was also used for an alien race that appeared
in the 2005 *Doctor Who* story *The Christmas Invasion*. And while
we're in outer space, I should mention that the influential 1956
sci-fi film *Forbidden Planet* was based heavily upon the plot of *The
Tempest* with Dr Morbius (Walter Pigeon) playing the role of
Prospero, his daughter Altaira (Anne Francis) as Miranda and even
Robby the Robot acting the part of the spirit Ariel.

When Bob Carlton wrote his award-winning stage musical *Return
to the Forbidden Planet*, he kept the plot of the movie but, under-
standing its origins, created the entire script out of lines from
Shakespeare's plays … albeit with some licence. For example, when
the alien monster is first detected on radar the operator utters the
line: 'Two beeps or not two beeps? That is the question.' The special
effects were designed by *Thunderbirds* creator the late Gerry Anderson. The show has more or less run continuously since the 1980s and
won the Laurence Olivier Award for Best Musical in 1990.

Laurence Olivier, of course, appeared as Zeus in Harryhausen's
*Clash of the Titans*. He was asked to appear by his great friend, the

Oscar-winning actress Maggie Smith, who was married to the film's screenwriter, Beverley Cross. Olivier seems to have been glad of the work as he was then suffering from dermatomyositis and leg thrombosis and couldn't do any stage work. With Smith and Olivier on board, a host of other famous actors (Clare Bloom, Ursula Andress, Burgess Meredith, Flora Robson, Siân Phillips, etc.) also signed up and the film became a blockbuster. It has recently enjoyed a modern remake and sequel.

The screenwriter for Harryhausen's adaptation of *The First Men in the Moon* was **Nigel Kneale**, most famous for his *Quatermass* serials. Kneale's cantankerous Professor Bernard Quatermass was the star of three BBC television series, one ITV series and three feature film adaptations. He has been played variously by Reginald Tate, John Robinson, André Morell, John Mills, Brian Donlevy and Andrew Kier. In 2005, a new version of the original *Quatermass* serial was made by the BBC starring Jason Flemyng. It was, unusually, broadcast live to recreate the feel of the original 1953 serial. Interestingly, Quatermass is referenced several times in the *Doctor Who* series, most recently in the aforementioned episode *The Christmas Invasion* where the 'British Rocket Group' is reported to be sending a manned mission to Mars; the British Rocket Group was the organisation headed by Quatermass.[62] And in an earlier story, 1988's *Remembrance of the Daleks* (when Sylvester McCoy drove the TARDIS), the military scientific advisor Dr Rachel Jensen remarks to her colleague Alison, 'I wish Bernard was here', to which Alison replies, 'The British Rocket Group's got its own problems...' Nigel Kneale chose the name 'Quatermass' from a phone book because it looked interesting and because it began with QU, as do many surnames from his native Isle of Man.

Nigel Kneale wrote screenplays for a number of films including adaptations of the novels *Lord of the Flies* by William Golding and *Brave New World* by **Aldous Huxley**.

Aldous Leonard Huxley was an English writer who produced a wide range of work from novels and essays, to short stories, poetry, travel writing, and film stories and scripts. Among his many works was a biography of François Leclerc du Tremblay – the infamous **Grey Eminence**.

---

62. This is not announced on the TV show itself but on the BBC's tie-in website.

Leclerc was a Capuchin friar who was known to have had a huge influence on Cardinal Richelieu's decision-making and, some claim, was the real power of the church in France at that time. Richelieu was known as 'The Red Eminence' or *l'Éminence rouge* due to his Cardinal robes. Therefore Leclerc quickly gained the nickname of the Grey Eminence or *l'Éminence grise* due to his dull-coloured monastic robes (which were more beige than grey but beige wasn't yet a named colour). Therefore the expression *l'Éminence grise* has come to signify a powerful advisor or decision-maker who operates secretly or unofficially as the 'power behind the throne'. Aldous Huxley's biography of François Leclerc was, appropriately, called *The Grey Eminence* (1941).

Huxley's best known work was the novel *Brave New World* (1932), a dystopian view of a future society – London in 2540 – where warfare and poverty are things of the past but have been lost only at the expense of the things we value today: family, art, literature, science and religion. The population exists in a state of hedonistic narcotic stupor brought about by use of a hallucinogenic drug called *soma*. The title of the book was taken from Miranda's speech in William Shakespeare's *The Tempest*, Act V, Scene I:

> '*O wonder!*
> *How many goodly creatures are there here!*
> *How beautious mankind is!*
> *O brave new world*
> *That has such people in't!*'

The play contains a number of mythological characters, such as the spirit Ariel who serves the sorceror Prospero because he rescued her from imprisonment. She had been trapped within the body of a tree by Sycorax, the African witch. Sycorax's son is the deformed 'freckled whelp' of a monster called Caliban, who is described as 'not honoured with a human form'. He is depicted as a wild beast of a man with aspects of fish or lizard. He is also referred to in the play as a mooncalf.

**Mooncalf** was a term used in past times to describe ...

# INVESTIGATION 13

How do you connect **The Canterbury Tales**
to **Jethro Tull** and
**flatulence**?

## Silent but not Deadly...

**Hydrocarbons** are combustible chemical compounds that, as the name implies, are formed from hydrogen and carbon. They usually consist of a 'backbone' of carbon atoms to which hydrogen atoms attach themselves and form the basis of many fuels including petroleum, coal and natural gas. The most commonly found hydrocarbon is **methane,** which consists of four hydrogen atoms and one carbon, hence its chemical symbol of $CH_4$.

Despite common belief, methane has no smell. When used as fuel, suppliers add a strong-smelling sulphur-based odour (*ethyl mercaptan* is a favourite) to alert the user of leaks. Methane is created by organic matter decomposing in an oxygen-free environment. It is often erroneously cited as the primary constituent (and smell) of flatus.

Flatus is the proper name for intestinal gas released from the anus and known colloquially as a **fart**. The origins of the word 'fart' are confused but it has been in common usage for centuries. Until recently it was considered to be vulgar or 'bad language' but increasing use in children's TV shows (particularly from America where 'fart' is considered more acceptable) has removed much of the taboo. It famously appears in **Geoffrey Chaucer**'s bawdy *Canterbury Tales*. In *The Miller's Tale* (lines 3806–3807), a character called Absolon is just about to be tricked into kissing the buttocks of a man called Nicholas when Nicholas breaks wind in his face:

'*This Nicholas anon leet fle a fart*  [This Nicholas then let fly a fart]
*As greet as it had been a thonder-dent*  [as loud as any thunder clap].'

Absolon's reasoned response to this insult is to attack Nicholas's buttocks with a red-hot poker. Chaucer wrote this in 1386 but the *Oxford English Dictionary* cites an example of 'fart' as a verb from as long ago as 1250.

So, was Absolon put in any danger as the result of Nicholas's dastardly rearguard action? In 2001, a serious study was conducted to discover whether flatus is harmful.[63] It started with an enquiry from an Australian nurse who wondered whether she was causing contamination by farting in an operating theatre. A Dr Kruszelnicki identified the fact that no one really knew the answer and set out to discover the truth. So he asked people to fart onto Petri dishes filled with a gel that encourages bacteria growth.[64] Some of the farting Guinea pigs were naked, others clothed. The Petri dish used by the naked farters sprouted growths of two types of bacteria that are usually found only in the gut and on the skin. Meanwhile the clothed farter's dish remained clear, proving that clothing acts as an efficient filter. As Kruszelnicki reported, 'Our final conclusion? Don't fart naked near food.' However, he was keen to point out that the bacteria that did develop were harmless and, in fact, similar to the 'friendly' bacteria found in yoghurt and health drinks.

That said, in very rare instances, a fart can be fatal. In a 1966 medical paper called 'Anal carriage as the probable source of a Streptococcal infection', authors William McKee, Joseph Di Caprio, C. Evans Roberts and John Sherris tell the tale of a 45-year-old doctor who was the probable source of a serious infection in 11 hospital patients due to a very rare asymptomatic anal infection by a bacterium that is normally only found in the throat. Any flatus would disseminate the infection.[65]

Farting is a constant source of amusement and, some would say, may even be the foundation stone of all British humour. But what we

63. As reported in *The British Medical Journal* December 22–29 2001; 323:1449.
64. Invented by bacteriologist Julius Richard Petri in 1887 although there are claims that both Emanuel Klein and Percy Frankland had created something almost identical a few years previously. This may be a simple case of an idea 'having its time' as the science of microbiology was rapidly expanding.
65. My thanks to Faraz Mainul Alam from Imperial College who found this for me along with Schaffner, W., Lefkowitz, L. B., Goodman, J. S. and Koenig, M. G. (1969) *Hospital outbreak of infections with Group A Streptococci traced to an asymptomatic anal carrier.* Vanderbilt University School of Medicine, Nashville, Tennessee.

find funny is the noise … the smell can be anything but funny. This is, as stated earlier, regularly blamed on methane … but wrongly so. The odour comes from low molecular weight fatty acids such as butyric acid, which has a smell like rancid butter, nitrogen compounds such as skatole and indole, or from sulphurous compounds such as hydrogen sulphide or carbonyl sulphide, which smell like rotten eggs. Flatus consists mostly of oxygen, nitrogen, hydrogen and carbon dioxide. Very little, if any, is methane. Hydrogen is the gas that thrill-seekers ignite when they set light to their farts. It too is odourless.

Farting can be a form of communication. A recent study (2003) by marine biologists in Canada and the USA suggests that herrings (*Clupeidae*) release staccato farts in order to keep their shoal together. These 'fast repetitive ticks' (making the humorous acronym of FRTs) consist of high frequency sound bursts of up to 22 kilohertz accompanied by a stream of bubbles from the anus. Herrings have excellent hearing and, as FRTs happen mostly at night among high densities of fish, it suggests that it is a method employed to keep the shoal together in unlit waters. Dolphins and other predators may be able to use these FRTs to home in on their prey.

Farting can also be an artform. The grandaddy of all flatulists or *fartistes* was Joseph Pujol or, as he was professionally known, **Le Pétomane** – The Farting Maniac. Pujol had remarkable control of his abdominal muscles and sphincter and could draw air into his rectum and expel it at will, thus ensuring an odourless performance. And perform he did, first in Marseille in 1887 and later at the famous Moulin Rouge in Paris, where his act was seen by such dignitaries as Edward Prince of Wales, King Leopold II of the Belgians and Sigmund Freud. Highlights of his act included farting *La Marseillaise*, blowing out a candle from several yards away, impressions of farmyard animals and playing the flute by way of a rubber tube inserted into his bottom. He left the Moulin Rouge to form a traveling show called the *Theatre Pompadour* but retired from the stage with the outbreak of the First World War. He returned to Marseille and his original trade as a baker.

There are modern day flatulists too. The erroneously named **Mr Methane**, the alter-ego of Paul Oldfield, has travelled the world appearing live at comedy festivals and on TV and radio shows dressed in a bizarre superhero-like green-and-purple skin-tight costume complete with cape and mask. Oldfield claims he discovered his talent while doing yoga aged 15. From 1991 until 2006, when he retired, he claimed to be the only performing professional flatulist in the world. He released an LP in 2000 called *Mr Methane.com*. It was produced by former **Jethro Tull** drummer Barriemore Barlow who was, for a time, his manager.[66]

Jethro Tull is a British rock band led by songwriter/performer Ian Anderson. Formed somewhere around 1968, the band has produced a large number of albums that encompass a range of musical styles from folk to jazz to blues to electropop (Curiously, they did release an album in 1999 with a similar title to Mr Methane's *magnum opus* called *J-Tull Dot Com*). However, whatever the style of music, they are always identifiable due to Anderson's distinctive vocals and flute playing. They are frequently included within the Progressive (Prog) Rock genre due to their often elaborately structured music, diverse influences, instrumentation and styles. Their name comes from a noted 18th-century agriculturalist.

**Jethro Tull** was one of the first people to apply scientific method to agriculture. He invented new tools, such as his patented seed drill, and suggested improved methods of farming like using horses instead of oxen for ploughing. He made it his life's work to understand the science behind such mundane tasks as fertilising the soil with **manure**.

Manure is the faecal matter of vegetarian animals such as cows, horses, pigs and chickens. Due to the low level of proteins in the animals' food, it is often odourless. Elephant dung, for instance, has almost no smell at all, which is why Turner Prize-winning British artist Chris Ofili has been able to use it in his work, albeit with additional chemical treatment, without offending gallery owners or patrons (and maybe why elephant coffee isn't tainted). Manure is rich in nitrogen and other nutrients that plants need in order to grow and dried manure can be burned as a fuel. Cowpats are used extensively across India and so-called 'buffalo chips' were burned by early American pioneers and settlers. In desert countries, camel dung serves the

---

66. Research by Greer Ramsay has found evidence to suggest that flatulists were operating in 16th-century Ireland. Known as *braigetóirí*, they were entertainers who most likely set their farts alight for the chieftain's amusement. Ramsay's 2002 paper on the subject is brilliantly called 'A breath of fresh air: Rectal music in Gaelic Ireland' *Archaeology Ireland* Vol. 16, No. 1, 22–23. Also among a king's or chieftain's retinue would be a *crossán* whose repertoire often included 'distending his cheeks and his bag (testicles/scrotum) for comic effect'. A kind of early 'Puppetry of the Penis'.

same purpose as does llama, kangaroo, horse and elephant dung in countries where these animals are found. Some dung is even used in paper production as non-ruminant herbivores pass intact undigested plant fibres out of their bodies.

In addition to manure, ruminants – such as cows – produce a lot of intestinal gas. This is due to their extraordinary digestive systems where four 'stomachs' – the *rumen, reticulum, omasum* and *abomasum* – process the tough vegetation to extract maximum nutrition. This causes fermentation leading to production of carbon dioxide and methane. Cows burp and fart a lot, but it is only recently that researchers have realised quite how much. It has been estimated that the cow population of the USA alone releases around 50 million tons of hydrocarbons into the atmosphere per year. To put that into perspective, the accumulated annual gas of ten cows could provide heating and cooking gas for a small house for a year. By using methane more effectively, we could also reduce global warming. Methane is a greenhouse gas that has 22 times the warming ability of carbon dioxide but when it is burned it converts to the less harmful carbon dioxide and water. Therefore, it could be used instead of our dwindling reserves of 'dirtier' hydrocarbon-based fossil fuels, such as coal and oil, for energy.

**Hydrocarbons** are combustible chemical compounds that ...

## INVESTIGATION 14

How do you connect **Uranus**
to **hair loss** and the
**Miranda Rights**?

### *What's on the telly? It's all Greek to me...*

The word **eruption** comes from the Latin *ruptūra*, from *ruptus*, the
past participle of *rumpere*, which means 'to break'. Consequently,
*rumpere* is also the root word of 'rupture'.

*La Rupture* is how the 2006 film *The Break Up* was distributed
in France and other French-speaking countries. The film, starring
**Jennifer Aniston** and Vince Vaughan, tells the story of the acrimoni-
ous breakdown of a relationship and the tit-for-tat bitterness that
ensues. At one memorable point in the film, Aniston teases Vaughn
by parading naked in front of him having had a '**Telly Savalas**' bikini
wax. I wonder how Savalas would have felt about the comparison?
He was Aniston's godfather.[67]

American-Greek actor Telly Savalas, birth name Aristotelis Savalas, specialised in playing villains and heavies until he was chosen to
play the genial shaven-headed cop Theo Kojak. Kojak first appeared
in a 1973 TV movie called *The Marcus-Nelson Murders*, which was
based upon the real story of the Wylie-Hoffert 'Career Girl Murders'.
On August 28th 1963, Janice Wylie and Emily Hoffert were
murdered in their apartment on the Upper East Side of Manhattan,
New York City. Both had been stabbed more than 60 times using
knives from their own kitchen. The suspect arrested for the offence
was one George Whitmore Jr, an unemployed 19-year-old black man
of below average intelligence. He was incarcerated for 1216 days on
a confession gained under duress and some very shaky evidence. A

---

67. Jennifer Aniston's father is Greek-American actor John Aniston – birth-name Yannis
    Anastassakis. He was one of Savalas's best friends.

separate investigation eventually exonerated him completely and, in 1965, a man called Richard Robles was arrested and convicted of the murders.

Whitmore's case was cited by the Supreme Court while they were reviewing the case of *Miranda vs Arizona*, where labourer Ernesto Arturo Miranda[68] had been convicted solely upon his confession and had not received legal advice. The review led to the introduction of the so-called **Miranda Rights**, whereby anyone arrested must now be informed of their right to remain silent and to have legal representation before anything they say becomes admissable in law.

*The Marcus-Nelson Murders* featured a tough and incorruptible New York Detective Lieutenant called Theodopolous Kojack, played by Savalas. The character proved so interesting that a TV series was developed. *Kojak*, with its new spelling, went on to become one of the most popular and iconic cop shows of the 1970s. With his catch-phrase of 'Who loves ya baby?' and his trademark lollipops (Savalas used them to help him quit smoking), Theo Kojak made a star of Savalas. The detective's other notable feature was his bald head. Savalas had shaved it in 1965 to play Pontius Pilate in the movie *The Greatest Story Ever Told* and liked it so much he kept it.

In ancient Egypt – around 1500 BCE – a shaved head was considered de rigueur ... for women. **Baldness** was the height of feminine beauty and women would pluck out every hair with gold tweezers and polish their heads to a high sheen with buffing cloths. Priests too would shave their heads and pluck the hairs from their body. In contrast, the Greeks regarded long hair as a symbol of wealth and power and it was common for slaves to have shaved heads. Therefore Grecian men desperately tried all manner of things to prevent hair loss. The physician Dioscorides suggested raw onion mixed with honey and applied to the scalp overnight. Hippocrates developed a series of treatments with ingredients such as cumin, nettles, horserad-ish and pigeon droppings. He also noted that castrated boys didn't suffer from hair loss as they grew up, but that was maybe a step too far as a baldness prevention strategy (suddenly a few nettles and

68. Miranda was re-tried without the now inadmissible confession but was still found guilty of kidnap, rape and armed robbery. He was released from prison on parole in 1975 and supplemented his meagre wages by selling autographed Miranda cards. He was fatally stabbed in a bar-room brawl in 1976. Miranda cards were found on his body. The killer was never caught.

pigeon poo doesn't seem quite so severe a cure, does it?).[69] Having a good head of hair was also seen as a sign of virility. However, such things were of little concern to one particular Greek called Mihailo Tolotos. When he died in 1938 at the age of 82 he was perhaps the only man in history to have never met anyone or anything recognisably female.

Orphaned at birth, Tolotos was adopted by monks from a reclusive monastery on the **Mount Athos** peninsula where no women are allowed to enter – not even female animals.[70] The rule was brought in when the monastery was established in order to reduce sexual temptation. Consequently, no female has been allowed to enter the building for nearly 1,000 years... although several have done so including the 1929 reigning Miss Greece, Aliki Diplarakou, who gained access dressed as a monk. She later married diplomat Sir John Wriothesley Russell, becoming Lady Russell.

Mount Athos lies on a peninsula in Macedonia that is known as the *Autonomous Monastic State of the Holy Mountain*. Although it is connected to the mainland, the peninsula can only be reached by boat and is home to 20 ancient monasteries supporting a population of some 2250 monks. Access to the peninsula is by ticket only and, even then, only to males over 18 who are preferably Greek Orthodox Christians.

Athos was one of the Gigantes, the children of Gaia and **Uranus**. In Greek mythology, Uranus was the primal sky god and Gaia the earth goddess.

Using the standard convention for naming planets in our solar system, the planet Uranus should rightly be called Caelus. All of the other planets (except earth) are named after Roman gods. Only Uranus is named after a Greek deity. That said, Uranus is infinitely better than the planet's original name. Discoverer Sir William Herschel wanted to name it *Georgium Sidus* or 'George's star' in

69. Hippocrates did correctly make the connection between baldness and 'maleness'. What he couldn't have known was that it is due to the action of the hormone testosterone.

70. I'm told that some female animals do live on Mt Athos to provide milk and eggs. However, the most penitent and fundamentalist monks will not allow themselves any contact with them. It is accepted that there will be contact with some female wild animals such as birds, fish and insects but they have no obviously female physical characteristics with which to tempt and beguile.

honour of King George III.[71] It was German astronomer Johann Elert Bode who suggested the more fitting Uranus as he was the father of Kronos (Saturn) and the grandfather of Zeus (Jupiter) – the two planets before Uranus. Why he plumped for the Greek rather than the Roman is a mystery.[72] The non-standard naming convention also extends to Uranus's moons. Unlike all the other planets (except earth) where the moons are named after mythological beings, the 27 known Uranian moons are named after characters from the works of William Shakespeare and Alexander Pope and include Titania, Oberon, Cordelia, Ariel, Caliban, Sycorax, Prospero, Ophelia, Setebos and Miranda.

The **giant** Athos was born as the result of Uranus impregnating Gaia. He had to do this with his blood after being castrated by his own son Kronos. (Did it prevent his baldness? He certainly didn't seem to suffer any loss of virility.) During an assault on Mount Olympus, Athos threw a mountain at Poseidon who deflected it into the sea where it still lies to this day, bearing his name and covered in monasteries. In another version of the story, Athos was buried under the mountain as a punishment. The same fate awaited the other Gigantes, most famously Enceladus who was buried under Mount Etna. To this day, the movements of the entombed giants cause earthquakes and **volcanic activity**.

There are many different kinds of volcanic activity: fissure eruptions occur when part of the volcanic cone splits; central eruptions occur in the centre of the cone sending debris straight upwards; submarine eruptions are where the volcanic activity is underwater and subglacial eruptions are under ice. Eruptions can be explosive or effusive (non-explosive flows). Large, explosive volcanic eruptions create steam and water vapour, carbon dioxide, sulphur dioxide, hydrogen chloride, hydrogen fluoride and ash. Severe eruptions can throw debris as high as 20 miles into the earth's atmosphere.

The word **eruption** comes from the Latin...

---

71. Latin has a number of words that all mean star. They include *sidus*, *stella* and *astrum*.

72. The best explanation I have found is that Caelus, although the Roman equivalent of Uranus, was not generally venerated as a god. Incidentally, the Greek names for the five visible planets – Hermaios (Mercury), Aphrodision (Venus), Areios (Mars), Dios (Jupiter) and Kronios (Saturn) – pre-date the Roman names so it may be that Uranus is actually the only correct name in current use.

How do you connect **Shakespeare**
to **penicillin** and the
number **23**?

## *Words and Numbers*

An average HB **pencil** has enough 'lead' to draw a line 35 miles long
or to write approximately 50,000 English words ... or so a common
internet 'factoid' states. In fact, it's more than double that. In 2007 a
group of people set out to hand-write the novel *To Kill a Mocking-
bird* by Harper Lee using a standard yellow pencil. Organisers
Kenneth Sheppard, Keith Eldred and a team of 26 volunteers managed to copy the entire book – all 100,388 words – and still had a
stub of pencil 1 and ³⁄₁₆ths inches long (3.09 cms) left over. But even
if every single one of those 100,000+ words were different, it would
hardly scratch the surface of the **English lexicon**.

It's hard to work out exactly how many words there are in the
English language because English is such a mongrel tongue. Many
words we use have been borrowed from other languages. Then there
is the additional complication that many words can be used in different ways. Take the simple word 'fly'. It can be an annoying insect, a
zipper in a pair of trousers and the name for a tent door-flap. It can
be a noun (the annoying insect), a verb (as in 'fly a plane') and an
adjective ('pretty fly for a white guy!'). And it gets even worse when
you start adding tenses. I fly. The plane flew. It was flown by me. It
flies very well. Flies fly but a fly flies. Another example is 'wind'.
There is wind (that which propels a sailboat), wind (to gather around
a spool), wind (abdominal gas), wound (having gathered around a
spool), wound (a form of injury), winding (meandering), winding
(the action of gathering around a spool), winding (releasing trapped
wind, usually from a baby) and winding (to punch someone in the
stomach). All are wholly different words despite their similar spell-

ings. The simple word 'set' is actually one of the most complex words in the language. It has 58 uses as a noun, 126 as a verb and ten as an adjective. It takes the *Oxford English Dictionary* 60,000 words to explain it. So do we count 'set' as one word or 194?

The second edition of the *Oxford English Dictionary* contains entries for 171,476 words in current use, 47,156 obsolete words and 9,500 derivative words included as subentries. That's at least a quarter of a million distinct English words. It's often claimed that around 1700 to 2000 of them were created (or popularised at least) by just one man – **William Shakespeare**. However, as has quite rightly been pointed out by the *Oxford English Dictionary* and other authorities, an examination of other 16th-century texts written by less well-known authors reveals that many words and phrases attributed to Shakespeare were already in use at the time. There is also the common sense observation that if Shakespeare had used a lot of new words in his plays then the audiences – many of whom were fairly uneducated to begin with – wouldn't have understood them.

However, the myth persists and provided the plot for a 2007 episode of *Doctor Who* (*The Shakespeare Code*) in which the Bard of Avon's genius with words was manipulated by an ancient species who use words, rather than numbers, as the basis of their science. And while we're mentioning numbers, Shakespeare was born on April 23rd 1564 and died on April 23rd 1616. This is often trotted out by a certain kind of conspiracy theorist who believes that **the number 23** is, in some way, significant.

In the early 1960s, the writer **William S. Burroughs** (*Naked Lunch*, *The Soft Machine*, etc.) knew a chap called Captain Clark who ran a ferry from Tangiers to Spain. One day, Clark said to Burroughs that he'd been running the ferry for 23 years without incident. According to Sod's Law, the ship sank that very day, killing Clark and his passengers and crew. Burroughs claims that he was thinking about the tragedy when he turned on the radio … and caught the news of a plane crash on the New York to Miami route. The pilot was another Captain Clark and the flight was listed as Flight 23. Convinced there was maybe something in this, Burroughs began collecting incidences of the number 23 in a scrapbook. Some of these incidents ended up in his writing.

Some claim that the number 23 has some disturbing associations with disaster. Hexagram 23 of the *I Ching* (P'o), translates as 'Splitting or breaking apart'. And in magician Aleister Crowley's *Cabalistic Dictionary*, he defined 23 as 'the number of parting, removal, separation, joy, a thread and life'. But, on a more positive note, there are any number of 'good' occurrences of 23 in nature. Humans have 46 paired chromosomes. Each parent contributes 23 chromosomes to the DNA of their child to make the total. Hermann Swoboda and Wilhelm Fliess, the two doctors who first came up with the concept of human 'biorhythms', state that the cycle is 23 days long. And around 23% of the universe is made up of so-called 'dark matter'. Nobody knows quite what it is, but it outweighs all the atoms in all the stars in all the galaxies in the universe, and may be what keeps the universe stable.

The supposed significance of the number 23 has not gone unnoticed by the makers of TV shows. In the cult TV series *Lost* the number pops up frequently, most notably in 'the numbers' that made chunky millionaire Hurley's – and everyone else's – life a misery (the numbers were 4, 8, 15, 16, 23 and 42). There are whole websites that list the appearance of the number 23 throughout the series. And if that's not enough for you, 2007 saw the release of *The Number 23*, a thriller starring Jim Carrey in which continued appearances of the number lead Carrey's character, Walter Sparrow, to uncover a terrible truth ...

Twenty-three is not the only number that appears to have some special significance. The number **seven** appears time and time again in popular culture (seven seas, seven dwarves, Magnificent Seven, seven Samurai, seven deadly sins, etc.) and is often called 'Lucky 7'. This may be simply because there are several different ways to throw a seven with two **dice**, making it statistically more likely to be thrown than some other numbers.

For example, there is only one way to throw a two or a 12: 1+1 and 6+6 – but there are two ways to throw a three: 2+1 or 1+2. There are three ways to throw a four (3+1, 1+3 and 2+2) and four ways to throw a five (2+3, 3+2, 4+1, 1+4). By the time we get to seven, you have six chances: 1+6, 6+1, 2+5, 5+2, 3+4 and 4+3. From that point on, the options begin reducing again; to throw an eight, for example, you have only five chances (4+4, 5+3, 3+5, 2+6, 6+2) and to throw a ten there are just three (5+5, 6+4, 4+6).

There are 36 possible combinations of two dice: 1+1, 1+2, 1+3, 1+4, 1+5, 1+6, 2+1, 2+2, 2+3, 2+4, 2+5, 2+6, 3+1, 3+2, 3+3,

3+4, 3+5, 3+6, 4+1, 4+2, 4+3, 4+4, 4+5, 4+6, 5+1, 5+2, 5+3, 5+4, 5+5, 5+6, 6+1, 6+2, 6+3, 6+4, 6+5, 6+6. Therefore, you have only a $\frac{1}{36}$ chance of throwing a 12 but a $\frac{6}{36}$ or $\frac{1}{6}$ chance of throwing a seven.

The dots – actually called pips – on opposing sides of a die always add up to seven.[73] Dice probably evolved from the ancient practice of divining or game-playing using the ankle or 'knuckle' bones (*talus* or *astragalus*) of animals like cows and oxen. Even today, dice are still sometimes known as 'bones'. They have become smaller as time has gone on – which is just as well as, during the 18th century, illegal English gambling dens employed people solely to swallow the dice if there was a police raid.

The oldest known dice were excavated as part of a 5000-year-old Backgammon set, at the Burnt City archeological site in South-Eastern Iran. The Romans used dice made of wood, bone, ivory and lead.

Lead is a soft, heavy and highly toxic metal that has the chemical symbol of Pb (from the Latin *plumbum*). It is a potent neurotoxin that can accumulate in soft tissues and bone over time.

Contrary to popular belief, pencil 'leads' have never been made from lead, although lead was used in the Roman *penicillus*, a slim stylus that left a grey mark when applied to paper. It is from penicillus that we get the word 'pencil' and also, oddly enough, the name penicillin. The Latin *penicillium* means 'paintbrush' and was applied to the antibiotic fungus due to its shape. Pencil 'leads' are made of a kind of graphite called *plumbago*, which means 'acts like lead'.

An average HB **pencil** has enough...

73. *Dice* is the plural of *die*. However, 'dice' is rapidly becoming the accepted singular term along with the clumsy and innaccurate 'dices' as the plural form. The English language is as plastic as ever.

# INVESTIGATION 16

## How do you connect **digital cameras** to **Rupert Bear** and **The Wizard of Oz?**

### *Factum Obscura*

A *Camera Obscura* (or Dark Chamber) is, essentially, a large pinhole camera. It consists of a room, closed to all light except for a small hole in one wall. Light passing into the room from outside will form a round image on the opposite wall. Curiously, the image is always upside-down. This can be corrected with a lens, which also allows the hole to be made larger; therefore the projected image can be brighter, sharper and the correct way up. Astronomers used the *Camera Obscura* to study the sun. Evidence of this is found in the records of people like the first Astronomer Royal, John Flamsteed, who reported that he 'observed the eclipse of the sun ... on a scene [screen] in a darkened room'.

By tracing the projected image onto paper, the *Camera Obscura* allowed artists to 'trace real life' and to complete drawings and paintings with accurate detail and correct perspective. Many of Canaletto's most famous Venetian landscapes started life in this way and his *Camera* still survives to this day in the Correr Museum in Venice. Sir Joshua Reynolds also used one and recent evidence suggests that Johannes Vermeer may also have done so. In his book, *Secret Knowledge: Rediscovering the Lost Techniques of the Old Masters*,[74] British artist David Hockney suggests that many of the great classical artists – such as Ingres, Van Eyck and Caravaggio – did not draw freehand from life but used optical devices like the *Obscura* and the *Camera Lucida* to project the live image onto their canvas before tracing it. This has become known as the Hockney-Falco thesis.[75]

74. Thames and Hudson, London, 2001.
75. The 18th-century British portrait and landscape artist Thomas Gainsborough had a

The *Camera Lucida* or 'Lit Room' was patented in 1807 by William Hyde Wollaston. The device uses a mirror and lens to super-impose an image of the person or thing it is aimed at onto the surface that the artist is using. The artist can therefore see both the 'model' and drawing surface simultaneously. It was a portable development of the *Camera Obscura*.

It was the invention of light-sensitive photographic film that led to the term 'camera' becoming associated with photography. Photo-graphic paper was simply used instead of drawing paper and the devices became smaller and more user-friendly. Despite no longer needing a room, the term 'camera' has remained in use.

As an aside, we can't talk about cameras without mentioning pioneer George Eastman. In 1884, he developed the prototype for a dry gel-coated photographic paper to replace the old photographic plates and chemicals that photographers had to carry around with them. This discovery led to the first production cameras going on sale, making photography available to anyone.

The name **Kodak** is interesting. Eastman liked the letter K, describing it as a 'strong, incisive sort of letter'. He and his mother invented the word by setting three rules: (1) the name should be short; (2) it should be hard or impossible to mispronounce; and (3) it does not resemble another word and therefore cannot be mistaken for anything else. Other stories, such as the idea that the name was originally Nodak (short for North Dakota) or that 'ko-dak' was the sound of a camera shutter, are urban myths.

The word 'camera' comes from the Latin for 'chamber' and the two words show their shared ancestry if you pronounce the 'ch' as a hard K sound (as in *chord*) and the 'b' is silent (as in *dumb*). The term *in camera* is still used in law to mean a Judge deliberating in his/her private chambers.

Therefore, **digital camera** is an altogether odd phrase as it literally translates as 'finger room' or 'chamber of fingers'. The Latin *digitus* means 'finger' or 'toe'.[76] When we learn to count and add and sub-tract on our fingers, we are engaged in *digital* activity. And we are *computing* – processing numbers to find a solution. Therefore, it was

fascinating technique that allowed him to paint and stand back from his canvas all at once. He painted with brushes attached to sticks sometimes up to six feet long.

76. Interestingly, it is closely related to *dicere* which means to 'tell, say or point out' which is the root of such words as *diction*, *dictionary* and *dictate*.

only natural that when we developed machines to do that for us, the terms transferred across. The word 'digital' came to us via the Middle English form of *digitus*, which also gave us **digitalis**.

The common **foxglove** (*Digitalis purpurea*) is a tall plant with purple flowers that emerge from tubular stems. The flowers are bell-shaped and fit snugly over a human fingertip, hence their scientific name, which means 'purple and finger-like'. Variant species can produce pink, white and yellow flowers. The *digitalis* plant produces a cardiac glycoside called digoxin which is used to treat irregular heartbeats (arrhythmia). In larger doses, however, it is a poison and, in 2003, US serial killer nurse Charles Cullen admitted killing as many as 40 hospital patients over 16 years using the drug. The plant is a major source of food for the larvae of a small British moth called the foxglove **pug** (*Eupithecia pulchellata*).

A pug is a toy dog breed recognisable by its dark wrinkly face and pale body. The name 'pug' may come from the same root as words like *pugilist* and *pugnacious* (Latin *pugnus* [fist]) as the dog has the look of a boxer who has taken one too many to the face. Or it may be a corruption of 'Puck', the character in Shakespeare's *A Midsummer Night's Dream*, because of the breed's mischevious nature. Originally bred for Chinese emperors during the Shang dynasty (1766–1122 BCE), they were known as *Lo-Chiang-Sze* (after their place of origin), Foo dogs or even Dragon dogs. In fact, stylised sculptures of pugs are sometimes mistaken for dragons. The alien Frank from the film *Men in Black* and its sequels took the form of a pug and 'Little Willie' was a pug that appeared regularly in the early days of UK soap opera *EastEnders*. Disney's *Pocahontas* featured a pug called Percy and Algy Pug was one of **Rupert Bear**'s best friends.

Rupert Bear is a long-running cartoon strip that first appeared – and continues to appear – in the British *Daily Express* newspaper. Rupert – a well-behaved young white bear dressed in a red jumper and a yellow plaid trouser and scarf combo – was created by Mary Tourtel in 1920. Rupert's best friends are Algy Pug, Bill Badger, Edward Trunk (an elephant), Podgy Pig, Pong-Ping (a Pekingese), Gregory Guinea-Pig, Bingo the Brainy Pup and Tigerlily (a young Chinese girl). His frequent tormentor is a creature made from sticks called Raggety.

Mary Tourtel was succeeded in 1935 by Alfred Bestall, whose brilliant artwork and clever storylines made the character even more popular. Bestall continued to draw Rupert until his retirement in 1973, when he was replaced by John Harrold. Every year, a *Rupert Annual* is produced which, curiously, always has a honey-coloured Rupert on the cover even though he is always otherwise depicted as white furred.[77] Rupert was also honey-coloured in the 2006 animated TV series *Rupert Bear: Follow the Magic*. In order to bring the character into the more politically correct 21st century, the producers swapped Rupert's boots for trainers and changed the other characters too: Raggety has become an elf, the Professor's assistant is no longer 'The Dwarf' but Bodkin, and the previously male Pong-Ping has undergone a sex change.[78]

Rupert Bear's darkest hour came in 1971 when he was cited in an obscene publications trial. *Oz* was a subversive underground magazine produced in London between 1967 and 1973. In 1971, the three editors – Jim Anderson, Felix Dennis and Richard Neville – were taken to court for 'conspiring to corrupt the morals of young children and other young persons' for printing a cartoon strip featuring Rupert Bear. A graphic cartoon strip drawn by the American artist Robert Crumb, in which a man is attempting sex with a virgin, was altered by pasting Rupert's head and scarf over the male character's head and rude rhyming couplets were then added underneath each panel to mimic the usual Rupert format. The finished result was a hit with the magazine's audience but not with the *Daily Express* and the more prudish elements of society. On August 5th 1971, after being refused bail and kept in custody for seven days (during which their long hair was cut off against their will), the editors were sentenced to fines, deportation (in the case of Australians Anderson and Neville) and prison sentences ranging from nine to 15 months. An appeal later quashed all of their sentences. The *Oz* trial was widely publicised and helped to promote the magazine, which, in turn, is said to have helped popularise Australia's common British nickname. It is, of course, in no way related to the fictional Land of Oz created by L. Frank Baum.

In the 1939 MGM film of *The Wizard of Oz*, Dorothy (Judy

---

77. Or white furred to our eyes anyway (remember the polar bears?). There is one exception to the honey-coloured covers and that was the 1973 annual cover on which Rupert keeps his usual colour.

78. A similar 'PC' revamping happened with Enid Blyton's *Noddy* – the naughty Golliwogs were replaced by goblins and his best friend and apparent co-habitee Big Ears was replaced with Greybear.

Garland) sings the classic song *Somewhere Over the Rainbow*. The song (and indeed all the songs in the film) were written by E. Y. 'Yip' Harburg and Harold Arlen who won an Oscar for their efforts. Harburg and Arlen also wrote a number of popular hits including *Lydia the Tattooed Lady*. In 2000, 'Somewhere over the Rainbow' was voted the 20th-century's Number One song by the Recording Industry Association of America (RIAA) and the National Endowment for the Arts (NEA). The song has been recorded by hundreds of famous singers but, in recent years, has become particularly associated with two singers who both died tragically young.

**Eva Cassidy** was an American singer who died in 1996 of melanoma at the age of only 33. She was almost unknown outside of her native Washington DC until her death but has since sold in excess of four million albums.

The other is Hawaiian singer **Israel Kamakawiwo'ole**, also known as Bruddah Iz, who died in 1997 from respiratory illness compounded by his obesity (757 pounds [54 stone] or 343 kg) at the age of 38.

Kamakawiwo'ole's gentle voice and ukelele version of the song appeared in the final episode of British time travel cop drama *Life on Mars* and references to the *Wizard of Oz* appeared all through the series. For example, Gene Hunt often called Sam Tyler 'Dorothy' and the mysterious Chief Inspector who leads Sam back to the present day is called Frank Morgan; the name of the actor who played the wizard in the film (and also four other roles – the city guard, taxi driver, Professor Marvel and the doorkeeper). There is a **rainbow** seen in the opening credits of the series and, when Sam and Annie finally kiss in the last episode, a rainbow appears in the sky behind them.

A rainbow can only occur when the light source – usually the sun – is less than 40 degrees above the horizon. That means morning or late afternoon, and usually not so much in winter time when the sun is low and water droplets in the air are often frozen. Rainbows in the middle of the day can usually only be seen from an elevated position such as on a mountaintop or in a plane. It's a curious thing to consider that no two people ever see the same rainbow; it is an optical effect created by the refraction of light through raindrops. Rainbows are made inside our eyes, just like the colour white is. Also, a rainbow's position is based upon where it is seen from. As you move closer to a rainbow it appears to move away but, actually, it is a continuous series of new rainbows being generated, which is why you can ever reach the Leprechauns' legendary pot of gold. Not that a rainbow has 'ends' anyway as every rainbow is, in fact, a circle. Perhaps it should more properly be called a rainring? How much of the circle we see depends upon the width of the band of rain and where the sun is at the time.

Studying the sun has always been impossible with conventional telescopes as it inevitably results in damage to the eye. Even staring with the naked eye can do some harm. Therefore, much early study of such things as eclipses and sunspots was done either while the sun was low in the sky near the horizon and thus diffused by the atmosphere, or by using a *Camera Obscura*.

A ***Camera Obscura*** (or Dark Chamber) is, essentially, ...

How do you connect **Wall Street**
to **Adolf Hitler** and
**Superman**?

## A Pocket full of Jadarite

**Kryptonite** is a fictional mineral that was created (or liberated) during the destruction of the planet Krypton, home world of Superman.[79] The most common form is green kryptonite which causes weakness, paralysis and, ultimately, death to Kryptonians. Gold kryptonite removes powers permanently. Red kryptonite is a lot more interesting as individual pieces affect Kryptonians in different ways. When exposed to it, Superman has become a giant, a dwarf and an ant-headed humanoid. He has also become hugely obese, his hair and nails have grown long, has aged rapidly, become psychic, grown extra arms and turned into a raving lunatic. Black kryptonite separates people into two personalities; good and bad. White kryptonite is deadly to plant life. Then there's pink kryptonite, seen just once in the *Supergirl* comic in 2003, which makes normally heterosexual Kryptonians gay.

'Kryptonite' was sort of found recently in the Jadar Valley in Serbia. The mineral, actually a white powder rather than a green crystal, was identified in 2007 by geologists and is officially named **Jadarite** (after the location it was discovered). Its chemical make up is sodium lithium boron silicate hydroxide ... which is why it has been nicknamed 'Kryptonite' because, in the 2006 film *Superman Returns*, Lex Luthor steals some Kryptonite from the Metropolis Museum and the scientific name displayed on the museum case is ... *sodium lithium*

---

79. Krypton is supposed to have been far away in another galaxy but in the earlier 1940s radio shows it was on the far side of the sun, permanently hidden from us. Which is appropriate as *kryptos* means 'hidden' as in cryptic, crypt and cryptography (the study of codes and ciphers).

*boron silicate hydroxide with fluorine.* Of course, the addition of fluorine would make it an entirely different substance, but it is oddly coincidental that the two names are so similar. It was noticed by Dr Chris Stanley from London's Natural History Museum who searched the internet using the mineral's chemical formula and discovered that it already existed, in fiction, as Kryptonite.

*Pocket Full of Kryptonite* was the 1991 debut album from US band **Spin Doctors**. The album – which contained the hit *Two Princes* – had several references to the Superman canon. The cover of the album featured a telephone box and the song *Jimmy Olsen's Blues* revolved around the life of Clark Kent's colleague at *The Daily Planet*.

**Klark Kent** was the alter-ego used by influential **Police** drummer Stewart Copeland when he released several singles in the late 1970s and an album in 1980. Copeland has cheekily claimed that the A&M record label only signed the Police so that they could get Klark Kent. Copeland enjoyed huge success with Sting and Andy Summers but has also written operas, ballets and the soundtracks to TV series, video games and feature films. Among them are *See No Evil Hear No Evil*, *Highlander 2*, *The Equalizer*, *Dead Like Me*, *Spyro the Dragon*, the pilot of *Babylon 5* and **Wall Street**.

Wall Street – originally *De Waal Straat* – is a narrow street in New York City that takes its name from the fact that it once formed the northern boundary of the Dutch-owned New Amsterdam (as the city was then called).[80] By 1653, it had grown to become a fortified 12-foot high wall made of timber and earth and was intended to keep the Native Americans (and the British) out. The wall was eventually pulled down by the British in 1699. Wall Street became associated with finance during the late 18th century when traders and speculators would informally meet there by a buttonwood tree. In 1792, these meetings were formalised by **The Buttonwood Agreement**, which led to the creation of the **New York Stock Exchange**.

The New York Stock Exchange is one of the most influential money markets in the world but it has had a chequered history. The infamous Wall Street Crash of 1929 caused widespread panic and, together with other events, led to the **Great Depression**. In some ways, it also sparked the outbreak of the Second World War.

80. An alternative but less popular theory states that the name is a corruption of *Walloon*. If you want to know about the Walloon people, skip on to Investigation 27.

The Great Depression was an economic collapse that started in America and spread across Europe. It severely damaged international trade and wages shrank. The events caused political upheaval and many voters moved their loyalties to the far left or far right. In Germany the ruling Weimar Republic suddenly found that they were no longer receiving loans from the USA to rebuild after the devastation of the First World War. Unemployment rose steeply and the people looked to the fascists for an answer, voting Hitler's Nazi Party to power in January 1933. The rest is history.[81]

Before World War II, the New York phone book boasted 22 people named 'Hitler'. By the end of the war, all of them had disappeared. The Hitler family, keen to disassociate themselves from the Führer, simply disappeared by changing their names. One such was Adolf's nephew, **William Patrick Hitler**.

William Patrick was the son of Adolf's half-brother, Alois, and his Irish wife Bridget Dowling. They had met in Dublin in 1909 and eloped to Liverpool where William was born in 1911. Anecdotal stories tell of the young boy being known as Willy or Paddy Hitler. After the outbreak of World War II, the Hitlers found themselves stranded in America while on a lecture tour. William subsequently served in the US Navy and the Naval Medical Corps. He was used in several propaganda films where he was seen berating and taunting his uncle. After the war, and with the Hitler name forever stained with the blood of millions, William became William Stuart-Houston. He married, had four sons and moved to Long Island, New York, where he set up a business analysing blood samples for hospitals. He died in 1987 and is buried alongside his mother, Bridget, at Holy Sepulchre Cemetery in Coram, New York. A Broadway show called *Little Willy* tells his life story. One of William's sons died in a car accident but the other three are alive and, according to a journalist who has met the family, have taken an extraordinary pact not to have children themselves and thus end the Hitler bloodline forever.[82]

81. Did you know that Fanta, the soft drink, was invented in Nazi Germany? Because Coca-Cola couldn't be produced or imported into Germany during World War II (due to shortage of ingredients and a trade embargo), the company made a new drink from what they could get. The name is derived from *fantasie*, the German for 'imagination'; something the company needed in order to produce something from next to nothing. It must be pointed out, however, that the drink was not made for, nor by, the Third Reich as some websites erroneously claim.

82. David Gardner's *The Last of the Hitlers* (2003) BMM.

It could be said that William Stuart-Houston was a **quisling** to his uncle Adolf because he collaborated with the 'enemy'. The term is named after a Norwegian fascist and supporter of Hitler called Vidkun Quisling. He was appointed Führer of Norway throughout the war but, ultimately, proved so unpopular that the Norwegians put him in front of a firing squad. After his execution, the name Quisling became synonymous with 'traitor'.

Other common euphemisms for traitor include 'Fifth columnist' and '**Benedict Arnold**'. The term 'Fifth column' originated during the Spanish Civil War of 1936–1939. During a radio address by Nationalist General Emilio Mola, he referred to his militant followers – who were busy trying to undermine the government – as his 'fifth column'. His army was, at that time, marching in four columns towards Madrid. Benedict Arnold meanwhile, was a notorious US Army general who is best known for betraying his own side to the British during the American Revolution. When his misdemeanours were noted he defected to the UK and ultimately moved to London. He is buried at St Mary's Church, Battersea, having died in poverty and bad health.

Benedict Arnold was a personal hero to the comicbook villain **Lex Luthor**. Luthor's HQ was based in an abandoned museum in the city of Metropolis and access was gained by shaking the hand of a statue of Julius Caesar at the entrance. Luthor had access to an amazing array of CCTV cameras fitted inside a giant statue on the museum roof that allowed him to see every part of the city. The statue also hid his personal spaceship. Inside the museum was Luthor's bizarre Hall of Heroes, in which he placed life-sized waxwork type figures of his personal role models. These included Benedict Arnold, Atilla the Hun, Al Capone, Nero, Blackbeard the pirate and Genghis Khan. Luthor claimed that he visited the Hall to be 'uplifted ... inspired to go on with my work!'

Luthor discovered, to his cost, that the ideal way to fight Superman was by acquiring a ring set with green kryptonite. However, his plan backfired when he discovered that prolonged exposure to the radiation it gave off had given him cancer. Firstly his hand was amputated, but later, as the cancer spread, he had his unaffected brain transplanted into a new cloned body.

**Kryptonite** is a fictional mineral that was created ...

How do you connect **Charles Lindbergh**
to **gypsies** and
**cooked testicles**?

## *Moth Balls*

To this day, **strippers** are sometimes employed at rural Chinese funerals to encourage larger crowds of mourners. The belief is that the more people who attend, the more the dead person is honoured. However, Chinese authorities have now clamped down on the 'obscene' practice and have even created a 'funeral misdeeds' telephone hotline to report incidents.

The origins of striptease as a performance art are disputed and various dates and occasions are given from ancient Babylonia to the 20th century. For example, there are claims that the 'Dance of the Seven Veils' that Salome performed for King Herod was the first striptease and that it was inspired by the ancient Sumerian story of the descent of the goddess Inanna into the Underworld (or *Kur*). Inanna had to remove an article of clothing or a piece of jewellery at each of the seven gates. However, although the Bible records Salome's dance, the first mention of her removing seven veils occurs in **Oscar Wilde**'s play *Salome* in 1893.

Oscar Wilde died in Paris of cerebral meningitis on November 30th 1900 (and not Syphilis as is sometimes claimed)[83] and was originally buried at the Cimetière de Bagneux outside Paris. Later, he was relocated to the city and the Père Lachaise Cemetery. His tomb was designed by sculptor Sir Jacob Epstein, and depicts an angel in the Modernist style. However, the angel's genitals were broken off by an unknown citizen and subsequently spent many years as an unnerving paperweight in the offices of the cemetery warden before vanishing

83. Wilde's physicians, Dr Paul Cleiss and Dr A'Court Tucker, reported that the condition stemmed from an 'old suppuration of the right ear'.

one day, never to be seen again. Artist Leon Johnson created a new set of genitals in silver and they were installed following a short ceremony in 2000 to commemorate the centenary of Wilde's death.

Angel's **penis** would certainly be the priciest item on the menu at the Guolizhuang restaurant in Beijing, China's speciality penis emporium. The restaurant's founder, Mr Guo, claims that cooked penis is low in cholesterol and tastes great. Chinese medicine also claims that penis can be used to treat all kinds of ailments: donkey penis is supposedly good for the skin; sheep, horse, ox and seal are excellent for the circulation; and virility issues involve the most expensive penis of all (barring angels) – tiger penis – which can cost upwards of £3000 per portion. The restaurant claims that all of its tiger penises are obtained from zoos and private collections where the animals have died naturally.[84]

Bull's perineum is also a delicacy, apparently, and so are **testicles**. They are often erroneously called sweetbreads but sweetbreads are actually the thymus glands found in the neck. Cooked testicles are more properly referred to as lamb fries, animelles or Mountain Oysters.

It's often reported that the word 'testicle' is related to the words *Testament* and *Testimony* as they all spring from the Latin *testis*, which means 'witness'. However, 'testis' is derived from the Indo-European word for 'three' and its context in relation to a witness is that they are a third party. The confusion may have been caused by the fact that the Bible does mention swearing on the testicles or, as it's more euphemistically described, 'swearing under the thigh' or 'grasping the thigh'. And, anyway, these Biblical references actually imply that the person is swearing on the testicles of the king, in the same way that people swear on a Bible today.

It is a popular belief (and the subject of a rather silly song) that **Adolf Hitler** only had one testicle. Until relatively recently, this was dismissed by many as a myth put about by British propagandists. However, in 2008, a document came to light that records a conversa-

---

84. It would be nice to believe that this is so. It is true that there are more tigers in captivity than left in the wild. The World Wide Fund for Nature suggests that there are around 3200 wild tigers left. The number in captivity is unknown as ownership is not regulated in many countries. However, estimates suggest there are over 4000 in China and 5000 in the USA alone.

tion with Dr Johan Jambor, a field doctor who treated Hitler for a groin wound during the Battle of the Somme, in which he states that Hitler did lose a testicle on the battlefield. Another myth was that Hitler was a vegetarian. While it is true that his diet mostly consisted of fruit and veg, he regularly ate pigs' knuckles and was known to eat up to 2lbs of chocolate per day. His diet was very heavy in carbohydrates and sugars, which may have been responsible for the depression he suffered. Hitler was voted *Time* magazine's 'Man of the Year' in 1938.

Since 1927, *Time* magazine has annually chosen a person who, for better or worse, is considered to have had the greatest impact during the previous year. The 'Man of the Year' has now become the 'Person of the Year' to include the other 50% of the human race, and the accolade can now also be awarded to an idea or object too. Over the past 50 years, the list has included Josef Stalin (1939 and 1942), Queen Elizabeth II (1952), JFK (1963), The Computer (1982) and You (i.e. the reader) in 2006. George W. Bush has been 'honoured' a total of three times in 2004, 2000 and jointly with his father in 1990. Irish rocker Bono shared the limelight in 2005 with Bill and Melinda Gates, and The Endangered Earth was the themed winner for 1988. One person who would have been pleased about the 1988 winner is **Charles Augustus Lindbergh**, who was the very first *Time* 'Man of the Year'.

In later life, Lindbergh became a strong advocate of balancing technological advances against the preservation of the natural world and worked tirelessly on a number of environmental projects including saving the humpback and blue whales from extinction. But he is far better known for his aviation skills, particularly for making the first solo, non-stop flight across the Atlantic from New York to Paris in 1927 in his plane *Spirit of St Louis*.[85] In later years, many of Lindbergh's innovations led to transcontinental air travel as we know it today. Less well-known is the fact that this great American patriot was once labelled a Nazi by President Franklin D. Roosevelt. While living in France in the late 1930s to avoid the media circus at home, Lindbergh made frequent trips to Germany to study their aircraft and

---

85. Lindbergh was not the first; a total of 81 people had crossed the Atlantic before him, starting with the British flyers Alcock and Brown. However, Lindbergh was the first to fly solo.

to meet with other pioneers such as Willy Messerschmitt and Ernst Heinkel. Lindbergh also shared many political views with the prevailing Nazi party including eugenics and the importance of racial purity. During one such visit in 1938, he was presented with the Service Cross of the German Eagle (the *Großkreuz des Deutschen Adlers*) by Herman Göring for his services to aviation (Henry Ford received the same award earlier in the year for services to the automotive industry). Lindbergh's acceptance of the award was initially overlooked at home but, once war was declared, was no longer viewed so kindly. Thus began the decline of Lindbergh's popularity and status. As another consequence of this (and Lindbergh's suggestion that America ally itself with Germany rather than Russia as Nazism was better than Communism), Roosevelt banned Lindbergh from joining the armed forces.[86]

Another pioneering young aviator from those times was **Sir Francis Chichester**. In 1931, he became the first man to fly solo across the Tasman Sea, from east to west, in a de Havilland **Gipsy Moth** Aircraft fitted with floats. The name of the plane obviously had great sentimental meaning for him as he was later to name his record-breaking yacht the *Gipsy Moth III*. It was in this boat that he became the first man to win the solo transatlantic race in 1960 ... despite his having a lung removed in 1958 and being told that he had six months to live due to cancer. He then went on to achieve his greatest feat in the specially designed *Gipsy Moth IV* – his record-breaking solo-circumnavigation of the world in 1967. By the end of the voyage Sir Francis had established a number of records, including travelling more than twice the distance of the previous longest passage by a solo sailor.

The **gypsy moth** (*Lymantria dispar*) is a small European moth that is unusual in that the males of the species operate during the day rather than at night like most other species of moth. They are a significant pest for hardwood trees and, in 1981, gypsy moth caterpillars alone defoliated 12,900,000 acres of US trees. The origin of the name 'gypsy moth' isn't known for sure but probably relates either to their

---

86. There is a small left-facing swastika painted on the inside of the Spirit of St Louis's cone-shaped propeller spinner. However, until the outbreak of WWII, this was a common good luck symbol. It is accompanied by written good luck messages from the staff of the Ryan Aircraft Co. who designed and built the plane.

tendency to travel around and not stay in any one place, or their colour; 'gypsy' was once used to describe a shade of brown. As the name 'gypsy' is a corruption of the Greek word *Aigyptoi* (Egyptian), the colour may be related to the practice of grinding up mummies for pigment (this colour was called *Caput Mortuum*). The Roma people were wrongly thought by Europeans to be Egyptian – hence the name – driven to a peripatetic lifestyle as a punishment for harbouring the infant Jesus.

**Gypsy Rose Lee** was the stage-name adopted by Rose Louise Hovick, an American actress and burlesque entertainer, who is sometimes credited as being the woman who popularised striptease as a form of entertainment. Her main innovation was to add entertainment to titillation, using a casual strip style while telling humorous monologues and gags. She became one of the biggest stars of Minsky's Burlesque Theatres in the late 1930s and was frequently arrested in raids on the premises for alleged obscenity. But public opinion was with her and Minsky's empire spread. His chain of Burlesque Theatres went on to launch the careers of such famous comics as Phil Silvers, Abbott and Costello and Red Buttons.

Gypsy Rose Lee died of lung cancer in 1970 in Los Angeles. Sir Francis Chichester also died of lung cancer, but two years later (so much for the six months prognosis). Chichester's main rival for the 'first around the globe' prize was Sir Alec Rose who, due to technical problems, had to set off on his voyage a year later. And 'Rose' is also the surname of the man who wrote the famous song 'The Stripper' in 1962 – David Rose.

To this day, **strippers** are sometimes employed at rural Chinese funerals ...

# INVESTIGATION 19

## How do you connect 'buckyballs' to Marilyn Monroe and the Eden Project?

### *Worth her Weight in Diamonds*

In the US State of **Kentucky** it was once (apparently) illegal for a woman to appear in a bathing suit on a highway unless she was either escorted by at least two police officers or weighed between 90 and 200lbs. You'll find many of these strange and quirky laws listed on websites and in books. But how true are they? The truth is that very few are. Some are simply made up. Others are not actually laws at all but local ordinances, some of which only affect a particular street in a particular town in particular circumstances. And most have been very loosely interpreted. One frequently quoted example from Michigan states that it is illegal to tie an alligator to a fire hydrant. However, a little digging soon reveals a State statute (Section 56-2-7) that orders that: 'No person shall in any manner obstruct the use of any fire hydrant in the city or have, place or allow to be placed any material or thing in front thereof or connect or tie thereto any object, animal or thing.' So yes, it is technically true to say that you may not tie an alligator to a fire hydrant, but it's also illegal to tie your dog or your bicycle to one. But that just isn't as funny is it?[87]

The same nonsense is just as rife on this side of the Atlantic. I'm sure you've all heard the old chestnut about it 'still being legal to shoot a Welshman with a crossbow within the city of Chester after sunset'? It is simply not true. That particular statute relates to a bloody uprising by Welsh forces (led by Owain Glyndŵr) that was suppressed in the early 1400s. To ensure it didn't happen again,

---

87. Do seek out *You May Not Tie an Alligator to a Fire Hydrant* (2002) by Jeff Koon and Andy Powell. It's a great book that debunks many of these silly stories.

Henry IV wrote to the Mayor, Sheriffs and Aldermen of the City of Chester, commanding that *'All manner of Welsh persons or Welsh sympathies should be expelled from the City; that no Welshman should enter the City before sunrise or tarry in it after sunset, under pain of decapitation.'* The king specified that these new laws should be *'proclaimed publicly in your bailiwick for the informing of the people'*. (Source: Chester City Council). No mention of crossbows or even bows and arrows you'll note. Also, although this royal order may not have been repealed or recinded, it has been superceded by every Act of Parliament since that deals with the subject of murder, specifically the Offences Against the Person Act 1861, Homicide Act 1957 and the Human Rights Act 1998. So no shooting of Welshmen I'm afraid. Sorry to be a spoilsport but the sad fact is that if it sounds ridiculous, it probably is.

I don't know if the Kentucky ruling I started this Investigation with is the truth or a twisted version of an original statute. But I do know that most Kentucky women could legally appear in a bathing suit on a highway because the **average weight of US women** is 164.7lbs (or 11st 10oz or 74.7kg).[88]

The weight of an average UK woman (according to the Department of Trade and Industry) is 10st 5lbs (147lbs or 66.7kg). She stands at 5'3.8" (162 centimetres) tall and has a Body Mass Index of 25.2. All of which equates to a UK size 16.[89]

To put that into some perspective, **Marilyn Monroe** – named the 'Number One Sexiest Star of the 20th Century' by *Playboy* magazine and 'Sexiest Woman of the Century' by *People Magazine* in 1999 – was somewhere between a UK size 12 and a size 14. Her 'official' size, as put out by her studio bosses was 37–23–36 and she was 5'5.5" tall. Her dressmaker claimed it was 35–22–35. Marilyn herself once said that her epitaph should read 'Here lies Marilyn Monroe, 38–23–36'. All of which means that in today's Hollywood, she would probably be desperately trying to diet. Model and actress Liz Hurley

---

88. The most recent verifiable source based on a large nationwide sample I could find was the US National Health and Nutrition Examination Survey (NHANES) conducted from 2003 to 2006. However, the National Center for Health Statistics, Maryland, conducted a survey in 2010 and found an average female weight of 166.2lbs.

89. Incidentally, the average UK male stands 5'9.5" (176.5 centimetres) tall and weighs 12st 5lbs (176lbs or 79.8kg) with a BMI of 26.0.

– a modern icon for female body shape – is on record as saying (rather cattily) to *Allure* magazine, 'I've always thought that Marilyn Monroe looked fabulous, but I'd kill myself if I was that fat'.

Marilyn once sang that *Diamonds are a Girl's Best Friend*. Now, it seems that she may actually become a **diamond**. Or a part of her will anyway. A Chicago company, LifeGem Memorials, creates diamonds by combining carbon from human remains with other minerals and subjecting the mix to intense pressure and heat. At the time of writing they have taken several strands of Beethoven's hair to create three diamonds, which will be sold at auction, with the proceeds going to military families. They plan to do the same with hair from Abraham Lincoln, Charles Dickens and Marilyn Monroe.

It may actually rain diamonds on the planets Uranus and Neptune. According to researchers at Berkeley University, both planets boast high levels of methane that can be converted into diamonds when subjected to high pressures and temperatures such as those found on both worlds. Once the diamonds form, they would fall to the ground like rain. The researchers recreated conditions on the planets in the lab and succeeded in creating diamond dust.

Diamonds and the soft graphite used in pencils are made of exactly the same element – carbon. The only difference between the two is the arrangement of the atoms. In diamond, every carbon atom is bonded to four other carbon atoms in a tetrahedral, or pyramid-shaped, structure. Every bond is the same length, and it is the strength and regularity of this structure that makes diamond so hard. Theoretically, a perfect diamond could be composed of one giant carbon molecule.

Carbon is the 15th most abundant element on earth and the fourth most abundant in the universe (after hydrogen, helium and oxygen). Lonsdaleite is the hardest naturally occurring form of carbon and is 58% harder than diamond (although it is very rare and is only created when a meteorite containing graphite strikes the earth). But other forms of carbon now exist that are even harder. Graphene is a man-made form of carbon – created in 2004 by Sir Andre Geim and Konstantin Novoselov – that consists of a hexagonal lattice of carbon atoms just one atom thick. It is the strongest tensile substance known to man; if you could get a piece of the material large enough to make a drum skin and tried to puncture it with a nail, you would need to push the nail with a force equivalent to the weight of a car. Fullerenes are also stronger than diamond and, like graphene, can only be created in the laboratory in microscopic proportions at present. Examples include beta carbon nitride and ultrahard fullerite C60. Fullerite and fullerenes are named after **Richard Buckminster Fuller**.

Richard 'Bucky' Buckminster Fuller was an American visionary who spent most of his working life trying to answer the question, 'Does humanity have a chance to survive lastingly and successfully on planet Earth? And if so, how?' To this end, he became a true Renaissance man; a writer, poet, designer, architect and inventor. He is best remembered for his work on geodesic domes and it is this that led to his name becoming attached to the new carbon molecules. Fullerite and other fullerenes take the form of hollow spheres, elipsoids or tubes which, due to their similarity to Fuller's dome designs became known as Buckyballs and Buckytubes. The first to be discovered was officially named buckminsterfullerene by researchers Harold Kroto, James R. Heath, Sean O'Brien, Robert Curl and Richard Smalley at Rice University, Houston, Texas. But, as more have been created, the family has been named 'fullerenes'.

Fuller's work on **geodesic domes** led to the creation of *Spaceship Earth* at the Epcot Center at Walt Disney World, Florida, the Expo '67 dome (now the Biosphere) in Montreal, Canada, the Fukuoka Dome in Japan (currently the world's largest), and the the **Eden Project** near St Austell, Cornwall.

The Eden Project's Humid Tropics 'Biome' has an area of 167,805 square feet (15,590 square metres), is 180 feet high, 328 feet wide and 656 feet long. It is the biggest greenhouse in the world and is high enough to hold the Tower of London or 11 double-decker buses stacked on top of one another. The Warm Temperate Biome has an area of 70,395 square feet, is 115 feet high, 213 feet wide and 443 feet long. Another extraordinary statistic is that each biome at the Eden Project weighs around the same as the volume of air contained within them.[90]

You'll also find Eden in the $27 million **Creation Museum** where a Biblical version of the history of the world in played out in a series of

90. We don't think of air as having weight but, of course, it does. It has mass and anything that has mass within a gravity field, has weight. There is an often quoted claim that if we could make a close-fitting cylinder large enough to encase the Eiffel Tower, the volume of air within would weigh more than the tower itself. The Eiffel Tower is 1063 feet high and sits on a square base with sides of 410 feet. It would

dioramas occupying 60,000 square feet. Many were designed by Patrick Marsh, the man who designed the *Jaws* and *King Kong* attractions at Universal Studios in Florida. In the Garden of Eden exhibit you'll find Adam and Eve, and the serpent of course, and also their children playing happily alongside dinosaurs. The museum asserts that the world is not billions of years old but just 6000. And it proudly displays fossilised dinosaurs and other animals as evidence of the Great Flood. The museum is situated in the city of Petersburg, Kentucky.

In the US State of **Kentucky** it was once (apparently) illegal for a woman ...

therefore fit inside a cylinder with a radius of around 288 feet and a volume of 35.3 million cubic feet. That much air would weigh just over 11,000 tons. The tower weighs around 7300 tons. However, the figures are difficult to verify and some calculations have the weight of metal as being slightly more than the air. Either way, it's an interesting demonstration of air's 'weight'.

How do you connect **Elvis Presley**
to **fingerprints** and
**leprosy**?

## *Skippy has Twice the Fun*

The nine-banded **armadillo** (*Dasypus novemcinctus*) is a scientific
curiosity in that it usually produces litters of four identical same-sex
quadruplets. And because they are genetically identical, they are useful
to science as behavioural or medical test animals. Litters (multiple
births) are common enough in mammals but the phenomenon of
multiple identical births, or *polyembryony*, is very rare. In humans, it
provides us with the spectacle of **identical twins**, triplets and quads.
Five identical children or more is extremely rare and usually results
from treatments using fertility drugs. It is estimated that there are
around ten million identical twins and triplets in the world.

Elvis Presley was one of a pair of identical twins. Tragically, his
twin – named Jesse Garon Presley – was stillborn on January 8th
1935. Had Jesse lived, it's interesting to speculate whether he would
have followed the same career path as his twin. Two Kings of Rock
and Roll? That would have been extraordinary. There is plenty of
evidence that they would have shared similar talents. You only have
to look at other identical twins such as Craig and Charlie Reid of
Proclaimers fame. Or Mary-Kate and Ashley Olsen. Or Ross and
Norris McWhirter, compilers of the *Guinness Book of Records*. Then
of course, there were the nefarious talents of Albert and Ebenezer
Fox.

The **Twin Foxes**, as they were known, were born in 1857 and
became skilled and very effective poachers around the area of Steve-
nage in Hertfordshire, England. They were as wily as their namesake
and made sure never to go poaching together, often escaping prosecu-
tion by providing alibis for each other. Because no one could tell

them apart, it was impossible to disprove their alibis. Eventually, they attracted the attention of Sir Edward Henry[91] who believed that all **fingerprints** – even those of identical twins – were unique. Using the Fox brothers and several other twins, he was able to prove his theory and, in doing so, put the Twin Foxes in prison.

Before computers allowed for complex scanning, all fingerprint identification was done by eye. Various systems were developed including the Roscher system (used in Germany and Japan), the Vucetich system (South America) and the Henry system (developed in India and used in most English-speaking countries). The Henry system looks for distinct patterns of arches, loops and whorls in the ridges of skin on the fingertips. These basic patterns are then broken down further, providing us with such wonderful terms as tented arches, ulnar loops, accidental whorls and central pocket loop whorls.

Contrary to popular belief, the ridges that make fingerprints are not to improve grip. Work by the University of Manchester has proven that fingerprints actually reduce friction. It is suggested that the ridges allow the skin to deform and thus stop blistering, which is why we get blisters on the smooth parts of our hands and feet but not often on our fingerpads. As any guitarist will attest, we tend to get callouses instead.

The idea that fingerprints are for grip probably grew from the fact that they are only found in primates – ourselves, lemurs, apes and monkeys – primarily tree-dwellers; some monkeys even have fingerprints on hairless areas of the tail. There is one notable exception to the primates-only rule, however – the **koala**. In fact, koala fingerprints are so similar to human fingerprints that it is very hard to tell them apart.

Early European settlers to Australia called the **koala** (*Phascolarctos cinereus*) the 'native bear' and it is still often erroneously called a koala bear. Of course, it is not related to bears at all. Bears are placental mammals like we are; they give birth to live, fully-developed young while koalas and their closest relatives, the wombats, are **marsupials**.

91. Commissioner of the London Metropolitan Police 1903–1918 and the man who introduced the use of police dogs. He became interested in the subject of fingerprints while Inspector-General of Police in Bengal, India, where Sir William Herschel had introduced inked palm prints as a form of ID some 40 years previously.

Marsupials are so named because the female typically has a pouch, or *marsupium*, in which it rears its young from birth.[92] For many years, scientists believed that they were an inferior, earlier form of mammal. However, it now appears that they were simply a different design that co-evolved and coexisted alongside us placental mammals. Certainly, the earliest known marsupial – *Sinodelphys szalayi* – lived around 125 million years ago; about the same time as the earliest placentals.[93]

Marsupials are different to placentals in other ways too. Their reproductive and excretion systems are kept separate, waste being disposed of via an orifice called a cloaca (a few placentals, such as tenrecs, also have a cloaca). Female marsupials have three vaginas and males have a two-pronged penis. Their brains don't have the 'bridge' – the *corpus callosum* – between left and right hemispheres that we have. They also have a singular lack of diversity. While placental mammals have evolved into forms as different as blue whales, bumblebee bats, elephants and sloths, most marsupials are remarkably similar. Current theories for why this is centre on the marsupial's front limbs. A newborn joey[94] is discharged from the womb after just four to five weeks and is blind and helpless. However, because it must climb up to its mother's nipples inside the pouch, its limbs develop much more quickly than the rest of its body. Consequently, they could never evolve into hooves, wings or flippers without endangering the future of the species.

Possibly the most famous marsupial of all time was *Skippy*, the

92. The pouch is quite versatile in design. In some marsupials, such as the kangaroo, it forms a pocket. In others, it is a simple flap of skin. Burrowing marsupials have a bottom-opening pouch to stop it filling with earth.

93. We tend to think that all marsupials live in Australasia. However, 100 of the 334 known species actually live in Central and South America and one, the Virginia opossum, in North America.

94. Newborn marsupials are tiny and hairless and known as pinkies. When they develop into recognisable baby animals, they're called joeys; all baby marsupials are called joeys although no one knows why. I'd like to report that Australia's baby monotremes (egg-laying mammals) have more inventive names. However, according to various official sources, including the Australian Natural History Museum, they are simply called 'young platypus/echidna'. The name 'puggle' has become attached to them in recent years. This seems to stem from the fact that young monotremes look like a well-known branded soft toy from the 1980s called a Puggle, made by Mattel and popular in Australia. The name is also used to describe a pug/beagle mixed-breed of dog.

bouncing star of 91 TV episodes made between 1966 and 1969. *Skippy the Bush Kangaroo* was set within Waratah National Park in Australia and centred on the adventures of the park ranger's son Sonny Hammond and his pet. Famously, Skippy spoke in a kind of tutting, clicking noise – a noise that kangaroos cannot actually make in real life. Other characters were Matt Hammond (Sonny's Dad), Sonny's brother Mark, helicopter Pilot Jerry King and Clarissa 'Clancy' Merrick. This was an early role for popular actress **Liza Goddard**.

Liza Goddard was born in Smethwick, England, but moved to Australia in 1965 when she was 15. Later she returned to the UK and enjoyed great success in series such as *The Brothers, Take Three Girls, Take Three Women, Give us a Clue, Bergerac, Woof* and *That's Love*. These days, she is married to producer and director David Cobham (*Tarka the Otter*) but before that she was married to 1970s glam rock star Alvin Stardust and, prior to that, actor Colin Baker who played the sixth *Doctor Who*. Goddard appeared as a space pirate called Kari in the series in 1983 during Peter Davison's era (Doctor Number Five).

In the serial *Terminus*, a sabotaged TARDIS arrives on a derelict space station positioned at the centre of the known universe. However, it turns out that the station is not as derelict as it appears. It is Terminus, the last stop and receiving point for people with Lazar's Disease, a thinly-veiled reference to **leprosy**.[95] The station is owned by a business corporation that claims a cure exists there ... but no one ever returns from Terminus.

Very few animals – other than humans – can contract leprosy. They include some monkeys, rabbits and mice (on their footpads) and armadillos. Armadillos are especially susceptible because the leprosy bacterium likes their unusually low body temperature. Wild armadillos can carry leprosy, but it is very rare that it is transmitted to humans.

The nine-banded **armadillo** (*Dasypus novemcinctus*) is a ...

---

95. 'Lazar Houses' were leper colonies run in the Middle Ages by the Knights of St Lazarus.

How do you connect **William Blake**
to **ravens** and
**Tourette's syndrome?**

## Pop Idle

*The Idler* is an annual magazine (now published in hardback book
form) founded in 1993 by Tom Hodgkinson and Gavin Pretor-
Pinney.[96] The magazine campaigns against the tyranny of the nine-
to-five job, the 40-hour week and the whole work ethic that robs us
of our valuable time. The magazine is named after a series of essays
published in the *Gentleman's Magazine* between 1758 and 1759 and
written by **Dr Johnson**.

Dr Samuel Johnson is, after William Shakespeare, probably the
most quoted British writer of all time. He was an essayist, poet, critic
and biographer but is best known for his famous dictionary. Between
1745 and 1755, Johnson attempted to catalogue and define every
word in the English language. However, contrary to popular belief,
his dictionary was not the first. Twenty or more had been produced
in the 150 years before Johnson. These include Thomas Elyot's
Latin–English dictionary (1538) and Robert Cawdrey's *Table Alpha-
beticall* (1604). Johnson's work is rightly held up as a masterpiece
because it was the first to include meticulously researched definitions
for all words – not just difficult or uncommon words – and examples
of their usage. The finished book was 18 inches tall and 20 inches
wide and contained 42,773 words.

Johnson was tall, obese, had bad eyesight and was partially deaf.
He also had a scarred face due to childhood scrofula and several tics
and twitches. It now appears, judging by the symptoms described by
his good friend and biographer James Boswell, that Johnson also

96. *The Idler*, coincidentally, is typeset by the same gentleman who typeset this book:
    Christian Brett.

lived with a degree of obsessive-compulsive disorder and **Tourette's syndrome.**

Tourette's syndrome (sometimes called Tourette's or GTS)[97] is characterised by physical and vocal tics. In rarer cases, it can result in involuntary shouting, often of abusive or obscene words or phrases. This is called *Coprolalia*. Tourette's is most common in children and some estimates place the figure between one and 11 children per 1000. However, the more common tic disorders (eye blinking, coughing, throat clearing, sniffing, etc.) tend to tail off in adolescence and adult Tourette's is a rarity. In 2006, Pete Bennett, a singer from Brighton with adult Tourette's was the winner of the UK reality show *Big Brother*. Meanwhile, another singer called Patrick Brannan adopted the stage name of **Donny Tourette** and fronted the bands The Tourettes and Towers of London.

The **Tower of London** – more properly called Her Majesty's Royal Palace and Fortress, The Tower of London – is a cluster of buildings surrounded by two concentric fortress walls and a moat on the north bank of the Thames where the borough of Tower Hamlets meets the City. At the centre of the complex stands the White Tower, built by William the Conqueror in 1078. The Tower has, at one time or other, been a fortress, a prison, a royal palace, an armoury, a public records office, a mint, a treasury, an observatory and, most surprisingly, a zoo.

The Royal Menagerie was established at the Tower in the 13th century, and contemporary accounts report seeing lions, leopards, lynxes and camels among the animals there. The zoo was opened to the general public in the 18th century, when the admission fee was set at three half-pence or the supply of a cat or dog to feed to the lions. This was probably where William Blake saw the tiger that inspired his poem *The Tyger*, the one that begins:[98]

> Tyger! Tyger! Burning bright
> In the forests of the night,
> What immortal hand or eye
> Could frame thy fearful symmetry?

97. Named after Georges Albert Édouard Brutus Gilles de la Tourette, the French physician and neurologist who first described the condition.
98. Published as part of his collection *Songs of Experience* in 1794.

These days the only animals at the Tower are the famous **ravens** (*Corvus corax*). The largest member of the crow family *Corvidae*, ravens are very intelligent birds with highly developed problem solving skills. Under laboratory conditions, they have learned a number of skills including how to use switches, handles and pull-strings to get a reward. In the wild they have been seen to manipulate others into doing work for them, such as by calling wolves and coyotes to the site of dead animals so that the larger mammals can open the corpse up. They watch other birds burying food and remember where it is so that it can be stolen later. They drop nuts onto roads so that cars can crack them open. And there are accounts of ravens sliding down snowbanks and apparently playing 'catch-me-if-you-can' with wolves and dogs just for the sheer fun of it.

No one knows for sure when they were first introduced to the Tower of London; earliest official records date to just 1895. However, there is a story that during the reign of Charles II (1660–1685), the king was warned that the monarchy would fall if the ravens ever left the tower.[99] So they may have been there for over 350 years. Charles's astronomer, John Flamsteed, complained bitterly that the ravens impeded the business of his observatory in the White Tower.

During the blitz in World War II all but one of the ravens (a bird called Grip) were either killed or flew away. And even today, despite excellent food and having one wing trimmed, some ravens do occasionally disappear. According to the Tower of London website, Raven Grog was last seen outside an East End pub called the Rose and Punchbowl in 1981, and Raven George was 'dismissed' in 1986 for eating television aerials. He was sent to live at a sanctuary in Wales where he turned out to be Georgina. There should be six ravens in

99. Charles was crowned King of Scotland in 1649 but was only able to assume the crown of England after the death of Oliver Cromwell. The restoration of the monarchy and the end of austere Puritanism led to the writing and performing of bawdy 'restoration comedies'. Charles was survived by his wife, Catherine of Braganza (the woman who introduced the British to the fork and the habit of drinking tea) but no heir. However, his many mistresses (including the famous Nell Gwyne) had borne him many illegitimate children. One of them, Henry Fitzroy, first Duke of Grafton, was a direct ancestor of Diana, Princess of Wales, meaning that Prince William, when crowned, will be the first monarch descended from both Charles II and Charles III (currently Prince Charles). We must discount Bonnie Prince Charlie, 'the young pretender', who referred to himself as Charles III, King of England and Scotland, because, officially he wasn't).

residence in lodgings next to the Wakefield Tower. At time of writing there are seven – Hugine, Erin, Merlin, Munin, Rocky, Pearl and Porsha – all looked after by the **Ravenmaster,** a duty given to one of the **Yeomen Warders.**

The Yeoman Warders act as tour guides and ensure the security of the Crown Jewels, which have been kept safe at the Tower since 1303. The Yeoman Warders are known by the nickname of Beefeaters and there are several competing theories as to why. One common theory, that it derives from the French *buffetier* (waiter), has been dismissed by the *Oxford English Dictionary*. It is more likely that the name comes from the practice of part-paying the wardens in meat. Count Cosimo, Grand Duke of Tuscany, visited the Tower in 1669 and commented that, 'A very large ration of beef is given to them daily at court...that they might be called Beef-eaters'. Another theory concerns the ravens. They are fed on raw meat bought at Smithfield Meat Market personally by the Ravenmaster. So it may be that it is the ravens themselves who are the Beefeaters? We may never know the exact origin.

Yeoman Warders have been patrolling the Tower since 1485, making them the oldest military corps in the UK, and are all retired non-commissioned officers from the Army, Royal Marines or Royal Air Force. In 2007 Moira Cameron became the first female Beefeater.

In earlier times, the Yeoman Warders were responsible for guarding prisoners. And it was generally only very important or dangerous prisoners that were incarcerated, tortured and executed at the Tower. These have included King David II of Scotland, King John II of France, Charles I de Valois Duke of Orléans, King Henry VI, Queen Elizabeth I, Sir Walter Raleigh, Guy Fawkes, Lord George Gordon, Rudolf Hess and The Kray twins – the last prisoners to be held there in 1952 for failing to report for national service. Many of these miserable souls made their entrance via one of the Tower of London's most famous structures – the **Traitors' Gate.** The gate was designed and built between 1275 and 1279 on the orders of King Edward I and was originally known as the Watergate, but was later changed when it was used to bring in high security or important prisoners. The gate lies at the base of St Thomas's Tower (named for Thomas Becket) and can be found at water level adjoining the **River Thames.** The journey along the Thames would have taken the prisoners under

London Bridge where the heads of previously executed traitors were impaled on spikes.

The River Thames has a rich literary history, featuring in plays, novels, poems and essays by some of the greatest writers in the English language. Perhaps one of the most famous – and certainly most entertaining – descriptions of the river can be found in Jerome K. Jerome's *Three Men in a Boat* (1889). Jerome spent several years as a jobbing but penniless actor before trying his hand at journalism, teaching, being a clerk for a solicitor and then working as a packer in a factory. However, in 1885, he enjoyed some success with a book called *On the Stage – and Off* and this launched his writing career. It was his honeymoon on the Thames with his wife Georgina (not a raven) that inspired his most famous book.

Jerome also wrote a series of humorous essays collected as *Idle Thoughts of an Idle Fellow* (1886) and in 1892 was therefore chosen to edit *The Idler* (over Rudyard Kipling), a satirical magazine catering to gentlemen who 'appreciated idleness'.

*The Idler* is an annual magazine ...

How do you connect **ammonites** to
**St Patrick**
and **John Dowland**?

## *Pearls of Melancholy*

The musician **Sting** (real name Gordon Sumner) has had a species of Colombian tree frog, *Dendropsophus stingi* named after him in recognition of his commitment and efforts to save the rainforest. Sting shot to fame in the late 1970s with his band the Police. In 2006, he released a classical album called *Songs from the Labyrinth* in which he and lutenist Edin Karamazov perform songs written by **John Dowland**.

John Dowland is best known for his 'melancholy songs' that bear such depressing titles as 'Flow My Tears', 'I Saw My Lady Weepe' and 'In Darkness Let Me Dwell'. *Melancholia* was a popular musical movement in Elizabethan times and Dowland could be considered the Morrissey of his day.

While a popular writer and performer, it appears that Dowland's Catholic leanings didn't ingratiate him with Elizabeth I and he initially failed to be offered a post at her court. Instead, he worked for Christian IV of Denmark. However, he did return to England in 1606 and, in 1612, was appointed as a royal lutenist to the court of King James I. It has been noted that no new compositions exist after this time.

The late science fiction author **Philip K. Dick** was a fan of Dowland's music and referenced the composer in several ways. He often assumed the pen-name of Jack Dowland. And he also incorporated the title of one of Dowland's best known pieces into the title of his novel *Flow My Tears, The Policeman Said*.

Philip Kindred Dick was an American writer whose work has been frequently used as the starting point for feature films. *Total Recall*

(1990), was based on Dick's short story *We Can Remember It For You Wholesale*. Other films include *Minority Report* (2002), *Paycheck* (2003), *A Scanner Darkly* (2006), *Screamers* (1995), *Next* (based on the story *The Golden Man*) in 2007 and, most famously, *Blade Runner* (1982) based on Dick's 1968 story *Do Androids Dream of Electric Sheep?*

Dick died on March 2nd 1982 following a stroke but his fans brought him back by creating a life-sized remote-controlled lookalike for the San Diego Comic Convention. However, in February 2006, an airline lost the 'android', and it has not been seen since.

In his early teens, Dick suffered from recurring bad dreams and visions which he described as 'laser beams and geometric patterns, and, occasionally, brief pictures of Jesus and of ancient Rome'. He began to imagine that he was living a double existence, one as Philip K. Dick in 1970s America, the other as Thomas, a Christian perse-cuted by Romans in the 1st century CE.

In many modern scientific and other secular works (including this book), the older terms AD and BC have been replaced by CE (common era) and BCE (before common era). However, both conventions use the same dates i.e. 1961 AD is the same as 1961 CE.

The abbreviation AD stands for *Anno Domini*, which is Latin for 'In the year of Our Lord' and is used to describe dates after the supposed year of Jesus' birth. The system was created by Dionysius Exiguus in the 6th century AD. He also suggested the term BC to mean dates 'Before Christ'.

BC was the name of a long-running strip written and drawn by American cartoonist Johnny Hart from 1958 until his death in 2007. Like Philip K. Dick, he died of a stroke. The strip features cavemen and various prehistoric beasts ranging from dinosaurs to mammoths all coexisting side-by-side, just like they do in Hollywood films like Ray Harryhausen's *One Million Years BC* and at Kentucky's Crea-tion Museum. Scientific evidence tends to support the idea that the last dinosaur (discounting birds) died a good 65 million years before the first human arrived.[100] The name of the BC cartoon strip obviously comes from the fact that it is set way before the birth of Christ. How-ever, it also references Hart's home of **Broome** County, New York.

100. Dinosaurs were around for a long time. The period of time between Stegosaurus becoming extinct and Tyrannosaurus rex appearing (85 million years) is greater than the time between T-rex dying off and humans appearing.

Broome is also the name of a town in the Kimberley region of Western Australia, 2200 km north of Perth. The town features Australia's most famous nudist beach, Cable Beach, which is bounded at one side by the amusingly named Willie Creek. The town's history revolves around the harvesting of natural **pearls**, always a dangerous profession. The town's Japanese cemetery has more than 900 graves of divers who died while collecting the valuable stones.

Pearls are produced by marine pearl oysters (family *Pteriidae*), freshwater pearl mussels (families *Unionidae* and *Margaritiferidae*) and, much less commonly, by clams, whelks, abalones and the queen conch (*Strombus gigas*) – a kind of giant snail – although these pearls lack the iridescence found in the more valuable oyster and mussel pearls. The inside of the mussel and oyster shells is coated in a substance called *nacre*, or mother of pearl, which is secreted by the animal within. A pearl is formed as a response to an irritant inside the mollusc's shell. The idea that the irritant is a grain of sand is very rarely true. Usually it is organic material like rotting food or a parasite that enters the shell when it is open for feeding. The animal secretes nacre to cover the intruder. Adding successive layers is what creates the pearl.

The largest 'pearl' ever found came from the Philippines in 1934. In fact, it is technically not a pearl at all, being a calcium-based secretion related to but not actually nacre. However, it does weigh in at a staggering 14 lb (6.4 kg). It was named The Pearl of Allah by the local Muslim tribal chief because it resembled a turbaned head.

The pearl has long been greatly valued as a gemstone and is one of only a very few decorative 'stones' produced by a living organism. The others are jet (aka *lignite*, made from compressed fossilised wood), amber (a fossilised tree sap) and **ammolite**.[101]

Ammolite is a rare and valuable opal-like gemstone found in the Rocky Mountains of the United States and Canada. It is made of the fossilised shells of ammonites, which in turn were originally composed of minerals including calcite, silica, pyrite and aragonite, the same mineral found in nacre. Ammonites are an extinct group of marine molluscs that were closely related to modern octopus, squid, cuttlefish and nautilus. They survived several major Mass Extinction

101. Other organic material is used as decoration too, such as shell, ivory, coral, etc. However, they have not been turned into gemstones by time and immense pressure.

Events, but disappeared along with the dinosaurs 65 million years ago in the Cretaceous-Paleogene extinction event (The K-Pg MEE).

Their fossil shells usually take the form of coiled flat spirals, which is why Pliny the Elder named them *Ammonis cornua* because they resembled the 'horns of Ammon', an Egyptian god. In mediaeval Europe, they were thought to be petrified snakes, or **'snakestones'** and were assumed to be evidence for the actions of saints such as St Hilda and **St Patrick**.

St Patrick is said to have banished all of the snakes from Ireland and, sure enough, there are no native species to this day. Despite his association with the revels of March 17th and all things Irish, Patrick was British. He was carried off by pirates as a child and spent six years in slavery before escaping and becoming a missionary. He is credited with almost single-handedly introducing Christianity to Ireland.

The only UK national **patron saint** who actually comes from the place he represents is St David of Wales. Scotland's patron saint, St Andrew, was from Israel. He is believed to have been a fisherman from Galilee who, along with his older brother Simon Peter (who later became St Peter), became disciples of Jesus. Cornwall's patron saint, St Piran – whose life and deeds are celebrated during the annual St Piran's Day celebrations on March 5th – miraculously floated across from his native Ireland on a millstone. St George, meanwhile, probably never even set foot on English soil.

He's a bit of a mystery man is our George. One story says that he was born to a Christian family in Turkey during the 3rd century. His father was killed in battle so his mother took him back to her native Palestine where he was raised. In time, George became a soldier and achieved the rank of Tribune under the Emperor Diocletian before he was 30 years old. However, when Caesar Galerius decided to embark upon a persecution of Christians, George refused to take part and criticised the Emperor's decision. Diocletian ordered that George be tortured to renounce his Christianity. George refused despite terrible punishment and was eventually beheaded on April 23rd 303. His martyrdom convinced many others to convert to Christianity.

But it was during his military career that he performed the feat for which he is most famed. A dragon lived in a lake near Silena, Libya, and demanded two sheep every day from locals. When it didn't get its portion of mutton, it demanded a young maiden instead. George arrived in the area just as the local village lottery had chosen a young princess to be future dragon poo. Despite the fact that whole armies had been destroyed while taking on the beastie, George crossed himself and rode into battle and killed it with one blow of his sword. As the result, everyone around about became Christians and George distributed his prize (a generous bounty from the princess's dad) among the poor before riding off into the sunset.

Of course, there are any number of spoilsports who'll point out that the story is just an allegory about the triumph of Christianity over other faiths. But the dragon story is a lot more fun and George soon became a bit of a cult figure because he was chivalrous, strong, generous and devoted. He was all of the things that men wanted to be and all of the things women wanted men to be. By the 15th century, his feast day was as popular and important as Christmas Day. And it's celebrated in many countries still.

The cult of St George probably reached the UK with the Crusaders returning from the Holy Lands in the 12th century. Edward III was keen to promote the ideals of chivalry and knighthood in his kingdom and so adopted George as the patron saint of England and dedicated the chapel at Windsor Castle to his honour. And so it continued, with George becoming the icon for all the things that the English aspired to. He was commemorated in song and poetry and prayer. The George Cross was founded as an award for extraordinary bravery in battle. And St George's flag – the red cross on white – became the English flag.

There's a patron saint for just about any activity or job you care to think of. Here are some of my favourites:

St Basil the Great – patron saint of hospital administrators;
St Fiacre – of taxi-drivers, venereal disease sufferers, horticulturists and haemorrhoid sufferers;
St Cassian of Imola – of shorthand writers;
St Abhai – of venomous reptiles;
St Foillan – of truss-makers;
St René Goupil – of anaesthesiologists;
St Gummarus – of lumberjacks;
St Isidore of Sevilla – of computer programming;
St Januarius – of blood banks;
St Albinus of Angers – against pirate attacks;

St Joseph the Betrothed – of fighting Communism;

St Olaf – of difficult marriages;

St Martha – of dieticians;

St Peter the Apostle – of fishmongers, clockmakers and virgins (and much more. Also called upon to tackle snake bites, rabies and demonic possession).

St Raymond of Penyafort – of medical record librarians; and

St Jambon – the patron saint of ham.

St Terese of the Andes is the patron saint of bodily ills, illness, sick people, sickness and young people in general. She is also known as Saint Juanita Fernandez Solar.

The word 'solar' derives directly from the Latin *solaris* ('of the sun'). The term **'solar power'** first appeared in 1908.

The comic book hero **Superman** is solar powered. The cells of his body absorb electromagnetic radiation from yellow stars (like earth's sun) and store it like a living solar battery. Green kryptonite interferes with this semi-photosynthetic process.

'Nothing Like the Sun' is a line from William Shakespeare's 130th sonnet (*My Mistress' Eyes are Nothing Like the Sun*) and was chosen as the title for Sting's 1987 solo album. The album was influenced by the death of his mother and work with the charity Amnesty International, one of several good causes that the singer has supported throughout the years.

The musician **Sting** (real name Gordon Sumner) has had ...

# INVESTIGATION 23

How do you connect **spermicide** to the
**Citroën 2CV** and the
**transmigration of the soul?**

## He ain't Heavy, he's an Electron

**Murder** is the deliberate, calculated and unlawful act of killing some-one 'with malice aforethought'. Most killings are nothing of the sort and result from sudden anger, self-defence or accident. Consequently, the term **homicide** is employed as a blanket term to distinguish it from murder. Homicide means, simply, 'the killing of a person' but makes no judgement about the perpetrator. Technically, it means the killing of a man – from the Latin *homo* (man) and *caedere* (to kill). Killing a woman should be referred to as femicide.

Related words are matricide (mother), patricide (father), fratricide (sibling), sororicide (specifically a sister – sometimes applied to so-called 'Honour killings'), filicide (a child), infanticide (baby), familicide (spouse and children), uxoricide (wife), mariticide (husband), feticide (foetus) and prolicide (killing offspring either before or soon after birth). Parricide means killing your father, mother or other close relative or a person whose role resembles that of a parent such as a stepfather, godmother, community leader, etc. Then there's genocide (a race of people), tyrannicide (tyrant), regicide (killing a king or queen), gendercide (killing of specific sex) and suicide (self).

The '-icide' suffix is also applied to things other than people. Spermicide and ovicide refer to the destruction of viable gametes. Then there's insecticide, lousicide (lice), termiticide, amoebicide and the generic pesticide, herbicide, fungicide and germicide.[102]

There are lots of names to describe the various categories of killing

---

102. The word 'decide' also has a similar theme of elimination. The term comes from the Latin *decidere* meaning to 'cut away' or 'eliminate'. A decision involves elimi-nating all but one choice.

but they all result in **death**. For most of history, death was assumed to be when the person appeared to stop breathing or had no pulse. Given that medical science has only developed instruments to help measure these things in the past 200 years, some people may have been declared dead who were actually comatose.[103] These days, death is said to occur when brain function ceases. The body can be kept alive and nourished by artificial means but once all electrical activity in the brain has gone, it cannot be 'rebooted'. At least not yet. Whatever measure is used, it is accepted within most religions that when the body is dead, the soul leaves the body. Some believe that it is reincarnated in a new body (transmigration), others that it goes to heaven or ascends to some higher plane of existence.

In 1901 an American surgeon called **Duncan MacDougall** conducted a series of experiments to see whether the soul could be detected leaving the body. In order to do this he enlisted the help of several terminal 'consumptives' (people dying of tuberculosis) and popped them and their bed onto a sensitive set of scales. At the moment of death, any sudden unexpected weight-loss might indicate the soul vacating the body, he reasoned.

His experiments did show a sudden loss in some of the subjects. However, MacDougall remained scientific and impartial and attempted to find logical explanations for the loss. These included his equipment malfunctioning, exhalation of air (which, as we know, has mass and weight), water evaporation or any number of other reasons more likely than the migration of a soul. He was unable to account for the weight loss. The figure most often quoted when referring to his experiments is 21 grams – it has become such a part of cultural history that it even spawned a 2003 film of that name. However, MacDougall's experiments yielded a range of results across six subjects. The weight they lost was:

¾oz (21 grams);
½oz (14.1g) rising to 1½oz (42.5g) during examination;
½oz rising to 1½oz during examination;
No result due to 'interference by people opposed to our work';
⅜oz (10.6g); and
No result due to patient expiring before equipment set up.

103. The stethoscope was invented as recently as 1816 by French doctor René Laennec in order to hear the heartbeat in very obese patients.

MacDougall's experiments are not held to be particularly significant within the fields of either medicine or philosophy but, in more recent years, they have piqued the curiosity of physicists. If MacDougall's findings were correct (and that is a big if), could the weight loss be the person's personality being discharged? We now know that much of our brain activity – what we would call personality, emotion, memory, etc. – takes the form of electrical signals and electricity, like all energy, cannot be created or destroyed, only converted from one form to another.[104] So, when electrical activity in the brain ceases, where does it go? Does it dissipate into the air? It's an intriguing idea, made all the more so by the fact that energy also has mass.

In 2007, Harvard University professor Russell Seitz asked himself the question, 'If energy has mass, how much does the internet weigh?' Of course, he wasn't including the infrastructure of the internet – the cables, servers, silicon chips, copper wire, etc. – but only the data itself. He calculated that the weight of all the electrons in motion that make up the internet at any one moment is equivalent to around 50 grams or 1¾ ounces or the equivalent of a decent-sized strawberry.[105] And yet, to drive that 50 grams around the world, it takes the equivalent of a staggering 50 million **horsepower**.[106]

Horsepower is a unit of measurement we use to define the power output of the drive component of a machine, e.g. a piston, engine or turbine. The measure was originally created to gauge the effectiveness of early steam engines against horses that had been doing the same work. Although there have been a number of different measures of horsepower used around the world, the mechanical horsepower measure we use here in the UK is 33,000 pounds of force per minute (a human can exert a maximum of around 1.2hp briefly and about

104. This is the *First Law of Thermodynamics: The Conservation of Energy*. The total amount of energy and matter in the universe remains constant, merely changing from one form to another.
105. So, if MacDougall was right, the internet has approximately twice the mass of a human soul (which weighs the same as half a strawberry).
106. Another scientist, Prof John Kubiatowicz of the University of California, Berkeley, recently suggested that a fully loaded Kindle electronic book reader weighs more than an empty one. Each e-book is about as heavy as a single molecule of DNA. Filling a 4GB Kindle to its storage limit would increase its weight by a billionth of a billionth of a gram (0.000000000000000001 g) or the weight of a small virus.

o.1hp indefinitely). It must be noted that horsepower has since been superceded by the watt and can only be used as a secondary measure. One horsepower is the equivalent of 745.699872w. And, oddly enough, the average horse produces less than 1hp.

In 1940s France you were taxed on the number of horses you owned. Therefore, as cars started to be introduced, it was decided to tax the vehicles on their equivalent horsepower. In 1948 this led to Citroën boss Pierre-Jules Boulanger creating a car specifically for the French peasant. He asked André Lefèbvre to design a low-priced 'umbrella on four wheels' for the mostly horse-using rural population. His brief was for a car that could transport four peasants and 50kg of potatoes for 100kms (78 miles) on three litres of petrol at 30mph. It also had to have a suspension system that would allow the car to be driven across a ploughed field with a basket of eggs on board without breaking any.[107] The result was the **Citroën 2CV** which stood for *deux chevaux vapeur*, or 'two steam horses'. With its 425cc engine, it was deemed to be the equivalent of two horses and was taxed as such. The car stayed in production until 1990.

During the German occupation of France in World War II Boulanger organised some delightfully subtle sabotage at the commandeered Citroën truck factory by changing the position of the notch on the oil dipstick. This resulted in engine seizure, infuriating the occupation troops. This small but powerful action supported the greater **French Resistance** movement.

In the UK, a similar resistance movement was formed in case a Nazi invasion force ever landed in Britain. Known as **Auxiliary Units,** these were men who were not in the regular army – most were in reserved occupations such as farmers or miners – who were sworn to utmost secrecy and trained in a variety of deadly guerrilla techniques such as bomb making and assassination. They had no uniform (although many were also members of the local Home Guard) and they were so secret that records at War Office level are almost non-existent. Group photographs from the war years were banned in case they fell into enemy hands and recruitment was by word of mouth and personal recommendation. Such was their secrecy of purpose, the men who formed, manned and operated the patrols were told

107. On seeing the prototype, Boulanger asked that the height of the roof be raised by a few inches so that he could drive the car while wearing a hat.

that they would never receive any recognition other than the nation's thanks. It is only relatively recently that the existence of the Auxiliary Units has been officially recognised and medals awarded.

Around 3500 such men were trained on weekend courses at Coleshill House near Highworth, Wiltshire, in the arts of assassination, unarmed combat, demolition and sabotage.[108] All were given a buff-coloured book called the *Countryman's Diary 1939*, designed to sit innocently on any bookshelf disguised as a seed and fertiliser catalogue. In fact it gave instructions on subjects like how to make nail bombs, how to kill someone with a knife and how to blow up railway lines, bridges and petrol dumps.

Patrols secretly reconnoitred local country houses, which might be used by German officers, in preparation. Extraordinarily, some survivors claim that they had orders to assassinate certain people if an invasion occurred who: (a) might be sympathisers; or (b) had knowledge that the Nazis could extract and make use of. High on the list was the local Chief Constable of Police. It was felt that such killings would be 'justifiable homicide'. During times of war, openly declared hostilities mean that killing enemy soldiers on the battlefield is not unlawful, as long as it abides by the rules of conduct laid down by the Geneva Convention. In this instance, although the victim was actually on the same side, their death would be justifiable because the killing of one person could guarantee the lives and safety of many. It would not be murder.

**Murder** is the deliberate, calculated and unlawful act of killing...

108. www.coleshillhouse.com

How do you connect **Pac-Man**
to **shoe sizes** and
**Pandora's Box**?

## Pandora's Shoe Box

The classic video game *Pong* – a kind of simplistic digital tennis – was invented in 1958 by William A. Higinbotham at Brookhaven National Laboratory, Long Island. It was originally played on an oscilloscope and was called *Tennis for Two*. It appeared as a video arcade game licensed by **Atari** in 1972 and is often cited as being the first ever commercial video arcade game. However, *Computer Space* by Nutting Associates had appeared a year earlier. So why did *Pong* take off when *Computer Space* didn't? Nolan Bushnell, one of the founders of Atari, claims that it was because the Nutting game required the user to read an instruction book first while *Pong* could be played immediately. Bushnell employed an electronics expert called Allan Alcorn to create a version of *Pong* as a game that 'any drunk in any bar can play'. Soon, a home *Pong* console became available and hundreds of thousands of units were sold. However, the public's interest in *Pong* consoles had tailed off by the late 1970s, when more sophisticated games like *Space Invaders* and *Pac-Man* became available.

Bushnell formed the Atari company with Ted Dabney with an investment of just $250 each. To begin with, they were going to call the company Syzygy, an astronomical term they found in the dictionary that means the alignment of heavenly bodies. But they discovered that a candle company already had the name, so they chose Atari, which is a term used in the game *Go* that roughly equates to 'check' in chess.

**Go**, also known as Igo, Goe, Baduk, Paduk or Weiqi, originated in China. Some legends place its origins as long ago as 2337–2258 BCE when Emperor Yao had the game designed to teach discipline, concentration and balance to his unruly son, Danzhu. The earliest written reference to the game appears in 424 BCE in the annals of Zuo Zhuan.

Go is played on a grid of black painted lines (usually 19 by 19). The playing pieces, white or black 'stones' (*goishi*), are played on the intersections of the lines. The aim is to control a larger part of the board than your opponent by placing your stones in a way that forms 'territories' that cannot be captured. It has been claimed that Go is the most complex game in the world and this is why it has proved resilient to computer programming. Consequently, although it may have inspired the name of the first commercially successful computer games company, there is still as yet no computerised Go that can beat a human. Because of the vast number of variations possible in every game, one numerical estimate claims that the number of possible games of Go far exceeds the number of atoms in the known universe.

One common estimate for the number of atoms in the universe is $10^{80}$. The entire universe may have as many as $10^{700}$. These are BIG numbers. But the universe is a big place. The **observable universe**[109] contains about 30 sextillion to one septillion (3 to 100 × 1022) stars grouped into more than 80 billion galaxies, which themselves form clusters and superclusters. The edge of the observable universe is currently calculated to be around 14.3 billion **parsecs** (about 46.6 billion **light years**) away.

A parsec is a unit of distance corresponding to 3.26 light years, or about 19,000,000,000,000 (19 trillion) miles (31 trillion kilometres).[110] A light year is the distance that light travels in a vacuum in one Julian year (365.25 days). As light travels at around 186,000 miles per second, a light year is therefore around 6,000,000,000,000 (six trillion) miles or ten trillion kilometres.

109. The 'observable universe' is getting larger. After the Big Bang (13.75 billion years ago), the universe expanded at speeds much greater than light speed (although within the universe, lightspeed is considered an absolute speed limit). Since then, everything in the universe has been rushing away from everything else. But because the earth is only 4.5 billion years old and light can only travel at a maximum speed of 186,000 miles per second, some objects have travelled so far from us that the light from them hasn't reached us yet.

110. Parsec is a contraction of 'Parallax Second' as it is the distance from the sun to an astronomical object which has a parallax angle of one arcsecond. Nope, me neither.

Metric units of distance measurement, such as kilometres, **metres** and centimetres, are based upon a mathematical dissection of the size of the earth. One metre is one ten-millionth of the distance from the earth's equator to the North Pole (at sea level) passing through the Paris meridian.[111] For most people, that's quite hard to visualise, which is one of the reasons why various pressure groups have fought hard to keep the older 'common-sense' measures of feet and inches. These were based not on fractions of the circumference of the earth but upon everyday things you could see, including the human body. One inch is approximately the same length as the width of an adult male's thumb, across the knuckle. Or three barleycorns. The distance across the palm is around four inches (the hand is still retained as a measure for the height of horses, although they are now officially measured in centimetres). Three hands make a foot, which is the same length as an adult male size nine foot.[112] This same measure can be found in the distance between the wrist bone and the elbow. A yard is approximately the distance from hip to ground or the length of a walking stick (or yard stick). And one thousand paces was the original Roman **mile** (from the Latin *mille passuum* – one thousand paces). A mile is now 5280 feet (1760 yards, or about 1609 metres). For that to equate to a 1000 paces, it would entail a stride of 1.76 yards or 5¼ feet. As the average stride is between two to three feet, you'd need to be about nine to ten feet (2.7 to 3.0 metres) tall, like the alien blue-skinned **Na'vi** people in James Cameron's 2009 film *Avatar* (who would probably take a UK **shoe size** of 17½ to 18).[113] The Na'vi inhabit a moon called **Pandora** that orbits a gas giant planet called Polyphemus.

In Greek mythology, Pandora was the first woman. Her name means 'all giving'. According to the writer Hesiod (ca. 8th–7th

---

111. Since 1983, it has been defined as the length of the path travelled by light in a vacuum during a time interval of 1/299,792,458 of a second.

112. The average UK foot was a size 8 until the start of the 21st century. Therefore a size 8 shoe would be around a foot long. UK size 9 is now the average shoe size. The US equivalent is size 10. Health experts put this down to increases in obesity across populations.

113. You get this figure by multiplying 15.5 (male) or 14.5 (female) by your height in inches and then divide by 100. This formula is for US shoe sizes so adapt accordingly. I am 5'10 (70ins) and, sure enough, I do take a size 9–9½ shoe (US size 10–10½).

centuries BCE), Zeus ordered that she be created as a punishment for Mankind. This was because we were mucking about with fire after it had been stolen by Prometheus using some dried fennel. Woman was Man's punishment for handling stolen goods. Pandora was given various traits by the gods: Aphrodite gave her 'cruel longing and cares that weary the limbs' and Hermes gave her 'a shameful mind and deceitful nature' and 'lies and crafty words'. But worst of all, Pandora was equipped with a jar containing 'burdensome toil and sickness that brings death to men'. And we all know what happened when she opened the jar…

'Jar?' I hear you cry. 'Surely you mean Pandora's Box?' Well, actually, no. She was known for carrying a *pithos* containing all the world's evils. The mistranslation of *pithos* as 'box' is attributed to a 16th-century humanist and theologian called Desiderius Erasmus of Rotterdam. He wrote extensively (he is credited with coining the adage, 'In the land of the blind, the one-eyed man is king') and translated many old reference works and epic poems into Latin. During one such translation of Hesiod's works he mistook the Greek word *pithos* – which is a kind of jar used for storing grain – for *pyxis*, meaning 'box'. The phrase 'Pandora's box' has stayed with us ever since.

The Pandora is an open-source gaming console created specifically to allow so-called 'homebrew' game development and play. It was designed by computer users for computer users and is not tied in to any major computer or software company. In fact it was funded entirely by pre-orders. The product name reflects the idea of releasing many more affordable games onto the market without paying the bigger corporations. Another feature is that the Pandora can run computer games designed originally for other platforms.

**Computer games** or video games rose in popularity with the arrival of microprocessor-driven personal computers in the late 1970s and 1980s. However, the earliest computer game was called OXO, a version of noughts and crosses (or tic-tac-toe) created in 1952 using Cambridge University's **EDSAC1** computer.[114] EDSAC1 was built in what had once been the dissecting room (and filled the whole room) of the university's anatomy school. This meant that it benefited from a large goods lift that had been designed to carry two cadavers. But it

114. Electronic Delay Storage Automatic Calculator.

also meant that the place stank of formalin that had soaked into the floorboards. It wasn't the healthiest of working environments and boasted frequent poisonous mercury spillages and an electromagnetic radiation output so high that it garnered complaints for interfering with local radio stations. EDSAC1 ran its first program in May 1949 and was the first computer to store both data and programs, paving the way for future machines. A version of EDSAC1 is currently being reconstructed at Bletchley Park at the UK's National Museum of Computing.[115] However, it cannot use the original memory storage units – five feet long columns of mercury – due to Health and Safety regulations.[116]

The first recognisable video game appeared a few years later in 1961 when MIT students Martin Graetz, Alan Kotok and Steve Russell created *Spacewar!* on the University's PDP-1 mainframe computer. The game showed a simple graphic of two spaceships both in orbit around a star and two players could then attempt to shoot each other's ship. It was predated by the game *Pong* by three years but *Pong* was not a program that could be run on computers. Rather, it was a game created using specially designed components and hardware.

The classic video game *Pong* – a kind of simplistic digital tennis ...

115. www.tnmoc.org
116. The first ever business computer was developed not by an electronics lab or a university but by Lyons' Coffee Houses. In 1951, LEO1 – Lyons Electronic Office – began calculating the company's weekly bakery distribution totals. The computer filled 5000 square feet of office space but was so successful that LEO2 machines were soon developed and sold to companies such as Ford and BOC and to Customs and Excise and the Post Office. In researching LEO1's construction, staff from Lyons met the creators of EDSAC1 and helped to fund it with a donation of £3000.

# INVESTIGATION 25

How do you connect **Michael Jackson**
to **yellow fever** and
**Pablo Picasso?**

## *On the Never Never*

Peter Pan lives in the fictional world of **Neverland**. It first appeared in
J.M. Barrie's play *Peter Pan* and his subsequent novel *Peter and
Wendy*. In the earliest drafts of the play, it was called *Peter's Never
Never Never Land*, but later versions reduced it to *Never Never
Land*. In the published play, it was shortened to *Never Land* and in
the novel, it mutated into a single word: *Neverland*. In Neverland,
people never get any older. Peter leads young Wendy Darling and her
brothers to Neverland by flying towards the 'second star on the right
and straight on 'til morning'.[117]

It's a common misconception that Peter Pan creator James
Matthew Barrie invented the name 'Wendy'. The name was already
in use, albeit uncommonly, in the USA, England and especially Wales
where it was a common contraction of Gwendolyne. However, the
publication of *Peter and Wendy* did popularise the name. Another
story claims that the character was originally called Mia but that
Barrie hit upon the name Wendy after hearing it from a friend's four-
year-old daughter.[118] The poet William Henley often called Barrie
'Friend' and his daughter Margaret would try to copy this, referring

---

117. Years ago, when I did a little stand-up, one of my gags was: 'As Never Never Land
is a double negative, did Peter Pan actually live in Always Sometimes Land?' I
didn't do stand-up for long.

118. Barrie's many friends included Arthur Conan Doyle (with whom he wrote a
musical that bombed), Robert Louis Stevenson, George Bernard Shaw, H.G.
Wells, Robert Falcon Scott, Thomas Hardy, G.K. Chesterton and Jerome K.
Jerome – who introduced Barrie to his future wife. Barrie also played in a cricket
team with *Winnie the Pooh* author A.A. Milne.

to Barrie as 'Fwendy-Wendy' in that endearing way that under-fives do.

Peter Pan shares his name with the Greek god of shepherds and flocks but, other than playing the pipes, has very little in common. The classical Pan was a goat from the waist down and sported a pair of horns much like Fauns and Satyrs. The name Pan is derived from the Greek *paein* which means 'to pasture'.

The late **Michael Jackson** was often called the 'Peter Pan of Pop' due to his constantly changing appearance and childlike personality. And, of course, his ranch in Los Olivos, Santa Barbara, California was called Neverland. Jackson also famously had a pet **chimpanzee** called Bubbles. In a curious coincidence, the Latin name for chimpanzee is *Pan troglodytes*.

A German art expert, Katja Schneider of the State Art Museum of Moritzburg, was once fooled into believing that a painting done by a chimpanzee was the work of Guggenheim Prize-winning artist Ernst Wilhelm Nay. It was, in fact, painted by a 31-year-old chimp called Banghi. A similar event took place in 1978 when 100 Frankfurt art critics were invited to the premiere exhibition of exciting new artist Yamasaki. Impressed by the 'convincing luminosity of his colours' and 'the excitement of his powerfully dynamic brushwork' the critics bought all 22 exhibits. The exhibition organiser, Behrend Fedderson, then produced the artist – a chimpanzee – and announced that proceeds of the sale would go to the circus that owned the chimp. And three paintings by a chimpanzee sold for a staggering £12,000 in 2005. They were painted by Congo, star of the Granada TV show *Zoo Time*, which was shown during the 1950s and 60s in the UK. During his lifetime, Congo completed around 400 drawings and paintings. One was owned by Pablo Picasso.

*HMS Congo* was the Royal Navy's very first steam-powered warship. Or, rather, it should have been. Built in 1816 at Deptford Dockyard in London, she was classified as a steam sloop and fitted with a 30 ton steam engine connected to a pair of paddles. However, the engine was so under-powered that the ship could only manage three knots at top speed. Therefore, it was re-equipped with sails and the engine was removed and used to pump out the docks at Plymouth. HMS *Congo* was originally commissioned to explore the African river that shares its name. However, its one and only expedition achieved nothing. All it proved was that the river was only navigable for about 100 miles. This fact cost the lives of 38 of the 56 expedition members who died of **yellow fever.**

Yellow fever is an acute viral disease spread by the bite of the yellow fever mosquito (*Aedes aegypti*). It causes fever, nausea, pain and jaundice, hence the name. Around 200,000 people a year are affected by yellow fever and the annual death toll is around 30,000. There is no cure for the disease but it can be prevented by vaccination. It is believed to have evolved in Africa but soon spread to South America and to some North American states by way of the Slave Trade.

It could be said that yellow fever helped shape American history. When the disease took hold along the Mississippi river and its tributaries in the last years of the 18th century it killed over 100,000 people. In 1793 Philadelphia suffered an epidemic that killed around 5000 people; 10% of the population in the first month alone. It was the final nail in the coffin for any hope that the city might have had to become the permanent site of the nation's capitol. It then became one of the factors that prevented Napoleon from maintaining a French stake in the New World. In 1802 he sent his brother-in-law, General Charles Leclerc, and an army to suppress a revolt in Haiti; then the French colony of Saint-Domingue. But two-thirds of his force – between 35,000 and 45,000 troops (and his brother-in-law) – soon fell to the humble mosquito. Already facing bankruptcy and an imminent war with Britain, Napoleon realised that his colonies in the Americas were no longer defensible and so was forced to realise his assets at a bargain-basement price of just three cents per acre. This was the Louisiana Purchase that effectively doubled the size of the United States. No wonder then that the disease was also once known as the American plague. It was also known as **Yellow Jack.**

The Yellow Jack is the nickname for a flag flown from vessels under quarantine while in harbour. It is divided into four equal squares with the top left and bottom right coloured yellow and the other two black. Ships in harbour carrying serious contagious disease were sometimes burned or anchored and turned into **Lazarets** or Lazarettos. The name is derived from Lazar Houses (leper colonies) operated by the Order of St Lazarus, a society of Knights Hospitallers who also had leprosy themselves.

One of the very first cinematic depictions of leprosy – more properly known as Hansen's Disease – was in Cecil B. DeMille's 1923 silent masterpiece *The Ten Commandments* when Moses' sister Miriam develops leprosy scars on her arms in real time. The groundbreaking special effects involved the use of coloured filters and were pioneered by **Roy Pomeroy** who won an Oscar for technical effects at the first ever Academy Awards in 1927. He then became one of the 36 founding members of AMPAS,[119] which has awarded the Oscars from 1929 to the present. Pomeroy's next success was *Peter Pan* in 1924; the first ever film adaptation of the stage play. The film is deemed of 'cultural significance' by the US Library of Congress, not least because of Pomeroy's innovative special effects. In this film he had to create the character of Tinker Bell the fairy, make the characters fly convincingly, make Peter's severed shadow come to life and show Peter sweeping up fairies – all played by real actors – with a broom.

Peter Pan lives in the fictional world of **Neverland**...

119. Academy of Motion Picture Arts and Sciences.

How do you connect **Idaho** to
**Medusa the Gorgon**
and **Futurama**?

## *United States of Controversy*

Many of **America's 50 states** were named using Native American words. For example, Connecticut comes from the Mohegan word *quinnitukqut*, meaning 'place of long tidal river', Michigan comes from the Ojibwe term *mishigami*, meaning 'large water' and Texas is named after the Hasinai word *táysha* which means 'friends' or 'allies'. Some states' names come from other languages: Alaska comes from the Aleut *alaxsxaq* meaning 'the mainland', or more literally, 'the object/place towards which the action of the sea is directed'. Florida is from the Spanish for 'flowery' and California takes its name from a fictional island called California, ruled by Queen Califia.[120]

Some states are named after people: North and South Carolina were named by King Charles II in honour of his father, Charles I (Latin – *Carolus*). Washington is named after the US president and Louisiana after King Louis XIV of France. Virginia and West Virginia were named after Queen Elizabeth I – the so-called 'Virgin Queen'. The traditional story of the name 'Pennsylvania' is that it means 'Penn's forest' and was named in honour of Admiral William Penn by his son William Jnr, the colony's founder. However, in a letter from Penn to his friend Robert Turner, he explains that his first choice of name 'New Wales' was turned down by the king who liked the idea of naming it after the admiral. William Jnr therefore chose Pennsyl-

---

120. It appeared in a novel written in 1521 by Garcia Ordóñez de Montalvo called *The Exploits of the Very Powerful Cavalier Esplandian, Son of the Excellent King Amadis of Gaul*. It described an exotic island that lay much where the west coast of America lies now. It is probable that many of the early explorers to the Americas knew of the book and Cortés is said to have owned a copy.

vania as *pen* is Welsh for 'head' or 'high' and *sylvania* means 'woodland'. The addition of the extra 'n' appeased the king as it looked as if his preferred name had been agreed.

And then there is **Idaho**.

In the early 1860s, when the United States Congress was considering organising a new territory in the Rocky Mountains, eccentric lobbyist George M. Willing suggested the name 'Idaho', which he claimed was derived from a Shoshone phrase meaning 'gem of the mountains'. Some time later, however, Willing claimed that he'd made the word up – that it had just popped into his head. But several sources claim that the Shoshoni exclamation 'Ee-dah-how' means 'Behold! The sun coming down the mountain' or that the name is derived from the Apache word for 'enemy': *idaahe*. The exact origin may never be known.[121]

Idaho is a place of hidden treasures. Ask anyone to name the USA's deepest river gorge and they will probably say 'The Grand Canyon'. And they'd be wrong. The deepest river gorge is Idaho's Hells Canyon – 7,900 feet deep (the Grand Canyon's deepest drop is around 6,000 feet). Highest waterfalls in North America? Nope, it's not Niagara. It's the Shoshone Falls in Idaho which, at 212 feet, drop 52 feet further than their more famous northern relative. Idaho is also where you'll find the world's first Alpine-style ski lift. Built in Sun Valley by Union Pacific Railroad engineers in 1936, it was based upon a device used for loading banana boats. And the world's first nuclear power plant, which created its first electricity in 1951, can be found within the Idaho National Laboratory (INL), near Arco.

Rigby, Idaho, is known as 'The birthplace of television' since it was also the birthplace of one **Philo T. Farnsworth**. Scotsman John Logie Baird may have invented the first television set but it was Farnsworth, and his contemporary Vladimir Zworykin, who developed the electronic means to transmit and receive television signals. So while he may not have invented the television itself, Farnsworth was the father of television transmission.

Professor Hubert J. Farnsworth is a fictional mad scientist who

121. The origin of the name Des Moines, Iowa, is even funnier. It is derived from the Peoria Indians' claim that their rival tribe in that area were called the Moingoana. It was only after the city had been named that white settlers discovered that *moingoana* was actually a term of abuse meaning 'shitfaces'.

appears in the animated TV series *Futurama*. He was named after Philo T. Farnsworth[122] and University of California philosophy professor Hubert Dreyfus who was tutor to Eric Kaplan, one of the show's early writers and producers. It is implied on several occasions that the fictional professor indulges in cannibalism. In one episode he entreats Fry to eat an enemy's heart to benefit from its 'rich, tasty courage' and, on several occasions, he seems overly keen to harvest people's organs. In the episode *Roswell That Ends Well* he orders '**Soylent Green**, with some Soylent Orange and some Soylent coleslaw' from a fast food delivery service.

*Soylent Green* was a 1973 sci-fi movie starring Charlton Heston and Edward G Robinson. Set in the year 2022, it provided us with a dystopian view of future New York society; overcowded, globally-warmed and short of food. The plot revolves around a police officer called Robert Thorn (Heston) and his aged researcher friend Sol (Robinson) who are investigating the murder of a senior officer within the multinational Soylent company. Soylent produces a number of different food products that are dispensed in rationed amounts to the public by the State. The name 'Soylent' is an amalgam of soya and lentil. One of these products – Soylent Green – is supposedly made from plankton. During his investigation, Thorn discovers a terrible truth; namely that Soylent is made by recycling the dead into food products. Hence Heston's iconic cry of despair at the film's conclusion... 'Soylent Green is people!'[123]

Another controversial subject covered by the film was the legalisation and, indeed, encouraged use of voluntary euthanasia for the old, infirm or just fed up with life. Charlton Heston's tears during the scene in which Sol chooses euthanasia for himself were quite real. Edward G. Robinson was terminally ill with cancer during filming

---

122. Farnsworth is also referenced in the US sci-fi series *Warehouse 13* where the agents use video communication devices called 'Farnsworths' that are more effective than mobile phones.

123. There once was an urban myth that Charlton Heston chose his stage name by stabbing a map of London twice with a pin. The truth is that he was born John Charles Carter in the wonderfully-named town of No Man's Land, Illinois, and adopted his mother's maiden name (Charlton) and step-father's surname (Heston). But I almost wish the urban myth were true. Then, had he stabbed differently, he might have been Morden Oval, Croxley Blackfriars, Kennington Penge or Leyton Mudchute.

and Heston was the only cast member that he'd told. Robinson died nine days after shooting was complete on January 26th 1973. *Soylent Green* was his 90th and final film.

The film was loosely based upon a 1966 short story called *Make room! Make room!* by prolific sci-fi author **Harry Harrison**. Harrison – born Henry Maxwell Dempsey – penned a number of bestselling book series in his lifetime. He invented Slippery Jim diGriz (better known as *The Stainless Steel Rat*) and *Bill the Galactic Hero*. He also wrote the accliamed *Deathworld* series. But perhaps his most extraordinary and most applauded work is the Eden Trilogy: *West of Eden*, *Winter in Eden* and *Return to Eden*.

The books are based on the premise that the Chicxulub asteroid/meteor failed to hit the Yucatan peninsula 65 million years ago and the dinosaurs were not wiped out. Instead, they continued to evolve, eventually becoming the self-aware **Yilané** people. They develop language and culture, art, and a technology based upon genetic engineering of other life forms to make weapons, transport and other items. The books chronicle the story of what happens when human Stone Age hunter-gatherers meet the Yilané for the first time and the culture clash that ensues.

In designing his Yilané, Harrison sought the advice of experts in the fields of palaeontology and genetics, most notably Professor Jack Cohen. He wanted his reptilian race to have a realistic and plausible origin and biology. This is undoubtedly because reptiloid humanoids or 'reptoids' have appeared in sci-fi for as long as sci-fi has been around and mostly they are ill-considered attempts to simply produce something 'alien' i.e. cold-blooded, scaly skinned, egg-laying, etc.

In 1982, as part of a thought experiment, Dale Russell – curator of vertebrate fossils at The National Museum of Canada in Ottawa – and colleague Ron Sequin also created a plausible reptiloid. It accompanied a paper they wrote entitled 'Reconstruction of the Small Cretaceous Theropod Stenonychosaurus Inequalis and a Hypothetical **Dinosauroid**' in which they described the discovery of a small dinosaur called stenonychosaurus and noted that if you compared it with older related species there was a clear indication of 'increased encephalisation' (brain development) over time. Taking this one stage further, they postulated that, just like Harrison's Yilané, brainier dinosaurs like stenonychosaurus and troodon might have evolved into intelligent reptiloids had they been given the chance. He even had a model of his dinosauroid produced for display in the museum.

Reptiloids frequently appear in world mythology, although more often related to snakes than lizards or dinosaurs. Cecrops I, the first mythical king of Athens, was half man/half snake and Medusa the Gorgon had hair made of snakes. The Aztec god of benefaction was Quetzalcoatl the feathered snake[124] and the native American Hopi believed in a race of 'snake brothers' called the *Sheti* that lived under their feet. In India, the *Naga* are reptiloids that also live underground and, in the Far East, the Chinese *Lóng* (*Yong* in Korean, *Ryu* in Japanese) people were dragons who could take the forms of men. The reptile's appeal as something 'alien' and often evil also appears in the Bible of course with Eve's temptation by the serpent in the Garden of Eden.

Many alleged **UFO** abductees have claimed that the aliens who took them were reptiloids. And **David Icke**, a former British footballer and TV sports pundit, has claimed that a race of blood-guzzling seven feet (2.1 metre) tall 'reptoids' from the star system of Alpha Draconis is behind a worldwide conspiracy to control the planet and its resources. Icke has published at least 20 books outlining his views. In one, he claimed that the late Diana, Princess of Wales knew that her in-laws were shape-shifting aliens and that her death was part of the reptoid conspiracy. He even goes as far as to suggest that the reptoids have already infiltrated governments and heads of state including the president of the United State of America.

Many of **America's 50 states** were named ...

---

124. Commemorated in the name of one of the largest flying pterosaurs yet discovered – *Quetzalcoatlus northropi* – which had a wingspan of something like 36 feet. The name also honours John Knudsen Northrop, founder of the Northrop aircraft company who pioneered tailess 'flying wing' aircraft such as the B-2 'Spirit' Stealth Bomber.

How do you connect **Blackbeard the pirate**,
**Belgium** and
**bipolar disorder**?

## *Sing a Song of Nonsense*

A **smell** or odour is any form of volatilised (i.e. reduced to minute particles or droplets) chemical compound that humans and other animals perceive using their olfactory systems. There are a lot of synonyms for smell, ranging from the pleasant fragrance, scent and aroma to the nasty stench, reek, stink and pong.

Breaking wind often creates an unpleasant smell and, in the case of **Edward de Vere**, the 17th Earl of Oxford, it led to royal embarrassment. As recorded in John Aubrey's joyous and ribald *Brief Lives*,[125] de Vere was meeting Queen Elizabeth I one day when he bowed low and accidentally popped one out. So loud and obvious was the noise that Oxford fled the court in embarrassment and put himself into self-imposed exile for seven years. When he finally did return and had to bow before Her Majesty again, he did so carefully and worriedly... at which point Good Queen Bess reportedly leaned forward and said, 'My Lord, I had forgot the fart.'

De Vere became the 17th Earl of Oxford when he was 12 following the unexpected death of his father in 1562. In 1567, when only 17, Oxford accidentally killed an unarmed cook called Thomas Brincknell while practising his fencing with a friend called Edward Baynam. De Vere was skilled in horsemanship (and became a tilting champion), combat, falconry and hunting. In the ensuing inquiry, it was decided that Brincknell had committed suicide by running onto the point of Oxford's sword.

125. Aubrey began writing his short biographies or 'Minutes of Lives' in 1669 and gave them all to the Ashmolean Museum, Oxford in 1693. The title 'Brief Lives' was first attached in the 19th century.

In 1571, he married 15-year-old Anne Cecil who produced five children ... and a sixth while Oxford was touring France, Germany and Italy. Consequently they divorced on grounds of her adultery. However, he then produced an illegitimate child of his own with Anne Vavasour in 1581, enraging her uncle Sir Thomas Knyvet (the man who arrested Guy Fawkes) and the squabble became violent leading to several duels and a number of deaths among the staff of both men. The queen put an end to the whole business by threatening all concerned with jail. He was eventually reconciled with his ex-wife in 1581 and they cohabited until her death in 1588 at the age of 32. He then married one of the queen's maids of honour, Elizabeth Trentham, in 1591 and they produced four more children.

But the drama was to continue as Oxford's mismanagement of his finances forced him into bankruptcy. The queen stepped in and awarded him an annual pension of £1000 for his services during the war of the Spanish Armada (where he had a command in Holland) and this was continued by her successor, King James I. After the bankruptcy Oxford seems to almost disappear from English history but it is during this time that he is known to have become involved in the theatre and to have written many plays and books of poetry. We know this because other writers of the time recorded as such but none of Oxford's plays exist today (at least under his own name) and very little poetry.

There is a sizeable movement among scholars that supports the idea that Oxford was the author of the plays and sonnets we now attribute to Shakespeare. The theory was first put forward in 1920 by a Durham scholar called J. Thomas Looney. He pointed out that Oxford had an advanced education; he spoke French and Latin, and was taught writing, drawing, music, dance and cosmography. He also had knowledge of aristocratic life, the military and the law, and a background in the theatre (Oxford maintained and funded several small theatre companies). Looney also points out the fact that it would have been considered disgraceful for an aristocrat in Elizabethan times to be seen writing for 'low' public theatre and, therefore, it would have been appropriate for Oxford to have used a pseudonym or to have adopted someone to be the public face of authorship. He also notes that the regular publication of Shakespeare's plays stopped in 1604 – the year of Oxford's death. The controversy over his authorship of the plays has garnered support from many very well-respected people including Sir John Gielgud, Jeremy Irons, Sir Derek Jacobi and Sigmund Freud and has become known as the **Oxfordian Theory**. Which is better than the Looney theory I suppose.

**Loony** (and spelling variants 'Loonie' and 'Looney'), is a coarse term for a person suffering from mental instability or illness, unpredictable behaviour or exhibiting extreme foolishness. It is a shortened version of *lunatic*, which, in turn, is derived from the Latin *lunaticus* which means 'affected by the Moon'. In past times there was believed to be a direct link between human behaviour and the phases of the Moon. This was dismissed for many years as Old Wives' Tales but recent studies have re-evaluated the stories. The modern world is a much brighter place at night than it was in the past and the Moon's phases are barely noticed. In darker, pre-street and home lighting times, the Moon would have had a greater impact upon people's sleep patterns than now, causing insomnia and broken nights. Sleep deprivation has a profound effect upon behaviour and some conditions, such as bipolar disorder (or *cyclothymia*), are affected by light.[126]

Loonie is also a slang name for the Canadian one dollar coin. On one side it has an image of Queen Elizabeth II, and on the other a common loon – the nickname for a common Canadian wild bird properly called the **great northern diver** (*Gavia immer*). It is the provincial bird of Ontario and also the state bird of Minnesota in the USA and has a number of other nicknames including big loon, black-billed loon, call-up-a-storm (due to the belief that excessive calling led to rain), ember-goose, greenhead, guinea duck, imber diver, ring-necked loon and **walloon**.

Walloon also refers to natives of Wallonia, which equates roughly

126. You might be interested to learn that Andy Warhol's penis is on the Moon. Artist Forrest 'Frosty' Myers approached NASA to ask if a small plaque – a 'Moon Museum' featuring works by six prominent artists – could be attached to the leg of Apollo 12's *Intrepid* landing module. When the idea was rejected, Myers enlisted the help of an unnamed engineer at the Grumman Corporation. Simple drawings by Robert Rauschenberg, Andy Warhol, John Chamberlain, Claes Oldenburg, David Novros and Myers himself were miniaturised and baked onto an iridium-plated ceramic wafer measuring just ¾" × ½" × ¹/₄₀". The unnamed engineer attached it to Intrepid and it was taken to the Moon where it remains to this day. It was only later that NASA discovered it, and that the supposedly 'stylised initials' drawn by Andy Warhol were, in fact, a drawing of a penis.

to the southern half of Belgium. French-speaking Walloons share their country with the Dutch-speaking Flemish and the German-speaking inhabitants of the 'eastern counties' (*Cantons de l'est*). The name Walloon is derived from *walhaz*, which means 'stranger'. It is also the common origin of the names Wales, Wallace, Wallachia and the latter half of Cornwall (once *Cornu-Wallas* or 'the horn [shape of the county] of strangers'). *Walhaz* was a term used by Germanic tribes to describe what we now refer to as the **Celts**.

Celtic is a relatively modern blanket term used to describe a diverse group of European Iron Age tribes. They did not operate as a single race or nation but are grouped together by the fact that they spoke one of the Celtic languages; distinct and unrelated tongues to all other major European languages. Today, the term is used to describe the languages and cultures of Ireland, Scotland, Wales, Cornwall, the Isle of Man and Brittany. The languages are formed from two branches of the Celtic mother tongue: Irish Gaelic, Scots Gaelic and Manx are Goidelic languages, while Welsh, Cornish and Breton are Brythonic languages.[127] While the two branches have diversified to the extent that they are now quite different, the three languages within each branch are remarkably similar and fluent speakers can often hold conversations with people from the other areas.

Celtic art is full of beheadings as is Celtic mythology. Connemara's St Feichin is said to have been decapitated by Vikings but to have carried his own severed head to the Holy Well on Omey Island where a quick dunking ensured that it could be reattached. The heads of enemies were sometimes embalmed with cedar oil and displayed. Others were kept in boxes or display cases like prized trophies. It was said that an enemy's head affixed to a pole would start crying if an enemy came near. And a great hero's head, when buried, would protect those who buried it. The buried head of **Bran the Blessed** apparently protected Britain from invasion.

Bran the Blessed (or in Welsh *Bendigeidfran*) translates as meaning 'Blessed Raven'. Bran was a king of Britain in Welsh mythology and a giant to boot. According to the Welsh Triads, Bran's head was buried in London on the site of the White Tower in the Tower of London.

---

127. Efforts are being made to reconstruct another Brythonic language once used in the kingdom of Hen Ogledd, which took in modern day Cumbria and some parts of lowland Scotland.

As long as it stayed there, England would be safe. But legend has it that King Arthur dug it up, declaring that his protection was all that the country needed. There have been attempts to link Bran's name with the tradition of keeping ravens at the Tower. However, the link is tenuous at best.

Ravens and **crows** form part of the *Corvidae* family of birds, which also includes rooks, jackdaws, jays, magpies, treepies and nutcrackers. There are over 120 species of corvids with crows and ravens accounting for a third of them. Crows and particularly young rooks were once commonly eaten in the UK (and still are overseas). Blackbirds apparently make reasonable eating (although it is illegal as they are songbirds) and old recipes suggest harvesting them after they've been eating grapes, olives or myrtle berries. However, there's not much meat on one and you'd need 'four and twenty' baked in a pie for a substantial meal.

A few years ago, the urban myth debunking website Snopes[128] invented a wholly spurious origin for the rhyme *Sing a Song of Sixpence*, claiming that it was a coded message created by **Blackbeard** the pirate to recruit new crew. It was complete rubbish but the story spread to a large number of websites very quickly where it was touted as fact. Snopes did this to demonstrate the dangers of **False Authority Syndrome**; the problem of people believing something to be true because it appears to come from a reputable source. Snopes wanted to graphically demonstrate the pitfalls of the 'I got it from X, therefore it must be true' mindset.[129]

The true origin of 'Sing a Song of Sixpence' is unknown but we can only hope that it doesn't describe real historical events. Taken in its literal sense, it would be the grim and ghastly tale of a poor laundry woman being savaged and mutilated by a large rapacious bird. Her subsequent lack of a nose would have seriously compromised both her looks and her sense of smell.

A **smell** or odour is any form of volatilised …

---

128. www.snopes.com
129. The story of HMS *Friday* is another oft-touted urban myth. It turns up time and time again as an example of bad luck associated with Friday 13th. However, there has never been an HMS *Friday*.

# INVESTIGATION 28

How do you connect **crossword puzzles** to
**Diana Dors** and the
**Witchfinder General**?

## *Sex and Gauls and Rock and Roll*

**Asterix the Gaul** is a comic character created by French writer and
artist team René Goscinny and Albert Uderzo. The brave little Celtic
warrior first appeared in 1959 but is just as popular today. Asterix
and his best friend Obelix (and pet dog Dogmatix) live in a small village in Roman-occupied Britanny. Well, not all of Britanny is occupied
... Asterix's village has a secret weapon; a magic potion brewed by
the druid Getafix that provides superhuman strength and allows the
indomitable Gauls to keep the Romans out. Across more than 30
books, we have seen the plucky Gaul travel all over the world in
defence of his precious village.

There are a number of very clever naming conventions in the
Asterix books. All Gaulish men's names end in '-ix'. And, usually,
there are puns built into those names: Geriatrix is an old man,
Cacophonix is a tone-deaf bard and Unhygenix is a fishmonger with
a reputation for smelly stock. The women's names mostly end in
'-a' such as Impedimenta, Bacteria, Influenza. All Roman men's
names end in '-us', giving us delightful names like Giantortus,
Crismusbonus, Sendervictorius and Appianglorius. Some brilliant
wordplay led to the naming of a Gaulish boxer with a penchant for
all things Roman being called Cassius Ceramix, a Spanish chief
becoming Huevos Y Bacon (eggs and bacon) and an Egyptian gladia-
tor having the splendid moniker of *Ptenisnet*. Many of these clever
puns were dreamed up by English translators Derek Hockridge and
**Anthea Bell** who were employed by publishers Hodder and Stoughton
to turn the French originals into English while retaining the humour.[130]

130. Similar puns are used in other translations. Huevos Y Bacon becomes Soupa-

Translator Anthea Bell's father Adrian Bell was a Suffolk-based author and was the man who invented *The Times* newspaper's famous cryptic crossword. Her son, Oliver Kamm, is a columnist for *The Times*. And her brother, **Martin Bell**, was a BBC war correspondent before becoming an independent MP and ambassador for UNICEF (originally the United Nations International Children's Emergency Fund, now shortened to UN Children's Fund).

Martin Bell OBE joined the BBC as a reporter in Norwich in 1962 and enjoyed a distinguished career as a foreign affairs correspondent that lasted over 30 years. He covered a number of major conflicts including Vietnam, the Middle East, Nigeria, Angola, Northern Ireland and Bosnia where he was seriously wounded by shrapnel.

Then in 1997, he left the BBC to stand as an independent candidate for the Tatton constituency in Cheshire; a supposedly safe Conservative seat. The sitting MP, Neil Hamilton, was involved in allegations of 'sleaze' at the time and Bell was so annoyed by events that he stood himself and, as '**The Man in the White Suit**', won with a majority of 11,077 votes.

*The Man in the White Suit* was a satirical comedy film made by **Ealing Studios** in 1951. In the film, Alec Guinness starred as Sidney Stratton, a brilliant chemist who works for a textiles company. He invents a new kind of fibre that is seemingly indestructible and impervious to stains and makes up a white suit as a prototype. It appears to be a major breakthrough … until clothing manufacturers and the unions suddenly realise that this will put them all out of business as people will no longer need replacement clothing. There then follows a series of dirty tricks campaigns and threats aimed at ensuring that Stratton's invention is never made public.

The film was produced by the legendary Sir Michael Balcon who was also producer or executive producer on such classics as *The Ladykillers* (1955), *The Titfield Thunderbolt* (1953), *The Lavender Hill Mob* (1951), *Whisky Galore!* (1949), *Kind Hearts and Coronets* (1949) and *Passport to Pimlico* (1949). Clubbed together with a number of other classics, these films became known as Ealing Comedies as that's where many of them were made.

Other notable Ealing Studios films include *The Blue Lamp* (1950)

loignon Y Crouton (onion soup with croutons) in French editions, Costa Y Bravo in German and Paella Y Peseta in Dutch.

whose lead character, George Dixon, was later resurrected to appear in the long-running BBC police drama *Dixon of Dock Green*, *Let's Go Ape!* (1951) featuring the famous Hollywood chimpanzee Cheetah, and *Dance Hall* (1950) which starred Petula Clark and **Diana Dors**.

Diana Dors was Britain's answer to the 'blonde bombshells' of Hollywood – Marilyn Monroe, Jayne Mansfield and Mamie Van Doren – also known as The Three Ms. Born in Swindon, Wiltshire, Dors was christened Diana Mary Fluck. Upon entering showbusiness she was asked to change her name. Dors explained that this was because: 'I suppose they were afraid that if my real name was in lights and one of the lights blew...'. There is a story that, later in her career, she was asked to open a fête in her home town and, before proceedings began, she had lunch with the local Vicar who was due to introduce her. During the course of the conversation he stated that he would introduce her by her birth name as many of his parishioners would have known her by that name as a child. But then he became worried that he would mispronounce her name and cause embarrassment so spent an hour or so fretting and rehearsing what he would say. He then marched out onto the stage and introduced Dors with the immortal words: 'Ladies and gentlemen, it is with great pleasure that I introduce to you our star guest. We all love her, especially as she is our local girl. I therefore feel it right to introduce her by her real name; Ladies and Gentlemen, please welcome the very lovely Miss Diana Clunt.'[131]

Her career took off in 1951 with the film *Lady Godiva Rides Again* ... but for all the wrong reasons. The film was a light-hearted and altogether innocent film about beauty pageants. However, the American Board of Film Censors did not agree and banned the film from US cinemas because Dors's navel was visible. Suddenly Diana Dors was big news. The story ran in all of the papers and soon caught the notice of a man called Robert Lippert who decided that here was an opportunity to cash in on the controversy and turn Diana Dors into an international sex-symbol. The rest, as they say, is history.

Diana Dors's life story could fill an Investigation in itself but I will

131. I have yet to find absolute proof of this story. It does appear on her official fansite but not in the biographies of her that I have read – including her autobiography. But it's too funny a story not to include it.

leave you with just a few interesting facts about her. Firstly, she is one of the iconic figures on the cover of The Beatles' *Sergeant Pepper's Lonely Hearts Club Band* album. Secondly, she was a close friend of Ruth Ellis, the last woman to be hanged in the UK (Ellis actually made a cameo appearance in *Lady Godiva Rides Again* four years before she was executed by Albert Pierrepoint). And thirdly... no one can find Diana Dors's missing millions.

Before she died, Dors claimed to have hidden two million pounds in banks across Europe. Knowing that she had ovarian cancer, she gave her son Mark a piece of paper upon which was a code that would lead him to the money after her death. Diana was an avid crossword fan – she would have enjoyed Adrian Bell's cryptic *Times* crossword – and delighted in codes and ciphers. She had lodged the key to translating the coded message with her husband, Alan Lake. However, Lake committed suicide five months after Diana died without revealing the key. Son Alan was therefore left with a page of apparently meaningless letters and numbers. He therefore contacted cryptographers to solve the mystery and the boffins at Inforenz discovered that the code was the 16th-century *Vigenère* cipher. Using a decryption key based on a ten letter code (in this case it turned out to be DMARYFLUCK), they decoded the message. This was a list of names and locations across the UK. This is the full list, in the same order as it appeared on Diana Dors's paper:

| | |
|---|---|
| Bowen | Stoke On Trent |
| Richards | Leeds |
| Woodcock | Winchester |
| Wilson | York |
| Downey | Kingston Upon Hull |
| Grant | Nottingham |
| Sebastian | Leicester |
| Leigh | Ipswich |
| Morris | Cardiff |
| Mason | Slough |
| Edmundson | Portsmouth |
| Padwell | London |
| Pyewacket | Brighton |
| McManus | Sunderland |
| Coyle | Bournemouth |

| Humphries | Birmingham |
| Dante | Manchester |
| Bluestone | Liverpool |
| Cooper | Bristol |

The first name led them to a bank statement found among the late Alan Lake's papers but there was insufficient detail to trace the money any further. It has been suggested that there may have been another sheet of paper that may have given bank details to match the names and locations but nobody knows. At time of writing, the money is still lost.

The name **Pyewacket** from Brighton is interesting as it was the name of the witch's cat in the play and film *Bell, Book and Candle* (1958) which is thought to have inspired the sixties sitcom *Bewitched*. And in the film *The Amazing Mr Blunden* (1972), Dors portrayed an evil old woman called Mrs Wickens who would shout 'Pyewacket, Pyewacket!' to scare children away.

Pyewacket appears in British folklore as a name for a witch's familiar. Matthew Hopkins – the self-appointed 17th-century Witchfinder General – arrested a woman in Manningtree, Essex, as a witch and used sleep-deprivation to make her confess her 'sins'. In doing so, she gave the names of her animal familiars: Holt, a white kitten; Farmara, a fat spaniel with no legs; Vinegar Tom, a long-legged greyhound with the head of an ox; Sacke and Sugar, a black rabbit or hare; Newes, a polecat; and Ilemauzer, Pyewacket, Pecke in the Crowne and Griezzel Greedigutt, four imps. Hopkins claimed that they were names that 'no mortall could invent'.[132] Pyewacket was also the name of one of singer **Kate Bush**'s pet cats.

Kate Bush shot to fame in 1978 with her first single *Wuthering Heights*, which went straight to Number One in the UK charts and stayed there for four weeks. She was the first woman to reach Number One in the UK charts with a self-penned song. She was just 16 when she signed to EMI records. Her career has since gone from strength to strength with Brit Awards, Grammy nominations and an Ivor Novello Award for outstanding contribution to British music. She stepped away from the limelight in 1993 and enjoyed a 12-year hiatus in which she raised her son Bertie. However, she returned in

132. As described in his book *The Discovery of Witches* (1647).

2005 with a new album, *Aerial*, and a single *King of the Mountain*.

In the video for *King of the Mountain*, Kate references several famous people and objects. She mentions 'Rosebud' the sledge from Orson Welles' *Citizen Kane* and, at one point, she dances with Elvis Presley's empty white Vegas-years jumpsuit as ridiculous newspaper headlines float by: 'I Had Elvis's Alien Baby', 'Sighting of Elvis in Yeti Colony', etc.

In 2000, when Gordon Forbes, a US TV producer, was making a documentary about **Elvis impersonators**, he discovered a startling statistic. Back in 1977 – the year Elvis died of a heart attack at the age of 42 – there were just 150 people impersonating him. But by the turn of the millennium, there were 85,000. Simple calculation revealed to Forbes that if Elvis impersonation carried on growing at the same rate, there would be three billion of them by the year 2019; half of the world's population would be mimicking the King.

There are many different kinds of Elvis imitator. There is the so-called 'Chinese Elvis' – Paul 'the wonder of' Hyu. There is also a group of skydiving Presleys in Las Vegas called The Flying Elvi. And in Florida the first openly Jewish Elvis, called Melvis, performs such classics as 'Blue Suede Jews'. And there is Cardiff's 'Rockin' Sikh' Peter Singh whose live shows include such classics as 'Turbans Over Memphis' and 'My Poppadum Told Me'.

It has been said that Elvis's fame has overshadowed some of the earlier pioneers of rock and roll music. One such is **Bill Haley**. Sadly, he is only really known for 'Rock around the Clock' and 'Shake Rattle and Roll', but Haley recorded hundreds of records and was already a big success before Elvis put voice to vinyl.

Haley was born in 1925 in Highland Park, Missouri, and was blind in one eye from birth. He played in a number of country bands as a teenager including the Downhomers, the Saddlemen and The Four Aces of Western Swing. Elvis was just 15 years old when Haley cut his first true rock and roll single – 'Rocket 88'. It was the first song of its kind recorded by a white artist. Until then, all rhythm and blues and proto-rock and roll had been labelled 100% black music. This change in musical direction meant a change in look; out went the cowboy paraphernalia and in came the jive outfits and on-stage acrobatics. And the name changed too. Punning on their lead singer's name, the band became Bill Haley and his Comets.

The fact that Bill Haley pronounced his surname as *hay-lee* may be the reason why people often mispronounce the name of **Halley's Comet**; the 'hall' part is properly pronounced to rhyme with 'call' or 'ball' or, indeed, 'hall'. Halley's Comet is a periodic comet that last visited us in 1986 and will be back in 2061. As you may recall from Investigation 4, comets were once seen as harbingers of doom and the word 'disaster' comes from the Latin for 'bad star'. That's why an **asterisk** is called an asterisk – it is a small star-shaped punctuation mark. It is sometimes even referred to as a 'star', particularly when being read as part of a piece of computer programming code. And the asterisk key on your telephone keypad or computer keyboard is nearly always referred to as 'the star button'.

Comic book character Asterix the Gaul's name is an obvious comic misspelling of the word asterisk. And he is, after all, the star of the books.

**Asterix the Gaul** is a comic character created by...

How do you connect **dolphins**
to **Dutch courage** and the
**White Cliffs of Dover**?

## *Keep Calm ... You Jerk*

**Nightmares about falling** are very common but you won't die if you hit the ground before you wake up. It's just a story. Dream experts claim that falling dreams are related to insecurity, failure, anxiety and/or instability in our lives. The dream is all about our inability to hold onto things as we plunge downwards. Sigmund Freud, predictably, had a slightly different take on the matter. He reckoned that falling dreams happen when we are contemplating infidelity or giving in to a sexual urge. We don't necessarily have to give in to the urge but the 'naughty boy/girl' inside us all is what makes us feel like we're free-falling and potentially out of control. Falling dreams often end with a violent jerk that wakes the sleeper up.

We sometimes also suffer a sudden, involuntary spasm during the first stage of **sleep** (the Hypnogogic State) or, occasionally, when just waking up (the Hypnopompic State). I'm sure you've experienced that feeling of just drifting off and then jerking suddenly awake with your heart racing. There are several names for this spasm. It is known as Benign Nocturnal Myoclonus. Or a Myoclonic, Hypnagogic or **Hypnic Jerk**. But, despite these various names, no one is entirely sure why they happen.

One theory is that hypnic jerks (I'll use the shortest name to save my typing fingers) are a natural step in the body's transition from wakefulness to sleep. Your breathing gets more shallow. Your heart rate decreases. Your muscle tone changes too and that may fire off the spasm. Another theory says that the ancient flight-or-fight software in our brains mistakes the signals from our relaxing muscles and thinks that we're falling over. We therefore get an adrenalin surge and throw out our arms and legs to break the fall.

Sleep is a curious thing. We all do it for about a third of our lives and yet no one is entirely sure why. It used to be thought that it was a way to conserve energy but the amount saved by a good night's sleep is only around 50kcal – the equivalent of a slice of toast. It isn't about 'resting our brains' either as research shows that the brain is just as active asleep as when awake. Nor is it clear why some people can thrive on just a few hours – both Napoleon and Margaret Thatcher famously claimed that they only ever slept for four hours per night – while others need at least eight.

There is some evidence to support the idea that the traditional 'eight hour sleep' isn't as natural as we think. Psychiatrist Thomas A Wehr of the National Institute for Mental Health, Bethesda, Maryland, conducted several experiments in the 1990s in which people were left in darkness for 14 hours every day for a month. By the fourth week, the groups had all established a regular sleeping pattern in which they slept for just four hours, then woke and moved around for two hours before returning to bed for a second four hour sleep.[133] Wehr suggested, therefore, that the normal human sleep pattern should consist of two distinct chunks separated by a period of activity. This supports 16 years of research by historian A Roger Ekirch of Virginia Polytechnic, Blacksburg, Virginia. He found more than 500 references – including within Homer's *Odyssey*, Dickens' *Barnaby Rudge* and Cervantes' *Don Quixote* – to a 'first sleep' and 'second sleep'. Many 15th-century prayer books contained special prayers for 'the hours in between sleeps' and a doctor's manual from 16th-century France advised couples that the best time to conceive was 'after the first sleep'. Ekirch believes that this is our natural pattern and one that we lost in the move from pastoral to industrial lifestyles.

The amount of sleep required differs slightly between people but differs hugely between species. Humans enjoy, on average, 7.75 hours and our closest relatives, the chimps, like 9.7 hours. Pythons sleep for 18 hours, tigers for 15.8 and cats for 12.1. Meanwhile, sheep are

---

133. Wehr, along with colleague Norman E Rosenthal, is credited with the discovery of Seasonal Affective Disorder (SAD) and pioneered the use of light therapy to tackle it.

happy with an average of 3.8 hours, African elephants with 3.3 and giraffes with a tiny 1.9 hours per day. As you may have surmised, animals that sit on the 'prey' side of predator–prey relationships tend to stay alert and awake for as many hours as possible as sleep makes them vulnerable.[134] During the REM (rapid eye movement) stage of sleep, our brains are often more active than when we are awake but our bodies are effectively paralysed.

Sleep is a bit of a problem for whales, dolphins and porpoises as they – unlike seals, walrus and other sea-going mammals – cannot come onto land to have a snooze. They are also 'conscious breathers'; in other words, it isn't an automatic reflex as it is in most mammals, which is why they can effortlessly hold their breath underwater for lengthy periods – over an hour in some species. They need to be conscious to know when the next breath is needed. The way they solve the sleep problem is to effectively shut down one half of their brain at a time while the other half remains active. Researchers have observed dolphins swimming or 'logging' in this calm, half-asleep state for approximately eight hours a day.

It could be said that whales and dolphins get by because they can 'keep calm and carry on'. This famous phrase was coined in 1939 by Sir Percival Waterfield[135] – his grandfather was Sir William Herschel, the man who discovered Uranus – and is often referred to as one of the great morale-boosting posters of World War II... but nothing could be further from the truth.

Waterfield, then the Deputy Director of the Ministry of Information, thought that the slogan was likely to annoy people because it suggested that the government didn't believe that the nation was being stoic and brave. Market research by a social research group called Mass Observation supported his fears; it found that more people disapproved of the poster than approved. The British, it seemed, resented the idea that they needed to be told to stand firm. So the poster, of which 2.5 million had been printed, was shelved and never displayed. It was re-discovered in 2000 by second-hand booksellers

---

134. Koalas sleep for up to 20 hours per day because they have no natural predators, though young joeys can fall prey to feral dogs and cats, dingoes and larger birds of prey.
135. Waterfield was a chess master and played for Oxford University and the Athenaeum Club. Not terribly relevant but quite interesting nonetheless.

in Alnwick, Northumberland who found a copy in their shop. It has since become a popular – if unofficial – slogan for the current atmosphere of economic recession and austerity.

There is a similar tale to be told about the popular wartime hit '(There'll be Bluebirds Over) The White Cliffs of Dover', made popular by **Vera Lynn**. Has it ever puzzled you why it's bluebirds? After all, they're not native to the UK. The story goes that the composers, Americans Walter Kent and Nat Burton, were asked to write a song that sounded like 'Somewhere over the Rainbow' with a similar chord progression and imagery (bluebirds, etc.). The idea was that this would boost the campaign to entice the USA into joining WWII. So Kent and Burton did just that and the two songs are remarkably similar. In a bizarre twist, however, the British government did consider banning the song for the same reason they shelved the 'keep calm and carry on' posters – because they feared it would undermine morale at home by causing homesickness among troops overseas.

Another way to boost morale that originated during wartime is so-called **Dutch courage** – using alcohol to fortify yourself. The origin of this phrase can be traced back to the **Thirty Years War** (1618–1648). Dutch gin (also known as Jenever, Genever or any of several variant spellings all derived from the Dutch for 'juniper') was originally developed as a diuretic medicine.[136] Its invention is often wrongly attributed to a 17th-century doctor called Franciscus Sylvius. However, it is actually a century older and was invented by Doctor Sylvius de Bouve. The confusion is understandable as the men had similar names and were both physicians and chemists at the University of Leyden.

The Thirty Years War was a massive conflict that took place mostly in what is now Germany but which involved armies from more than a dozen countries. English soldiers fighting on the battlefields noted that the Dutch troops would have a drink before going into battle. A quick investigation revealed it to be Jenever and the English brought it home, delighting in its warming properties and happy to suggest to all and sundry that 'Dutch courage' came from a bottle. King William III,[137] smartly spotting both a tax opportunity and a chance to slap

136. Rather humorously, one of the modern Dutch producers of Jenever is called Van Wees. Another, in France, is called Loos [inserts puerile snigger].

137. Better known as William of Orange.

his European neighbours, imposed a heavy duty on all imported spirits but allowed unlicensed home production of gin. English gin – known as London dry gin and quite different from jenever – then became the drink of choice for many, especially as drinking water was generally unclean and carried diseases like cholera.[138]

The **Gin Craze**, as it came to be known, saw thousands of gin shops open all over the UK. By 1690, the people of London alone were consuming 500,000 gallons per year. By 1743 an average of 2.2 gallons (ten litres) of gin was being drunk annually per head of population and gin production had eclipsed beer brewing by some 600%. Gin was much stronger and cheaper than beer, and the poor consumed it with gusto. Such was the demand for 'Madame Geneva' that it was sold from wheelbarrows in the street. The surfeit of gin created a wave of social problems such as crime and drunken disorder, alcoholism, alcohol poisoning, miscarriages and depression. In no time at all, phrases like 'Mother's ruin' came into the language to describe the drink. One of satirist William Hogarth's most famous engravings is *Gin Lane*. The picture was completed in 1751 as one of a pair, the other being *Beer Street*. In the latter, beer is promoted as a healthy drink that encourages good behaviour and happiness while the former shows the effects of being gin-sodden: madness, lechery and even infanticide. Hogarth drew them to accompany attempts by Parliament to control gin production. Several Gin Acts were passed but, as most of them were built upon excessive taxation, it simply drove the distillers underground and provoked citizen riots. However, the Gin Act of 1751 (that Hogarth had supported with his pictures) found a solution by forcing distillers to sell only to licensed retailers. The gin palaces and gin joints slowly disappeared and the craze was over.

Gin also had the Victorian nickname of Strip Me Naked, presumably for the drink's ability to lower inhibitions, though quite why gin

---

138. For a while, tea was also seen as a 'foreign invader' that encouraged idleness in men and harlotry in women. Jonas Hanway suggested that, 'Men seem to have lost their stature, and comliness; and women their beauty. Your very chambermaids have lost their bloom, I suppose by sipping tea.' But the most fervent rants came from reformer William Cobbett who decried tea as, 'a destroyer of health, an enfeebler of the frame, an engenderer of effeminacy and laziness, a debaucher of youth and a maker of misery for old age'. His solution, unsurprisingly, was good English beer.

was singled out over any other spirit in that respect is unknown. The Victorians were undoubtedly involved in as much sexual activity as people are today but the prudish times they lived in meant that an entire lexicon of genteel euphemism and low **slang** evolved to keep private matters private. On the more poetic side, breasts were called things like 'Cupid's kettle drums' or 'one's dairy'. A lady's intimate area became a 'commodity' or 'crinkum crankum' and to 'tup' or 'occupy' a woman was as polite a way to say 'have sex with' as any I've seen. But best beware sailing on a 'fire ship' as that was a woman with the clap. There is also the wonderfully descriptive phrase 'melting moments' that described a fat man and woman in the act of sexual congress.

The harsher, bawdy slang produced a range of terms for prostitutes starting with 'bunter' – a prostitute who is also a beggar (also known as a 'hedge-whore') – and moved up the scale of charges to a 'three penny upright,' a 'buttered bun' (a lady who has recently lain with another man), 'laced mutton' and the wild and wanton 'dirty puzzle' and classy 'toffer'. Then, as now, there seems to have been a plethora of terms to describe the penis and testicles including the arbour vitae, bawbles, gaying instrument, plug tail, tallywags and whore-pipe. Then there's the 'rantallion' – a man whose testicles hang lower than his penis, possibly because of 'the whiffles', a relaxation of the scrotum.

Throughout history, there has been a constantly growing and ever-changing list of nicknames for the testicles. Not so popular these days but very popular in the 1970s was 'goolies', which is possibly derived from the Hindi word 'goli' meaning 'ball'. Other terms that have risen and fallen in popular speech include balls, nuts, cojones, nads, back wells, cobblers, cods, love spuds, nadgers, pods, conkers, plums, knackers, pills, family jewels and bollocks. In Japan they're called *kintama,* in Spain *pelota* and in Denmark *klodser.* Filipinos refer to their *betlog,* the Tamils their *kotai* and the Finns their *pallit.* In Hebrew, a common term is *beytzim.* Its direct equivalent in Arabic is *Baydat.* Meanwhile, the Spanish say *huevos,* the Germans say *eier* and Polish men talk about their *jaja.* All of these words translate as '**eggs**'.

A **Balut** is an egg-based foodstuff with, to Western sensibilities, a grisly twist. It is in fact a fertilised duck (or occasionally chicken) egg with a nearly fully-developed chick inside that is boiled alive and eaten in the shell. They are popular throughout Asia, especially in the Philippines, Cambodia and Vietnam where they are sold from trays of warm sand. Eaten with salt and accompanied by beer, they are considered both a high protein delicacy and an aphrodisiac. The shell is first broken and the 'juice' is sipped from inside the egg. Then the shell is removed and the egg and foetus eaten whole (the bones of the bird are soft). Such is the shock value of Balut to us here in the West that it frequently features in programmes about so-called 'freaky foods' and has made several appearances in episodes of reality shows like *Survivor*, *Fear Factor* and *I'm a Celebrity, Get Me Out of Here!* where contestants are often forced to face their worst nightmares.

**Nightmares about falling** are very common but ...

How do you connect **Dick Van Dyke**
to the **Millennium Falcon** and
the *Carry On* films?

## *Act your Age!*

British actress **Sally Thomsett**'s first major film role was in the 1970 film *The Railway Children* for which she received a BAFTA nomination for 'best newcomer'. Thomsett played an 11-year-old girl called Phyllis. Her older sister, Bobby, was played by Jenny Agutter. However, Thomsett was actually 20 years old at the time; two years older than Agutter. During the filming, Thomsett's contract stated that she was not allowed to do 'adult things' while in public. Therefore she was banned from going to pubs and had to be very careful about when and where to have a cigarette. Coincidentally, the film's director and screenwriter – veteran actor **Lionel Jeffries** – was also subject to an unusual age role-reversal in the 1968 film *Chitty Chitty Bang Bang*. He played Caractacus Potts's (Dick Van Dyke's) aged father... even though Van Dyke was actually six months older than him.[139]

*Chitty Chitty Bang Bang* was based on the 1964 novel of the same name by James Bond creator Ian Fleming. The book is very different from the film, being the story of Commander Caractacus Potts's renovation of a three time Grand Prix winning *Paragon Panther* racing car. Once repaired, Potts takes his family to the coast where they get involved in an adventure involving gangsters and gun-running across the channel in France. The car comes to life and saves the day.

1964 was also the year in which Lionel Jeffries starred in the film version of *The First Men in the Moon*, which was based on the book

139. I also find it hard to believe that veteran performer Sir Bruce Forsyth (born 1928) is older than Anne Frank (born 1929). Oh, and as was mentioned on the humorous website Popbitch recently, Gary Oldman is two weeks younger than Gary Numan. [Sniggers.]

by **H. G. Wells**. The film featured spectacular effects by Hollywood animation legend Ray Harryhausen. Other H. G. Wells books have also been made into films. *The Invisible Man* has been filmed many times, has spawned several TV series and inspired the 2000 Oscar-nominated film *Hollow Man* starring **Kevin Bacon**. *The War of the Worlds* was filmed in 1953 and 2005 and *The Time Machine* in 1960 and 2002. The latter book is credited with popularising the concept of time travel, although the first time machine to appear in fiction was created by Enrique Gaspar y Rimbau in his 1887 book *El Anacronópete*.

Time travel is the central theme of Cartoon Network's highly original animated series *Samurai Jack*. Created by Genddy Tartakovsky, the show features a mighty warrior torn from his own time in feudal Japan by Aku, an evil demon, and thrown far into the future. Jack's sole purpose in life is finding some device or magic that will allow him to travel back in time in order to defeat Aku. The show's highly stylised art and pacy cinematic direction drew Tartakovsky to the attention of *Star Wars* creator George Lucas, who was looking to develop an animated film to bridge the gap between *Star Wars Episode II: Attack of the Clones* and *Star Wars Episode III: Revenge of the Sith*. The two animated movies – known as the *Clone Wars* films – were released between 2003 and 2005 and were followed in 2008 by a new CGI (computer-generated imaging) movie and several new TV series.

CGI wasn't available to Lucas when he made the first three *Star Wars* films between 1977 and 1983. Therefore, the 3D chess game sequence aboard the Millennium Falcon spacecraft was filmed using stop-motion animated alien **chess** pieces.

Chess is an ancient game believed to have originated in India somewhere around the 5th century and was originally called *Chaturanga*. Legend states that that it was invented by King Gav so that he could re-enact some of his great battles for his friends and courtiers. It supposedly reached Europe sometime in the 9th century.

King, Queen, Knight and Bishop are all self-explanatory names for chess pieces. But what about rooks and pawns? The rook piece was originally depicted as a war chariot and was called a *rokh* (which is Persian for 'chariot'). Persian war chariots were heavily armoured and often built up with high side and rear walls to protect the chari-oteers so that they looked like small mobile fortresses. However, when the game found its way to Italy, the name mutated into the Italian *rocca* which means 'fortress'. It is from this that the modern design of the piece evolved. Pawns, meanwhile, take their name from the mediaeval word *Paon* or *Paeon* which means 'foot soldier'. Interestingly, there was an attempt in mediaeval times to give each pawn an individual title. They were:

**City guard** (standing before a knight piece as knights trained them);
**Worker/Farmer** (before a castle/rook that represented their employer's property);
**Blacksmith** (before the other knight as they shod the knights' horses);
**Weaver/Clerk** (before the bishop, for whom they worked);
**Merchant/Moneychanger** (before the king);
**Doctor** (the queen's pawn);
**Innkeeper** (before the other bishop – draw your own conclusions!); and
**Gambler** (placed at the far left, or *sinister* square and representing the lowest ranks of society).

The idea of individually named pawns did not catch on, however. And that's maybe a good thing as chess is a complex game enough without having to remember which pawn is which.

The origin of the name 'chess' is more difficult to pin down. It may have been derived from the plural of the Persian word for kings – *shah* – and the term 'checkmate' may come from *shâh-mât*, the full title of a Persian king.

Chess sets are very popular gifts and come in all kinds of themes. You can buy sets where the various pieces become *Muppets*, characters from *The Simpsons*, *South Park*, *Lord of the Rings*, the *Harry Potter* books ... there are even pornographic figures. One popular set is based upon the **Lewis Chessmen**.

The Lewis Chessmen were carved by Norwegian craftsmen some time during the 12th century. They are mostly carved from walrus ivory although a few are carved from whale teeth. They are currently displayed in the Royal Museum in Edinburgh and also at the British Museum in London.

They were discovered on the island of Lewis in the Outer Hebrides of Scotland sometime before 1831; the exact circumstances are unknown although it is believed they were found by a shepherd from the village of Bhaltos. We do know that they were found in a sand-bank near the Bay of Uig and comprise 93 pieces including two complete sets. It is likely they were on way to wealthy clients when they mysteriously ended up being buried.

Not far from Uig on the same west coast stands the imposing structure of Calanais – better known as the **Callanish Stones**. The Callanish site consists of an oval of 13 tall, thin stones, ranging from three to 16 feet in height. The oval itself measures 43 feet by 37 feet. At the centre is a tall stone (15 feet 6 inches) and a burial chamber in which human remains were found. There is a long avenue of stones to the north that leads to the 'circle', and shorter stone rows to the east, south and west. From the air, it is said to look a little like a Celtic cross. Callanish is one of the more imposing stone circles to be found in the UK. Others include the Rollright Stones in Oxfordshire, the Merrie Maidens in Cornwall, Swinside in the Lake District, Avebury in Wiltshire and, of course, **Stonehenge**.

Stonehenge is unusual in that instead of just being a group of standing stones arranged in a circle, the stones were meticulously shaped and arranged in trilithons (three stones – two upright and a lintel on top). It is this arrangement that gave the monument its name as 'henge' derives from the Old English word *hencen* which means 'gallows' as that's the shape gallows used to be.[140] This is where we also get the word 'hanging' when used in reference to execution. As it derives from a different source than the word 'hanging' in its putting things up on a wall sense (from Old English *hangian*, meaning 'to be suspended'), it is correct English to say that a person is 'hanged' while a picture is 'hung'.

*Stonehenge* is also a song by spoof UK heavy metal band **Spinal Tap**. In Rob Reiner's superb 1984 'rockumentary' *This is Spinal Tap*, the band are followed by director Marti di Bergi (Reiner) on their ill-fated tour of the USA. In one memorable sequence during a performance of the song, a prop trilithon is lowered onto the stage. However, due to a mistake during the planning stage, the fake stones are just 18 inches high instead of 18 feet. Consequently, the stones are

---

140. There was a notorious three-sided gallows sited at Marble Arch in London which became known as the 'Tyburn Tree' or 'The Three Legged Mare'.

shorter than the dwarfs who then come on stage to dance around them while dressed as pixies.

In another great live performance – this time of the song *Big Bottom* – all three of the regular band members are playing bass guitars. Derek Smalls (Harry Shearer) is actually playing a twin-necked bass; possibly the most pointless guitar imaginable.

Rob Reiner also directed *When Harry Met Sally* (1989), *Misery* (1990) and military courtroom drama *A Few Good Men* (1993) starring Jack Nicholson, Tom Cruise, Demi Moore, Keifer Sutherland and Kevin Bacon. Incidentally, Bacon was the star of *Hollow Man* (2000), which did not score too well with most film critics. However, one critic – David Manning – seemed to love the film. And well he might as it was later discovered that Manning did not exist; he was invented by Sony to create fake publicity for the film.

As I mentioned earlier, *Hollow Man* is loosely based on H. G. Wells's *Invisible Man*. Wells also wrote *The War of the Worlds* in which **martians** in their tripod attack craft attempt to subdue and conquer the earth. Tim Burton's 1996 film **Mars Attacks!** also featured a martian invasion and was based upon a series of trading cards produced by the Topps company in 1962. The cards caused outrage at the time as the painted artwork by Norman Saunders (over pencils by Wally Wood and Bob Powell) was very visceral with martian soldiers destroying dogs, burning US soldiers and cows and generally creating violent, bloody mayhem. The writers of *Mars Attacks!* – Len Brown and Woody Gelman – managed to include all of the images on the cards in their script and also some sci-fi B-movie staples such as giant robots and the inevitable flying saucers. Tim Burton based his flying saucers on the ones that appeared in the 1956 film *Earth vs. the Flying Saucers*.[141] In that film, the saucer effects were created by Ray Harryhausen – he who animated the Selenites and the mooncalf in *First Men in the Moon*. In that film, Professor Cavor (Lionel Jeffries) invents a substance that repels gravity, allowing his spaceship to fly to the Moon. Thus Cavor and his Victorian travelling companions become the first spacemen.

*Carry On Spaceman* is the title of an aborted film in the popular British **Carry On** series of films. Had it been made, it would have

---

141. He also used the same sound effect for the martian guns as the heat ray in George Pal's 1953 film version of *War of the Worlds*.

appeared after *Carry On Regardless* (1961). The *Carry On* films was a long-running series of low-budget comedies mostly directed by Gerald Thomas and produced by Peter Rogers. Drawing on a tradition of satire and saucy British seaside postcard humour, they turned regular cast members Sid James, Kenneth Williams, Joan Sims, Kenneth Connor, Bernard Bresslaw, Barbara Windsor, Hattie Jaques, Jim Dale, Peter Butterworth and Charles Hawtrey into stars.

There were 29 films and one compilation made between 1958 and 1978 with a 30th film (*Carry on Columbus*) made in 1992. Several films that did not get made (other than *Carry on Spaceman*) include *What a Carry On …* (1961 – set during an amateur dramatic production of *Romeo and Juliet*), *Carry On Smoking* (1961 – set in a fire station), *Carry On Flying* (1962 – set within the Royal Air Force), *Carry On Escaping* (a war-time drama spoofing the Colditz story), *Carry On Dallas* (aka *Carry On Texas*) (1987 – spoofing the famous US TV series), *Carry On Down Under* (1988 – based on Australian soaps *Neighbours* and *Home and Away*) and *Carry On Again Nurse* (1988) which was due to star popular TV comedian **Richard O'Sullivan**.[142] O'Sullivan had achieved fame by appearing in several ITV comedy series of the 1970s and early 80s including *Doctor in the House*, **Man About the House**, *Me and my Girl* and *Robin's Nest*. It would have been his second appearance in a *Carry On* film, having played a pupil in *Carry on Teacher* in 1959 (when he was 15 years old).

*Man About the House* ran for six seasons between 1973 and 1976 and is the series for which O'Sullivan is best known.[143] In the series (and the sequel *Robin's Nest*), he played single, randy chef Robin Tripp who ends up sharing a flat with two attractive young women,

142. There were some other films also directed by Gerald Thomas and produced by Peter Rogers and using the same writers and cast and crew of the *Carry On* films. However, for legal or copyright reasons they couldn't wear the *Carry On* label. They are *Please Turn Over* (1959), *Watch Your Stern* (1960), *No Kidding* (1960), *Raising the Wind* (1961), *Twice Round the Daffodils* (1962), *Nurse on Wheels* (1963) and *The Big Job* (1965). There is an unrelated film *Carry on Admiral* (1957) starring Joan Sims that predates the *Carry On* series.

143. A US version starring John Ritter, Joyce DeWitt and Suzanne Somers was called *Three's Company* and ran from 1977 to 1984. The US Ropers – Helen and Stanley – got a spin-off series called *The Ropers*, just as the UK Ropers – *George and Mildred* – did.

Chrissy and Jo, let by George and Mildred Roper. Much of the programme revolved around sexual frustration and Robin's various attempts to score with his flatmates. Chrissy and Jo were played by Paula Wilcox and Sally Thomsett.

British actress **Sally Thomsett**'s first major film role was ...

In this bonus Investigation I was challenged by Christina Broughton to connect **Paul Anka** to **Screech Owls** and **Moonflowers**. Can you do it?

## *The Holly and the Anka*

The term 'screech owl' is sometimes used in the UK as an alternative name for the Barn Owl (*Tyto alba*). However, Screech Owls are, in fact, a distinct genus – *Megascops* – that only live in the Americas.

There are more than 20 species including the Eastern *(Megascops asio)* and Western (*M. kennicottii*) Screech Owls, the Bare-shanked (*M. clarkii*), Bearded (*M. barbarus*), Rufescent (*M. ingens*), Cinnamon (*M. petersoni*), Long-tufted (*M. sanctaecatarinae*) and Whiskered (*M. trichopsis*) Screech Owls.

Despite their common name, they only screech when frightened. Normally their call is a trill or tremolo with a descending, whinny-like quality. It sounds, at times, remarkably like a lady opera singer rapidly descending a scale.

One lady opera singer who screeched more than a screech owl was **Florence Foster Jenkins** whose attempts to reach notes just beyond her limited range were almost painful to hear. Despite this, she had a very successful career.

Jenkins was born Narcissa Florence Foster in Wilkes-Barre, Pennsylvania and, from an early age, developed an abiding passion for music...if not the talent to perform it. She expressed a wish to study opera in Europe but her wealthy father refused to foot the bill. So she eloped with a doctor called Frank Thornton Jenkins and took singing lessons. However, the marriage lasted only seven years. She then formed a relationship with the actor St. Clair Bayfield and they stayed together for the remainder of her life.

Upon inheriting her father's wealth in 1909, she embarked on the career she'd longed for all her life. She soon became part of the musical social circle of Philadelphia before moving to New York. Her mother's death in 1928 gave her even more money to indulge her passions.

Jenkins was laughably bad with little facility for keeping either time or pitch. Her long-term accompanist, the excellently named Cosmé McMoon, became an expert at continuous adjustment to compensate for variations in tempo. But despite all this, Jenkins was a hit. Her concerts were hilariously funny, augmented as they nearly always were, with lavish costumes and bizarre gimmicks. One such was throwing flowers into the audience from a basket (on one occasion she hurled the basket too) while fluttering a fan. Curiously, Jenkins never seems to have realised that she was being mocked. She referred to the laughter she heard as 'professional jealousy' and once proudly said to a critic: 'People may say I can't sing but no one can ever say I didn't sing'. After being involved in an accident with a taxi in 1943 she discovered that, as the result, she could sing 'a higher F than before'. Rather than sue the cabbie, she sent him a box of expensive cigars.

Most of her performances were restricted to smaller venues and select audiences (she insisted on selling the tickets directly to the customers herself) but in 1944 – when she was 76 – she was persuaded to perform at Carnegie Hall. Tickets for the event sold out weeks in advance, but it was to be her swan song; Jenkins died a month later.

Her recitals were a mix of well-known operatic arias and pieces that she co-wrote with McMoon. Among her more popular pieces were 'Clavelitos' ('Little Carnations') during which she threw her flowers, and Mozart's 'Königin der Nacht' aria ('Queen of the Night') – properly called 'Der Hölle Rache kocht in meinem Herzen' – from *The Magic Flute*.

'Queen of the Night' is a popular name for a species of night-blooming *Cereus* cacti (*Selenicereus grandiflorus*), also known as the **Moonflower**. This is somewhat confusing as several other unrelated genera of plants are also called 'Moonflowers'. They are: the *Datura*, a group of flowering plants that includes the traditional 'witch weeds' Deadly Nightshade, Henbane and Mandrake; the *Ipomoea*, also known as 'Morning Glory' or the less glamorous 'Bindweed'; and *Mentzelia*, several species of American flowers also known as 'Evening Stars' or 'Blazing Stars'.

All stars blaze, of course, because they are gigantic balls of plasma held in shape by gravity and, for much of their lives, radiate heat, light and other forms of energy as the result of thermonuclear fusion of hydrogen at their cores. A 'star' is also the common name for a geometric shape – usually a pentagram (five pointed) or a heptagram (six-sided). When just an outline shape, it is sometimes called a 'hollow star'.

Stars Hollow is a fictional town in Connecticut in which US comedy drama *Gilmore Girls* is set. The series focuses on the lives of single mother Lorelai Gilmore (Lauren Graham) and her young adult daughter 'Rory' Gilmore (Alexis Bledel). Lorelai's Polish Lowland Sheepdog, for reasons never adequately explained, is called **Paul Anka**. In Season 6, the real Paul Anka makes a guest appearance during a dream sequence and when he and the dog meet, the town disappears in a flash of white light. Appropriately perhaps, Anka also wrote the song *Puppy Love*, which became a worldwide hit for Donny Osmond in 1977.[144]

Anka also wrote the hits 'Diana', 'She's a Lady', 'My Way' and one of **Buddy Holly**'s greatest hits, 'It Doesn't Matter Any More'. In fact, it proved to be Holly's final hit as it was released just a few days before his death. He was just 22 years old and newly married, and so the 17-year-old Anka insisted that, despite the song becoming a massive posthumous hit, all of his royalties from record sales should go to Holly's young widow, Maria Elena.

Born Charles Hardin Holley in Lubbock, Texas, Buddy Holly began his professional recording career in 1957 when he was signed to Decca Records. A typo on the contract led to him taking on the stage name of 'Holly'. He was an overnight sensation and was soon in great demand. In February 1959, during a three week tour across the Midwest with several other popular acts, Holly chartered a light aircraft to take him and fellow performers Ritchie Valens and J.P. 'The Big Bopper' Richardson on to the next venue. The plane crashed soon after take-off, killing all aboard.

For many decades afterwards, Holly's bass player Waylon Jennings was haunted by his last words to his friend. As he headed for his plane, Holly had jokingly said, 'I hope your ol' bus freezes up!' Jennings had replied 'Well, I hope your ol' plane crashes!'

144. Coincidentally, Paul Anka (human) originally comes from Ontario, Canada and the pilot for *Gilmore Girls* was shot in Ontario … although the series thereafter was shot on the Warner Brothers' studio lot.

Had Buddy Holly survived, he would, at time of publication, have been 77 years old alongside contemporaries Albert Finney, Bruce Dern, Glen Campbell, Englebert Humperdinck, Jackie Mason and Kris Kristofferson. Others born in 1936 who are no longer with us include Roy Orbison (d. 1988), Dennis Hopper (d. 2010) and **Lane Smith** (d. 2005), fondly remembered for his roles as Perry White in the series *Lois and Clark: The New Adventures of Superman* and also as Jim Trotter III, the town prosecutor who stands against Joe Pesci's character in the excellent 1992 movie *My Cousin Vinny*.

In one famous scene, city boy Vinny and his girlfriend are spending their first night in a cabin in the woods and he becomes very jittery about strange noises outside; so much so that he loads his pistol, storms out of the cabin in his underwear and fires several shots into the dark. In the foreground of the shot, an owl appears quite oblivious to his actions. According to director Jonathan Lynn, the scene involved a real owl that had been trained not to be frightened by the gunfire.[145] The owl was prompted to open its mouth at the right moments by offering it pieces of meat and the screeches were added later because screech owls don't make a screeching noise, despite their name.

The term **'screech owl'** is sometimes ...

145. When horses are trained to be confident and not to be startled by sudden unexpected events or loud noises, they are said to be 'bombproof'. This curious term, which comes to us from the Army's use of horses, led to a book called *Bombproof Your Horse* by Rick Pelicano and Lauren Tjaden winning the 2005 Bookseller Diagram Prize for oddest book title of the year. It narrowly beat such titles as *Detecting Foreign Bodies in Food*, *The Aesthetics of the Japanese Lunchbox* and *Applications of High Tech Squids*. What we may be seeing in *My Cousin Vinny* is the first bombproof owl.

# INVESTIGATION 32

Here's another bonus Investigation, this time for Ken Plume.
How do you connect **Rolls-Royce** cars
to **ostriches** and **The 'F' Word**?

## *Flucking Jezebel!*

**Peter Fluck** and his working partner Roger Law were the caricaturists behind the popular satirical British TV series *Spitting Image* that ran from 1984 to 1996. The series used 3D puppets of celebrities, politicians, the royal family and other newsworthy individuals to perform sketches based upon current events. Over time several of the caricatures started to develop their own curious idiosyncrasies: Prime Minister Margaret Thatcher was always seen in a gents' pin-striped suit and her successor, John Major, was a permanent dull grey monotone. Liberal leader David Steel appeared as a mouse-sized figure in the pocket of SDP[146] leader Dr David Owen (a fact that Steel later claimed seriously affected his political credibility). Pope John Paul II played the banjo and anti-immigration politician Enoch Powell was shown as black. The show featured many of the UK's top writers and impressionists, many of whom went on to fame in their own right such as Steve Coogan, Chris Barrie, Rory Bremner, John Sessions, Ben Elton, Jon Culshaw, Jan Ravens, Harry Enfield and Alistair McGowan. The show was the brainchild of John Lloyd the man who also gave us *Not The Nine O'Clock News*, *Blackadder* and *QI*.

*Spitting Image* was the perfect title for the show; it meant 'a good likeness' while also suggesting 'spitting acid' in the form of satire. Formic acid (also called methanoic acid) is 'spat' by certain formidable species of **ants** as a defence mechanism. The acid was named after the insects' family name: *Formicidae*.

---

146. The SDP or Social Democratic Party was a new political party formed in 1981 by members of the three major political parties as an alternative. In 1988 it merged with the Liberal Party to create the Liberal Democrats.

The *Formicidae* are some of the most numerous creatures on the planet and it has been estimated that ants account for somewhere between 15 and 20% of the entire animal biomass of this planet. Many ants can deliver formic acid by biting, but some species, such as the British Red Wood Ant (*Formica rufa*), can also squirt or spit it from their abdomens. All such ants are of the species **Formica**.

*Formica* – the building material – has nothing to do with either ants or acids. The name is a coincidence. It is a plastic laminate invented in 1912 by Daniel J. O'Conor and Herbert A. Faber, who, at the time, were developing it as an electrical insulator for the Westinghouse Corporation. The idea was to develop a cheaper substitute 'for mica' hence the name they gave to their new plastic. Mica is a heat resistant silicate mineral that can be split into flat sheets. Because of its colour and semi-transparency, it has been used throughout history as a substitute for glass. The Padmanabhapuram palace in India, built around 1601, has beautiful windows made from thin sheets of mica.

The Latin for 'window' is 'fenestra' (meaning 'little opening'), from which we get the term autocide-defenestration – the act of committing suicide by leaping from a high window. It is often shortened to '**defenestration**' although, technically, this just means 'to throw out of a window' and could be applied to any object or person. It seems to have been quite a popular activity in Czechoslovakia at one time. In 1419 a group of Hussites[147] showed their disdain for the way that they were being persecuted by the Catholic Church by throwing several members of the Prague Council out of the window of the town hall onto some spikes below. Then in 1618, just before the Thirty Years War, rebels opposed to the ruling Habsburgs threw two of the king's vice-regents out of the window of Prague Castle. Thankfully, on this occasion, their fall was broken by piles of garbage or manure. Then in 1948, Foreign Minister Jan Masaryk was found dead below a high window. It is not known whether he committed autocide-defenestration or if he was 'given a hand' by Communist agents.

There is a notable defenestration to be found in the Book of Kings in the Bible. Queen **Jezebel** of Israel, widow of Ahab and mother of Ahaziah and Jehoram, had turned her people from the God of

147. A Christian movement that became one of the forerunners of the Protestant Reformation. It followed the teachings of John Huss (circa 1369–1415).

the Israelites towards pagan gods like Baal. God was furious and instructed Jehu to deal with her. Consequently, he ordered her to be thrown out of the window by her servants where she was eaten by feral dogs. Jezebel's name is forever asociated with naughtiness of a sexual nature because she encouraged lewdness and impropriety.

Which nicely segues into 'The "F" Word'. So much has already been written about it elsewhere that I wondered what to tell you about the word 'fuck'. And then I found myself listening to the radio adaptation of **Douglas Adams**'s *The Hitchhiker's Guide the Galaxy: Tertiary Phase*,[148] which corresponds to book three in the series: *Life, the Universe and Everything*. In this phase of Arthur Dent's story, the robot warriors of Krikkit have to assemble a key to free their world from imprisonment. One of the component pieces turns out to be a silver rod that is used as the *Rory Award For The Most Gratuitous Use Of The Word 'Fuck' In A Serious Screenplay*.[149] It made me wonder what the winner would be if such an award was held for real.

At Number One, with 857 incidences of the word in a 93 minute film is *Fuck* (2005); a documentary about the use of the word (which appears on average 9.52 times per minute). Maybe this isn't a fair inclusion in the list[150] but the point the film makes is that fuck has had a bad press. Why should such a flexible word be considered a bad word? Why is this particular arbitrary group of four letters any worse than flan, fork, from, feel, funk, form, food, fuel, fain, farm or fool? As Stephen Fry once wrote in his book *Paperweight* (Mandarin, 1992): 'If school teachers describing animals talked about the way in which they *fucked* rather than "the mating process", if barristers and judges used "fuck" in court cases where penetration is an issue, instead of relying on those strange forensic phrases "intimate contact" and "physical relationship", if parents used it when explaining reproduction to their children, then a generation would grow up for whom the word held no more mysterious guilty terrors and strange dirty thrills than the word "omelette". What would that do to the sex

148. The aforementioned John Lloyd was a very close friend of Douglas Adams and co-wrote two episodes of the original *Hitchhiker* radio series.
149. When the book was published in the USA, the word 'Belgium' was substituted for 'Fuck'. I'm sure the Belgian people felt honoured by this.
150. The top five (barring *Fuck* itself) are *Gutterballs* (2008) with 625, *Summer of Sam* (1999) with 435, *Nil by Mouth* (1997) with 428, *Casino* (1995) with 398 and *Alpha Dog* (2007) with 367.

crime statistics? Were we to have taboos about the word "kill" or the words "maim" and "torture", however, it might perhaps be healthy: cruelty and homicide are things we really should be ashamed of.'

Such is the taboo surrounding the word that people use curious variants instead like freck, frack, frag, fook, frick and the much beloved Irish feck. There are quite a few other 'F' words that sound rude but aren't. They include futtock, which is the name given to the rib of a ship, farctate (full, stuffed to capacity), fipple (a plug used in the mouthpiece of woodwind instruments), flench (to cut up blubber from a whale), fossick (to turn over earth in search of something) and **furcula**, which is the correct name for a wishbone. It is V-shaped and is made from the fused clavicles (collar-bones) found in birds. It used to be believed that only birds have them but a study of fossils has shown that some theropod dinosaurs also had them – thus strengthening further the assertion that birds developed from dinosaurs.

The custom of breaking a wishbone can apparently be traced back to the **Etruscans** of pre-Roman Italy who fervently believed in the soothsaying power of chickens. After all, a cockerel could predict the dawn and hens squawked before the miraculous appearance of an egg. Therefore, the science of **Alectryomancy** was born – chicken fortune-telling. It worked like this: A circle was drawn on the ground. This was then sectioned off into 20 segments – one for each letter of the Etruscan alphabet. Then, some food was placed in each segment and the chicken was loosed. Her chosen route would take her through a sequence of letters – like a living, clucking Ouija board – and a priest of some kind would interpret the message. Then, when the chicken was eventually killed, its wishbone was saved and dried. After all, it was special; no other animal had a V-shaped bone. And the V-shape symbolised the crotch and the crucible of life. Any Etruscan wanting to extract some post-mortem prognostication would rub the bone and make a wish.

It was several hundred years later, when the Etruscan civilisation had been fully absorbed into Roman culture, that people started to break the wishbones for luck. The Romans brought the superstition to the UK where the wishbone became known as a 'merrythought'. And the Pilgrim Fathers took the tradition to the USA where it quickly became established as an integral part of Christmas and Thanksgiving.

Curiously, ostriches do not have a wish bone. They have a flat breastbone and lack the characteristic 'keel' found in most birds. Ostriches are extraordinarily useful birds. They can be ridden like horses (Cleopatra is said to have enjoyed riding one), and their meat and eggs are delicious – although it does take at least 40 minutes to boil one. Ostrich feathers are used in the top end of the automotive industry on special rollers to remove dust before paint is applied to the metal of the bodywork. Interestingly, there are wishbones on cars too. The wishbone joints form part of the suspension system, and posher cars – of the kind that would get feather dusted – have double wishbone suspension.

The credit for us being able to afford a car lies with **Henry Ford**. Ford may not have invented the motor car but he was the first to mass-produce them and bring the cost of ownership down.

Ford began producing his Model T in 1908 and by the time the model was discontinued in 1927, over 18 million had rolled off the assembly line. Ford was a brilliant businessman; he invented the modern system of manufacture using assembly lines, he offered good wages and working packages for his staff – so-called 'Welfare capitalism' – as long as they worked hard and kept production running high. He is credited with creating the concepts of the 40 hour working week and minimum wage.

Another innovative car manufacturer responsible for inventing some everyday household items was Frederick Henry Royce. He started his working life as a newspaper and telegram delivery boy but, following an apprenticeship with the Great Northern Railway Works in Peterborough, developed an interest in electrics. After working for the Electric Light and Power Company, he set up his own firm with his friend Ernest Claremont making small electrical components. But the company soon showed itself to be more than just a manufacturer. In just a few short years, Royce Ltd had created and patented the three wire electrical wiring system and plug, and the bayonet fitting light bulb – both still in use to this day.

Royce had bought himself a series of cars but had been hugely dissatisfied with their shoddy performance and unreliable electrics. So, being the kind of man he was, he designed and built his own. Among his innovations were a new type of smoother clutch, a three-speed gearbox driving a live rear axle, a rear footbrake and a handbrake. Word soon got around and eventually reached Charles Stewart Rolls, an importer of foreign cars based in Fulham, London.

Rolls had been frustrated by the lack of innovative and well-built British cars on the market and was fascinated by Royce's designs. The two met in the dining room of Manchester's Midland Hotel in 1904 and decided to go into business together. The **Rolls-Royce** Motor Car Company was born. Rolls agreed to sell as many cars as Royce could build but Royce was determined not to follow the Henry Ford path of mass production. His mission, in his own words, was to 'to turn out the best car in the world regardless of cost, and to sell it to those people who could appreciate a good article, and were able and willing to pay for it'. No one could argue that Rolls-Royce achieved their aim.

Many celebrities have owned Rolls-Royce cars as they are an obvious symbol of wealth and success. The 1960s was the car's height of popularity. John Lennon had his 1965 Rolls-Royce Phantom V controversially painted with psychedelic patterns by a group of travellers and river people. This enraged many people including one old lady who attacked the car with an umbrella while Lennon drove it through London. The car is now kept on display in the Henry Ford Museum. A 1937 Rolls-Royce Phantom III was one of the stars of the James Bond film *Goldfinger*. Auric Goldfinger and his henchman Odd Job used the car to smuggle gold between the UK and Switzerland by having solid gold car parts made and fitted. During this heyday of the Rolls-Royce, the youngest registered keeper in the UK, at just 20 years old, was a successful young actress called Diana Dors. And, as you know from a previous Investigation, her actual surname was Fluck.

**Peter Fluck** and his working partner...

# THE INDEX

### Investigation 5

capuccino

coffee

Palm civet

SARS

sneezes

bubonic plague

Bubo

R2-D2

James Earl Jones

Robin Williams

capuchin monkey

### Investigation 6

Caesar salad

Lucrezia Borgia

Buffalo Bill

*Les Misérables*

Napoleon

French Revolutionary Calendar

Julius Caesar

### Investigation 7

Six Degrees of Separation

Bacon Number

Fred Ott

*OTT*

Rick Wakeman

Nina Carter

Lycanthropy

Arcadia

Duran Duran

*Barbarella*

### Investigation 8

l'Académie Française

Georges Cuvier

Mass Extinction Events

Milky Way

*The Three Musketeers*

Cardinal Richelieu

### Investigation 9

Leo Tolstoy

White

Carolus Linnaeus

King Philip II of Macedon

Ptolemy Elrington

shopping trolleys

*The Six Million Dollar Man*

Charing Cross

*Oranges and Lemons*

### Investigation 10

blue whale

Asian elephant

Sitting Bull

Ghost Dance

Jack Wilson

Jackie Wilson

Jocky Wilson

dentures

## Investigation 16

*Camera Obscura*

*Camera Lucida*

Kodak

digital camera

digitalis

foxglove

pug

Rupert Bear

*Oz*

'Somewhere Over the Rainbow'

Eva Cassidy

Israel Kamakawiwo'ole

*Life on Mars*

rainbow

## Investigation 17

Kryptonite

Jadarite

Spin Doctors

Klark Kent

Police

Wall Street

The Buttonwood Agreement

New York Stock Exchange

Great Depression

William Patrick Hitler

quisling

Benedict Arnold

Lex Luthor

## Investigation 18

strippers

Oscar Wilde

*Salome*

penis

testicles

Adolf Hitler

*Time*

Charles Augustus Lindbergh

Sir Francis Chichester

Gipsy Moth

gypsy moth

Gypsy Rose Lee

## Investigation 19

Kentucky

average weight of US women

Marilyn Monroe

Diamonds

Richard Buckminster Fuller

geodesic domes

Eden Project

Creation Museum

## Investigation 20

armadillo

identical twins

Twin Foxes

fingerprints

koala

marsupials

## Investigation 30

Sally Thomsett
*The Railway Children*
Lionel Jeffries
*Chitty Chitty Bang Bang*
*First Men in the Moon*
H. G. Wells
*The Invisible Man*
*Hollow Man*
Kevin Bacon
*The War of the Worlds*
*The Time Machine*
*Samurai Jack*
*Clone Wars*
chess
Lewis Chessmen
Callanish Stones
Stonehenge
Spinal Tap
*A Few Good Men*
martians
*Mars Attacks!*
*Carry On*
Richard O'Sullivan
*Man About The House*

## Investigation 31

screech owl
Florence Foster Jenkins
*Queen of the Night*
Moonflower
*Gilmore Girls*
Paul Anka
Buddy Holly
Lane Smith
*My Cousin Vinny*

## Investigation 32

Peter Fluck
*Spitting Image*
ants
Formica
defenestration
Jezebel
The 'F' Word
Douglas Adams
furcula
Etruscans
Alectryomancy
Henry Ford
Rolls-Royce

# THE CONNECTOSCOPIC INDEX

As we've discussed, everything in the universe (the multiverse too, if it exists) is connected to everything else. It's therefore no surprise that all of the facts in this book can be connected together, regardless of what Investigation I've included them in. What's more, they can also be connected to all of the facts that I included in my previous book, *Joined-Up Thinking* (Pan Macmillan, 2008). It is, in fact, quite possible to pick any fact from either book and follow an unbroken chain of connections to every other fact in both books. Mind boggling, eh? Welcome to my world.

Here is a list of the connections that I've spotted. There are undoubtedly many more. The numbers in square brackets relate to the chapters in the previous book.

**Investigation 1** mentions *Jerome K. Jerome* as do Investigations 21 and 25. *Eden* is mentioned as a name and as a place here and in Investigations 19 and 26. *Jim Henson* is mentioned here and in Investigations 4 and [30]. Animator *Genndy Tartakovsky* appears here and in Investigation 5 and his series *Samurai Jack* is here too and in Investigation 30. Here be *witchcraft* and *witches* and they be in Investigations 2, 28, 31, [1], [12], [20] and [28] too. *Murder* and *homicide* crop up here and in Investigations 3, 11, 14, 23 and 26. *LSD* is mentioned here as it is in Investigation [20]. *Peter Pan* flies in here and in Investigation 25. There's a Samurai *Jack* and a donkey *Jack* here and a Yellow *Jack* in Investigation 25. The seemingly omnipresent *BBC* turns up here and in Investigations 3, 4, 9, 10, 12, 28, [6], [8], [16], [22], [24], [25] and [30]. And *Chris Barrie* pops up here and in Investigation 32.

**Investigation 2** mentions the *Olympics* and *Greece* as do Investigations 4, 5, 14 and [5]. We also find the *Mars* confectionery company here, as it is is Investigation 8. *Witchcraft* gets a mention as it does in Investigations 1, 28, 31, [1], [12], [20] and [28]. Here we find mention of the *Louisiana Purchase* which is also mentioned in Investigation 25. Both *Prometheus* and *fennel* appear here and in Investigation 24.

**Investigation 3** mentions *Charlton Heston* as do Investigations 4 and 26. It also mentions *Caliban* and *Sycorax* as do Investigations 12 and 14. *Jennifer*

*Aniston* makes an appearance here and also in Investigation 14. There is *murder* and *homicide* here and in Investigations 1, 11, 14, 23 and 26. *Suicide* makes an appearance here too, as it does in Investigations 23, 27, 28 and 32. *Soylent Green* appears here and in Investigation 26. *Cannibalism* is a tasty theme here as it is in Investigation 25. The *Welsh Triads* are mentioned here and Investigation 27. Our first sighting of *William Shakespeare* occurs here and he turns up again in Investigations 11, 12, 14, 15, 16, 21, 27, [1] and [8]. What a busy bard. The *BBC* tunes in here and in Investigations 1, 4, 9, 10, 12, 28, [6], [8], [16], [22], [24], [25] and [30].

**Investigation 4** has mentions of *Greece* and *Olympic Airlines* linking it to Investigations 2, 5, 9, 14 and [5] and *Greek Mythology* links it to Investigations 12 and 14. *The Sweeney* links it to Investigation 3. Investigation 4 mentions *Charlton Heston* as do Investigations 3 and 26. It also mentions *David Bowie* who appears in Investigation 4. *Halley's Comet* appears here and again in Investigation 28, as do *stars* that also appear in Investigation 31, [21] and [22]. Investigation 4 also mentions *Doctor Who*, just as Investigations 12, 15, 20, [6], [10] and [22] do. The *sun* shines here and in Investigations 7, 8, 10, [1], [9], [10] and [21]. *Jim Henson* is here and in Investigations 1 and Investigation [30]. The *BBC* turns up here too and in Investigations 1, 3, 9, 10, 12, 28, [6], [8], [16], [22], [24], [25] and [30]. *William of Malmesbury* appears here and in Investigation 21. Mars is mentioned here as it is in Investigations 12, 16, 30, [1], [4], [19] and [21] ... and as a chocolate bar in Investigations 2 and 8. *Apollo* appears here and in Investigation 10. *Bulls* charge in here and in Investigation 10.

**Investigation 5** mentions *Robin Williams* and *Ewan McGregor* who both appeared in Investigation [4]. It also talks about *Capuchins* as does Investigation 12. *Ray Harryhausen*, *Clash of the Titans* and *Theodore Roosevelt* all appear in Investigation 5 and in Investigations 11, 12, 19 and 30. *Owls* are also mentioned in Investigations 12 and 31. *The First Men in the Moon* also appears here and in Investigation 30. Another *Roosevelt* appears in Investigation [29]. *Star Wars* appears here as it does in Investigations 30, [4], [29] and [30]. *Genndy Tartakovsky* directs the action here and in Investigation 1. *Monkeys* swing in here here and Investigations 20, [21], [24] and [27]. *Sneezing* appears here and in Investigation [28]. The *Olympics* feature here and in Investigations 2, 4, 5, 14 and [5]. *Elephants* appear here and in Investigations 10, 13, 16 and [11].

**Investigation 6** features *Buffalo Bill* as does Investigation 10. Investigation 6 has a footnote relating to *La Marseillaise*, which appears in Investigation 13. *Caesar* marches in here and in Investigations 15, 17 and 22. *Les Miséra-*

*bles* is mentioned here and in Investigation [6]. *Napoleon* bullies his way into this Investigation and Investigations 8, 25, 29, [19] and [29].

**Investigation 7** mentions *Rick Wakeman* who also features in Investigation [4] and [8] and *Yes* in Investigations [4] and [15]. *The Young Ones* cause havoc here and in Investigation [14]. The *sun* shines here and in Investigations 4, 8, 10, [1], [9], [10] and [21].

**Investigation 8** mentions the *Mars* confectionery company as does Investigation 2. *Cardinal Richelieu* makes an appearance here in Investigation 8 and in Investigation 12. *Marsupials* nuzzled up to us here and in Investigations 20 and 29. *The Three Musketeers* appear here and in Investigation 14. So does *volcanic activity*. The *sun* shines here and in Investigations 4, 7, 10, [1], [9], [10] and [21]. *Napoleon* charges his way into this Investigation and Investigations 6, 25, 29 [19] and [29]. The *Chicxulub* meteor/asteroid lands here and in Investigation 26. *Starfish* sprawl here and in Investigations [27] and [29]. *Darwin* is mentioned here and in Investigations 11 and 27. *Fossils* are discovered here and in Investigations 13, 22 and [2]. *Spiders* appear here and in Investigation [17]. I've got *Crabs* here and in Investigation [3].

**Investigation 9** links *Greece* (in the mnemonic) to Investigations 2 and 14. *Native Americans* settle here and in Investigations 10, 26 and [11]. *Macedonia* (Macedon) appears here and in Investigations 1 and 14. *Spectrums* (or *Spectra*) appear here and in the form of *rainbows* in Investigations 16, 29 and [1]. *Bears* prowl here and in Investigations 20 and [28]. *Cyborgs* appear here and in Investigation [26] as does the *Six Million Dollar Man*. The *Great Fire of London* burns furiously here and in Investigation [28]. The *BBC* repeats itself here and in Investigations 1, 3, 4, 10, 12, 28, [6], [8], [16], [22], [24], [25] and [30].

**Investigation 10** mentions *Buffalo Bill* and *General Custer* as does Investigation 6. The *Blue Whale* swims in here as it does in Investigation 18. *Mice* appear here and in Investigation 20. *Native Americans* feature prominently in this Investigation and in Investigations 9, 26 and [11]. The *sun* appears in Investigations 4, 7, 8, [1], [9], [10] and [21]. The *BBC* is here and in Investigations 1, 3, 4, 9, 12, 28, [6], [8], [16], [22], [24], [25] and [30]. *George Washington* is sworn in here and in Investigation 26. *Apollo* appears here and in Investigation 4. *Ivory* appears here and in Investigation 15. There's a tiny species of *Bat* here and *Bat out of Hell* in Investigation 23. *Bulls* appear here and in Investigation 4. *Elephants* charge through here and Investigations 5, 13, 16 and [11].

**Investigation 11** features *Laurence Olivier* as does Investigation 12. Investigation 11 briefly mentions *Charles Dickens* as does 19, [15] and [18]. *Blenheim Palace* appears here and in Investigations [14] and [15]. *Roosevelt* appears here and in Investigations 11 and 12. *Newton* gravitates towards this Investigation and Investigations [1] and [18] and there's a *Jerome Newton* in Investigation 4. *William Shakespeare* appears here and in 3, 12, 14, 15, 16, 21, 27, [1] and [8]. *Rutherford* is buried here and he and his namesakes appear also in Investigation [18]. *Darwin* appears here and in Investigations 8 and 27. *Chaucer* has a tale to tell us here and in Investigation 13. *Oscar Wilde* is mentioned here and in Investigation 18. And *murder* and *homicide* appear here and in Investigations 1, 3, 14, 23 and 26. *Yellow fever* is mentioned here and in Investigations 25 and [15].

**Investigation 12** mentions the *BBC* as do Investigations 1, 3, 4, 9, 10, 28, [6], [8], [16], [22], [24], [25] and [30]. *Laurence Olivier* is here and in Investigation 11. *William Shakespeare* also appears here and in Investigations 3, 11, 14, 15, 16, 21, 27, [1] and [8]. *Cardinal Richelieu* makes an appearance here and in Investigation 8. Investigation 12 mentions *Capuchins* as does Investigation 5. *Caliban* is here as he is in Investigations 3 and 14. *Greek Mythology* links this to Investigations 4 and 14. *Ray Harryhausen* and *Clash of the Titans* also appear in Investigation 5 and *Owls* in Investigations 5 and 31. *Doctor Who* appears here and in Investigations 4, 15, 20, [6], [10] and [22]. *Roosevelt* appears here and in Investigations 5 and 11. The *Wizard of Oz* and *Frank L. Baum* appear here and in Investigations [1] and [13]. *Zeus* gets a mention here as he does in [9], [15] and [21]. *The Oscars* are mentioned here and in Investigations 16, 25, 30, [6], [7] [14] and [21]. *Gerry Anderson* appears here and in Investigation [10]. The *moon* looms here and in Investigation 27. *Mars* gets a mention here and in Investigations 4, 16, 30, [1], [4], [19] and [21].

**Investigation 13** features *La Marseillaise* as does a footnote in Investigation 6. *Farts* blow in here and in Investigation 27. *Carbon* itself is the element upon which all earthly life is based so maybe that's why it so commonly appears in these books, namely here and in Investigations 19, [2] and [6], *Carbon Dioxide* blows through here and Investigations 14 and [6], and *Hydrocarbons* appear here and in Investigation [2]. *Fossils* appear here and in Investigations 8, 22 and [2]. *Chaucer* has a tale to tell us here and in Investigation 11. *Sigmund Freud* appears here and in Investigations 27 and 29. *Methane* wafts in here and in Investigation 19. *Elephants* charge through here and Investigations 5, 10, 16 and [11]. And *Belgium* and *Belgians* appear here and in Investigations 27, 32 and [14].

**Investigation 14** mentions *Jennifer Aniston* as does Investigation 3. *Greece* appears here as it does in Investigations 2, 4 and 9. *Volcanic activity* appears here and in Investigation 8. Investigations 1 and 9 both mention *Macedonia*. *Greek Mythology* links this to Investigations 4 and 12. And Shakespeare gets a mention as he does in Investigations 3, 11, 12, 15, 16, 21, 27, [1] and [8]. *Murder* and *homicide* get mentioned here and in Investigations 1, 3, 11, 23 and 26. *Uranus* appears here and in Investigations 19 and 29.

**Investigation 15** features *Doctor Who* as do Investigations 4, 12, 20, and Investigations [6], [10] and [22]. *Graphite* appears here and in Investigation 19. *Lead* appears here and in Investigations 10 and 19. Investigation 15 mentions *William Shakespeare* as do Investigations 3, 11, 12, 14, 16, 21, 27, [1] and [8]. *Oxford* appears here and in Investigations 27, [9], [14], [18], [22], [25] and [28] (and that's not counting numerous references to the *Oxford English Dictionary*). *UFOs* get mentioned here and in Investigations 26 and [10]. *The Beatles* play here and in Investigations 28 and [21].

**Investigation 16** mentions *William Shakespeare* as do Investigations 3, 11, 12, 15, 21, 27, [1] and [8]. *Pong-Ping* appears here while *Pong* appears in Investigation 24. *Elephants* trumpet here and Investigations 5, 10, 13 and [11]. *Oz* and its creator Frank L. Baum are mentioned here as they are in Investigations [1] and [13]. *Mars* is in the ascendant here and in Investigations 4, 12, 30, [1], [4], [19] and [21]. *Rainbows* also appear here and in Investigations 29 and [1]. *Spectrum* appears here and in Investigations 9 and [1]. *The Oscars* are mentioned here and in Investigations 12, 25, 30, [6], [7] [14] and [21]. *Portrait Painting* is mentioned here and in Investigation 32.

**Investigation 17** mentions *Hitler* as do Investigations 18 and [29]. It also mentions *Nazis* as do Investigations 23, [16] and [29]. *Superman* and *Clarke Kent* appear here and in Investigations 22, 31 and [7]. *Sting* and *Police* storm into Investigation 17 and also Investigation 22. *Blackbeard* the pirate sails into this Investigation and Investigation 27. *The Natural History Museum* gets a mention here and in Investigation [30]. *Walloons* appear here and in Investigation 27.

**Investigation 18** has a plethora of *penises* and *testicles* as does Investigation 29. *Adolf Hitler* is here as he was in Investigation 17 and [29]. *Oscar Wilde* is mentioned here and in Investigation 11. The *Blue Whale* swims in here as it does in Investigation 10. *Time* magazine appears on the newsstands here and in Investigation [3].

**Investigation 19** mentions *Charles Dickens* as does 11, [15] and [18]. *Graphite* appears here and in Investigation 15. *Lead* weighs in here and in Investigations 10 and 15. *Eden* is mentioned as a name and as a place here and in Investigations 1 and 26. The *Creation Museum* is sited here and in Investigation 20. *Carbon* feature is here and in Investigations 13, [2] and [6]. *Marilyn Monroe* looks gorgeous here and in well-rounded Investigations 19, [8] and [26]. *Diamonds* feature in this Investigation and Investigations 1 and 25. *Uranus* features here and in Investigations 14 and 29. *Methane* blows in here and in Investigation 13. *Dinosaurs* appear here and in Investigations 20, 26 and [23].

**Investigation 20** features the ever popular *Doctor Who* as do Investigations 4, 12, 15, 23, [6], [10] and [22]. *Armadillos* and *leprosy* both appear here too as they do in Investigations 25 and [17]. *Monkeys* are here as they are in Investigations 5, [21], [24] and [27] and *bears* are here and in Investigations 9 and [28]. *Mice* squeak in here and in Investigation 10, and *marsupials* are here and in Investigations 8 and 29. *Elvis* swings his hips here and in Investigations 28, [4], [13] and [21]. *Twins* appear here and in Investigations 21, [21] and [22]. The *Proclaimers* sing their way into this Investigation as they did into Investigation [22]. *Sir William Herschel* pops up here and in Investigations 14 and 29. *Dinosaurs* appear here and in Investigations 19, 26 and [23]. *Ray Harryhausen* is mentioned here and in Investigations 5, 12 and 30. The *Creation Museum* is built here and in Investigation 19.

**Investigation 21** mentions *Jerome K. Jerome* as do Investigations 1 and 25. *Queen Elizabeth I* appears here as she does in Investigations 22, 26, 27 and [8]. The *Tower of London*, *The White Tower* and *ravens* all flock here and to Investigation 27. *William Shakespeare* makes an entrance here and in Investigations 3, 11, 12, 14, 15, 16, 27, [1] and [8]. *William of Malmesbury* is here as he is in Investigation 4. *Twins* appear here and in Investigations 20, [21] and [22]. *Big Brother* is watching you here and in Investigation [8]. The *River Thames* flows through here and Investigation 1 and *Charles II* reigns over this Investigation and Investigation 26.

**Investigation 22** features *Queen Elizabeth I* who also appears in Investigations 21, 26, 27 and [8]. *Sting* and *Police* appear here and in Investigation 17. *Superman* is super here and in Investigations 17, 31 and [7]. *Fossils* are found here and in Investigations 8, 13 and [2].

**Investigation 23** mentions *Nazis* as do Investigations 17, [16] and [29]. There is *murder* and *homicide* here and in Investigations 1, 3, 11, 14 and 26. And *suicide* here and in Investigations 3, 27, 28 and 32.

Investigation 24 mentions the game of *Pong* while *Pong-Ping* the Pekingese appears in Investigation 16. *Chess* is played here and in Investigations 29 and 30. Both *Prometheus* and *fennel* appear here and in Investigation 2.

Investigation 25 features *Jerome K. Jerome* as do Investigations 1 and 21. *Leprosy* also features as it does in Investigation 20. *Napoleon* marches in as he does in Investigations 6, 8, 29, [19] and [29]. *Peter Pan* appears here and in Investigation 1. This Investigation mentions a kind of *Jack* as does Investigation 1. The *Louisiana Purchase* gets a mention here and in Investigation 2. *Yellow Fever* is mentioned here and in Investigations 11 and [15].

Investigation 26 features *Charlton Heston* as do Investigations 3 and 4. *Soylent Green* is mentioned here and in Investigation 3. *UFOs* hover here and in Investigation 15. *Queen Elizabeth I* appears here as she did in Investigations 21, 22, 27 and [8]. *George Washington* is sworn in here and in Investigation 10. *Eden* is mentioned as a name and as a place here and in Investigations 1 and 19. *Native Americans* set up camp here as they do in Investigations 9, 10 and [11]. *Cannibalism* is a theme here as it is in Investigation 3. *Louis XIV* flounces into this Investigation and Investigations [9] and [15]. *Dinosaurs* are here and in Investigations 19, 20 and [23]. There is *murder* and *suicide* here and in Investigations 1, 3, 11, 14 and 23. *Charles II* pops up here and in Investigation 21.

Investigation 27 and *Queen Elizabeth I* appears here as she did in Investigations 21, 22, 26 and [8]. *King James I* also appears here and in Investigation 22. *William Shakespeare* makes an entrance here and in Investigations 3, 11, 12, 14, 15, 16, 21, [1] and [8]. *Darwin* appears here and in Investigations 8 and 11. The *Tower of London,* the *White Tower* and *ravens* all appear here and in Investigation 21. *Sigmund Freud* analyses this Investigation and Investigations 13 and 29. The *Welsh Triads* are mentioned here and Investigation 3. *Farting* appears here and in Investigation 13. *Oxford* appears here and in Investigations 15, [9], [14], [18], [22], [25] and [28]. *Suicide* occurs here and in Investigations 3, 23, 27 and 28. The *moon* features heavily here and also in Investigation 12. *Blackbeard* the pirate weighs anchor here and in Investigation 17. *Cornwall* is here as it is in Investigations [15], [29] and [30]. *Walloons* appear here and in Investigation 17. *Wales* is also here as it is in Investigations 13, 20 and [25]. *Scotland* appears here and in Investigation 4, 21, 22, [17] and [22]. *Ireland* is here and in Investigations 22, [17] and [30]. And *Belgium* and *Belgians* appear here and in Investigations 13, 32 and [14].

**Investigation 28** mentions *Elvis* as do Investigations 20, [4], [13] and [21]. *Halley's Comet* whizzes by here and Investigation 4 and *stars* get a mention in Investigations 4, 31 and Investigations [21] and [22] as well. *Alec Guinness* is mentioned here and in Investigations [4] and [30]. *Witchcraft* is here and also materialises in Investigations 1, 2, [12], [20] and [28]. The *BBC* repeats itself here and in Investigations 1, 3, 4, 9, 10, 12, [6], [8], [16], [22], [24], [25] and [30]. *Marilyn Monroe* is gorgeous here and in Investigations 19, [8] and [26]. *The Beatles* love you (yeah yeah yeah) here and in Investigations 15 and [21]. *Diana Dors* is magnificent here as she is in Investigation 32. And there is *Suicide* here and in Investigations 3, 23, 27 and 32.

**Investigation 29** features *Napoleon* who also invades Investigations 6, 8, 25, [19] and [29]. *Chess* is played here and in Investigations 24 and 30. *Marsupials* swing by here and in Investigations 8 and 20, *Rainbows* light the sky in Investigations 9, 16 and [1]. *Testicles* dangle here and in Investigation 18 as do *penises* and *Uranus* is spectacular here and in Investigations 14 and 19. *Sir William Herschel* signs in here and in Investigations 14 and 20. *Sigmund Freud* appears here and in Investigations 13 and 27. *Margaret Thatcher* is here and in Investigation 32.

**Investigation 30** features *James Bond* as do Investigations [6], [24] and [25]. It also mentions *Ray Harryhausen* who appears in Investigations 5, 12, 20 and the film *The First Men in the Moon* which is mentioned in Investigation 12. *H.G. Wells* appears here and in Investigations 1, 12 and 25. *Samurai Jack* fights his way in here and in Investigation 1. *Star Wars* occur here and in Investigations 5 [4], [29] and [30]. *Mars* gets a mention here and in Investigations 4, 12, 16, [1], [4], [19] and [21]. *Chess* appears here and in Investigations 24 and 29. *The Oscars* are mentioned here and in Investigations 12, 16, 25, [6], [7] [14] and [21]. And the ubiquitous Mr *Kevin Bacon* ends this epic journey here and in Investigation 7.

**Investigation 31** mentions *owls* as do Investigations 5 and 12. *Stars* get a mention in Investigations 4, 28 and Investigations [21] and [22] as well. *Witches* swoop in here and in Investigations 1, 2, 28, [1], [12], [20] and [28]. *Superman* gets a brief mention here and in Investigations 17, 22 and [7].

**Investigation 32** mentions *Chris Barrie* who also gets a footnote mention in Investigation 1. *Diana Dors* is here and in Investigation 28. *QI* and *John Lloyd* get a mention here and in Investigation [25]. *Portraits* appear here and in Investigation 16 and *Belgium* and Belgians pop up here and in Investigations 13, 27 and [14]. *Margaret Thatcher* is here and in Investigation 29. *Stephen Fry* gets a mention here and in Investigations [25] and [30], while

*Douglas Adams* appears here and in Investigation [25]. *Ants* swarm here and in Investigation [3]. *Suicide* is painless here and in Investigations 3, 23, 27 and 28.

# GRATEFUL THANKS

Good research means tracing a fact back to the earliest and most authoritative source that you can find. I have tried to ensure that all of the facts in this book are accurate by doing exactly that. However, there is always the possibility of a genuine mistake on my part or of new information becoming available that changes what we know about a particular subject. As Samuel Arbesman says, many things we think of as facts have a kind of 'half-life'; everything we know has an expiration date. There have also been instances where there has been more than one source for a fact and they have disagreed. In these cases, I've opted for the version that carries the most weight of evidence to support it. If you do spot any errors please let me know – my email and Twitter addresses appear at the end of the book. I'm always delighted to learn from my mistakes. I'd also love to hear about any new and unlikely connections that you find.

Poor research, in contrast, means dipping into a few internet sites and lifting the content, word for word, and assuming that it is accurate. Sadly, it sometimes isn't. To make matters worse, lazy researchers can perpetuate the inaccuracy and give it a false degree of authority by including the duff fact in their own works.[151] Because of this, it's become quite a common practice for authors and editors to plant mountweazels[152] somewhere in their books to catch the lazy researcher out.

A mountweazel is a copyright trap; a deliberately false fact, name or word that the author inserts into a work so that they can track plagiarism. One of the most famous appeared in Fred L. Worth's *Trivia Encyclopaedia* in the late 1970s when he deliberately (and wrongly) stated that shabby TV detective *Columbo*'s first name was Philip.[153] This 'fact' subsequently appeared in questions for the board

151. See Investigation 27 to learn about 'False Authority Syndrome'.
152. Named after the wholly fictitious lady photographer Lillian Virginia Mountweazel (1942–1973) whose biography was included in the 1975 edition of the *New Columbia Encyclopedia* in order to catch out the lazy editors of other encyclopaedias.
153. In fact, Lieutenant Columbo's first name was never revealed during the entire run

game Trivial Pursuit in 1984 and Worth tried to sue the game's creators. However, in this case, the courts ruled that it was acceptable for
a game about trivia to source its facts from books of trivia as facts are
common property and not owned by anyone. But it does show how
these things spread.

So I thought it might be fun to include a mountweazel in this book.
If you spot it, do let me know... but don't tell the world, eh? It'll be
our dirty little secret.

Now, let's get on to the important job of thanking some splendid
people.

I am hugely lucky to have a small but perfectly-formed gang of
friends who support and encourage my blatherings. In alphabetical
order I'd like to especially thank my brother Si, Marc Abrahams, Mo
McFarland and Huw Williams for always being invaluable sources of
fascinating information and friendly criticism. Huge thanks also to
Chris Addison, Jimmy Carr, Dave Gorman, Robin Ince, Helen Keen,
Graham Linehan and Robert Llewellyn for their encouragement.

And then there are the many friends and associates who help to
keep me sane and on track. They include Alex Andreou, Jason
Arnopp, Tony Bannister, Ram and Jane Badrock, Piers Beckly and all
at the London Writers' Group, Terry Bergin, Gordon Bibby, Mr
Bingo, Sue Black, Maria Boyle, Christina Broughton, John Butler,
Warwick Cairns, Ben Cameron, Paul Campbell, Sarwat Chadda,
George Chopping, Neil Denham, Neil Denny, Julian F. Derry, Kathy
Eaton, Ptolemy Elrington, Kate Fantham, Jane Farmery, Charles
Fernyhough, Irving Finkel, Richard Foreman, Matt Fox, Mrs Edna
Fry, Ash Gardner, Dave Gavin, Darren Goldsmith, Lara Greenway,
Chris Hale, Paul Hargrove, Faye Hartley, Jo Haseltine, Neil Henson,
Steve Hills, Debbie Hodson, Sarah Hook, Keith Kahn-Harris, Chloe
Kembery, Andy Kerr, Alex Kew, Khandie Khisses, Eric Lampaert,
Alasdair MacDonald, Mark Mason, Faraz Mainul Alam, Mick
Masters, Erica McAlister, Iain McCulloch, Ross McFarlane, Joel
Meadows, Barry Miller, Michael Moran, James Murphy, Mark Page,
Lizzie Pain, Stuart Peel, Ken Plume, Jackie Potter, Martin Robbins,
Sid Rodrigues, Helen Scales, Mikael Shields, Helen Smith, Janet
Smith, John Soanes, Naomi Stolow, Adrian Teal, Paul Thompson,

of the show. However, in one episode when Peter Falk shows his badge, the name
Frank can be quite clearly seen. However, that hasn't stopped the 'fact' that he's
called Philip spreading across any number of books and websites.

Tom Truong, Dave Turner, Kerry Underhill, Simon Watt, Cordy Williams, Julian Williams, Geoff Williams, John Williams, Stuart Witts and my many, many blogging pals and Twitter chums.

I cannot thank enough the following people: Alex Bell, Rob Blake, Will Bowen, Xander Cansell, Mat Coward, Jenny Doughty, Ilana Fox, Isobel Frankish, Stephen Gash, Justin Gayner, Christopher Gray, Caitlin Harvey, Rachael Kerr, Dan Kieran, John Lloyd, Sarah Lloyd, Piers Fletcher, James Harkin, Anne Miller, Deirdra McAllister, John Mitchinson, Andy Murray, Molly Oldfield, Justin Pollard, Jenny Ryan, Dan Schreiber, Liz Townsend and Rich Turner. Some work for *QI*, some for *The Museum of Curiosity* and others for Unbound. Some work for more than one of the three. They are truly interconnectible people and their support and friendship is very dear to me.

Special thanks to James Harkin and Kate Greig for their sterling work on the manuscript, to Mark Ecob (design), Emma Hudson (proof reading), Christian Brett (typesetting), Tom Gauld (for my amazing book cover), and to Cathy Hurren who steered the book towards physical reality.

Massive corduroy-clad thanks are due to Stephen Fry for kicking the ball – in his deliciously uncoordinated way – and getting it rolling in the first place.

And finally, as always, I am gobsmacked by the energy and support of my agent Ben Mason at Fox Mason who works tirelessly to make me look less incompetent than I probably are.

Am.

Twitter: @stevyncolgan
Blog: http://colganology.blogspot.com
Email: stevyncolgan@me.com
Website: www.stevyncolgan.com

# SUBSCRIBERS

Unbound is a new kind of publishing house. Our books are funded directly by readers. This was a very popular idea during the late 18th and early 19th centuries. Now we have revived it for the internet age. It allows authors to write the books they really want to write and readers to support the writing they would most like to see published.

The names listed below are of readers who have pledged their support and made this book happen. If you'd like to join them, visit:

www.unbound.co.uk

Wyndham Albery
Hazel Alexander
Mike Allen
Rich Anderson
Helen Armfield
Daniel Atkinson
Paddy Baker
Mummy Barrow
Paul Bassett Davies
Jo Bathie
Emma Bayliss
Carla Becci
Richard Bennett
Max Bergin
Terry Bergin
Ekaterina Berova
Gordon Bibby
Tracey Binns
Janet Bishop
Sue Black
Peter Borthwick
Edward Bowyer
Caroline Bramwell

Jennifer Brant
Andrew Brenton
Michele Brenton
Ben Brignell
Christina Broughton
A. Brown
Cathy Brown
Laura Elizabeth Brown
Robert Bruce
Martha Brummer
Gill Buchan
Joseph Burne
Pauline Burney
Christine Burrows
Mario Cacciottolo
Andy Cairns
Flor Cam
Ben Cameron
Paul Campbell
Andy & Joy Candler
Xander Cansell
Marianne Cantwell
Glenn Carey

Neil Carhart  
Derek Carrillo  
Joe Cassels  
Steven Cassidy  
David Chamberlain  
Claire Chambers  
Deborah Charlton  
Thomas Chubb  
Sarah Churchwell  
Emma Clifford  
Gordon Climbs  
Pat Colledge  
Mick Collins  
Robert Collins  
Kacie Connors  
Anthony Cooke  
Quentin Cooper  
Jessica Coover Adelman  
Balloffet Corinne  
Linda Corrin  
Alastair Craig  
John Crawford  
Oliver Cross  
Iain Cullum  
Heather Culpin  
Silas Currie  
Ruth Curtis  
James Dale  
Sarah Darling  
Charlotte David  
Debbie Davies  
Louise Davies  
Martyn Davies  
Benjamin Davison  
Lottie Davison  
Moira Davison  
Gary Day-Ellison  
David Dempsey  

Thomas Dempster  
Neil Denham  
J F Derry  
Mar Dixon  
Stephen Donnelly  
Lawrence T. Doyle  
Daniel Drozdzewski  
Ian Dryland  
Julie Dryland  
Ali Dunlop  
Vivienne Dunstan  
Nick Efford  
Kay Elliott  
Chris Emerson  
Tahnee Evans  
Gary Fellows  
Charles Fernyhough  
Catherine Forward  
Ilana Fox  
Matthew Fox  
Isobel Frankish  
Captain Salty Freckletits  
Dominic Frisby  
Sue Fuller  
Alison Garner  
Richard Garner  
Barry Geddis  
Alan Gibson  
David Gilray  
Martin Glassborow  
Darren Goldsmith  
Jessica Gooch  
Dave Gorman  
Peter Govan  
Darren Govey  
Voula Grand  
Katherine Green  
Mike Griffiths

Matthew Gumm

Andy Hall

Donna Hall

Matt Hall

Denis Haman

Samyogita Hardikar

Pam Hardiman

Paul Hargrove

Pat Harkin

Jennifer Harris-Frowen

Faye Hartley

Steve Hartley

Caitlin Harvey

Joanna Haseltine

Jo Hawkins

Ludy Hills

Steve Hills

Anne Hitchman

Rob Hitchman

Charlotte Hooson-Sykes

Stephen Hoppe

Nicola Horlick

Andrew Horne

Andy Horton

Clive Howard

John Howe

Vince Hudd

Matt Huggins

Lucy Hunt

Elizabeth Hunter

Cathy Hurren

Sarah Jackson

Fadi Jameel

Karolien Jaspers

Simon Johnson

Gail Jones

Julie Jones

Keith Kahn-Harris

Caroline Kay

Helen Keen

Andrew Kelly

Jared Kelly

Scott Kennedy

Andrew James Kerr

Alison Kershaw

Dan Kieran

Meg Kingston

Doreen Kirker

Richard Lalchan

Cheryl Lancaster

Stephanie Langston

Jason Le Page

Angela Lord

Stuart Lowbridge

Catriona Macaulay

Pamela McCarthy

Susan McClymont

Iain McCulloch

Karen McDonnell

Mo McFarland

Dustin McGivern

Aven McMaster

Cait MacPhee

Julie Maddison

Gaynor Maher

Wendy Mallas

Peter Maloy

Dave Mansfield

Rhodri Marsden

Michael Masters

David Maxwell-Lyte

Audrey Meade

Joel Meadows

Rob Medford

John Melhuish

Deborah Metters

Irene Mikheeva
Gia Milinovich
Barry Miller
Lesley Miller
Suzie Miller
Margo Milne
Danny Molyneux
Merlin Montgomery
Tom Moody-Stuart
Cate Moore
Sami Mughal
Neil Mumbray
Ann Murgatroyd
Shamus Murphy
Richard Neville
David Newsome
Andy Nichol
Al Nicholson
Chris Nicholson
Greg Norman
Henry Earl Norman
Lauren O'Connell
Suzanne O'Leary
Ben Oliver
Niall Olsen-Dry
Jan O'Malley
Mark O'Neill
Monica Ormonde
Asta Ottey
Louise Paddock
Mark Page
Keith Paine
Michael Paley
Sarah Pannell
Yianni Papas
Mark Parker
Rebecca Pascoe
Jenette Passmore

Sarah Patmore
Stuart Peel
Ian Pendegrass
Su Pendegrass
Tannice Pendegrass
William Penman
Cindy Penney
Laura Perehinec
Ken Plume
Justin Pollard
Casey Poon
William Pope
Jacquelynn Potter
Huan Quayle
Mikael Qvarfordh
Sam Randall
Mary Rather
Paul Rawcliffe
Katie Rawlins
Stephen Reeves
Brian Reiter
John Richards
Christopher Richardson
Sid Rodrigues
Felicitas Rohder
Debbie Ruddy
Allan Russell
Benjamin Russell
June Russell
Emma Ryal
Marie Ryal
Keith Ryan
Seb Sander
Natalie Shaw
Mikael Shields
Murray Skinner
Anne Skulicz
Sophie Slater

Sarah Smith
Nat Snell
Fiona Sothcott
Max Sothcott
Rafe Staples
Bernie Stefan-Rasmus
Ed Stenson
David Stevens
Jeremy Stimson
Naomi Stolow
Caroline Streek
Eric & Edmund Sundaram
Mark Sundaram
Mark Sunner
Trina Talma
Helen Taylor
Kathryn Taylor
Adrian Teal
Caz Thomson
Carl Tipple
James Tobin
Donna Tranter
Sarah Tregear
Charlie Trewella
Kilgore Trout
Thomas Truong
Laura Tryphonopoulos
Twisty
Louise Udall-Waring
Mirjam Veenker
Mark Vent
Michelle de Villiers
Jose Vizcaino

Donna Waite
Danielle Walker
James Walker
Dave Wardell
Nerys Watts
Richard Webber
Julius Welby
Simon West
Chris Weston
Paul Whelan
Levin Wheller
Matthew Whittaker
David Whittam
Heather Wilde
Alan Williams
Anthony Williams
Dylan Williams
Geoff Williams
Julian Williams
Sally Williams
Sean Williams
Russ Willis
Elliot Wilson
Keeley Wilson
Stuart Witts
Ian Wolf
Steve Woodward
Liz Wooldridge
Daniel Wright
Marilee Wyman
Simon York
Jonathan Young

# A NOTE ABOUT THE TYPEFACES

Jan Tschichold (1902–1974) was a German calligrapher, typographer, book designer, teacher and writer, skills he shared with the English sculptor and stonecutter Eric Gill (1882–1940). This book has been typeset using digital representations of their designs, namely, Linotype Sabon and Monotype Gill Sans.

Sabon-Antiqua, designed by Jan Tschichold for both hand- and machine-composition, was issued simultaneously by the Linotype, Monotype and Stempel type foundries in 1967. The designs for the roman were based on the type designs of Claude Garamond (c.1480–1561) and the italics on those by Garamond's contemporary, Robert Granjon. Gill Sans was drawn on the basis of the classical Roman capitals (such as those found on the column of Trajan in Rome) and was inspired by Edward Johnston's sans serif 'Johnston' typeface designed for London Underground. Gill's design originally appeared in a hand-painted sign over a Bristol bookshop opened in 1926 by his friend Douglas Cleverdon. Stanley Morison, then adviser to the UK arm of Monotype, commissioned him to produce a full font family, released in 1928. It swiftly became a British design classic, used by British Rail, the BBC and as the main font on the cover of Penguin paperbacks.

Between 1947 and 1949 the designer for these books was Jan Tschichold. Tschichold, accused of communist leanings by the Nazis, witnessed the suppression of all the books he had designed and in 1933 was arrested and held in Neudeck Prison for around six weeks before being released under a general amnesty. Upon release he fled to Switzerland with his wife using forged passports. During his time at Penguin he oversaw the design of 500 paperback covers and produced a four-page booklet of precise guidelines called the Penguin Composition Rules. It wasn't an easy process and Tschichold became the scourge of Penguin's typesetters and printers, demanding the highest levels of consistency. 'Every day I had to wade through miles of corrections (often ten books daily). I had a rubber stamp made: "Equalize letter-spaces according to their visual value." It was totally ignored.'